1001
QUESTIONS
AND
ANSWERS

Books Are Fun ®Ltd

Text: Simon Mugford (Weather and Climate; The World Around Us)
and Alexander Gordon Smith (Space)

Designer: Amanda Hawkes
Production designers: Mike Croll (Kingpin Media), Amy Barton

Editors: Sally Delaney, Nicola Baxter

Illustrators: Julian Baum, Peter Bull Art Studio, David Blundell, Robin Carter,
Stefan Chabluk, Tom Connell, Michael Langham Rowe,
Sally Launder, Terry Pastor, Sandra Pond

Photographs: Atlas Collection: 185ct; Corel Professional Photos; Digital Vision: 126r, 126bc, 128br,
134t, 134bl, 135b, 136t, 138t, 139t, 141br, 143t, 143bl, 144t, 144bl, 145t, 145b, 154t, 155c, 155b,
156t, 157t, 160t, 160b, 161b, 163c, 164c (all), 165t, 166c, 169tl, 169b, 173t, 173bl, 173br, 174b,
176t, 178t, 178b, 179t, 180t, 182t, 185cb; European Space Agency/CNES/Ariannespace: 167t;
Mary Evans Picture Library: 162c, 162b;
Natural History Museum: 152t; NASA: 151cl, 167br, 174t; Courtesy of NASA/JPL/Caltech: 133cb,
136c, 139cb, 141cl, 144br, 145cl, 146cl, 146cr, 147tr, 151tr, 153b, 172t, 172b, 184bl;
NASA/NSSDC: 142t, 147ct, 147cl, 148 (inset), 151tl;
remaining photographs ©˙Stockbyte™. Every effort has been made to ensure that all photographs
have been credited. If there are any unintentional omissions or errors, we will be happy to correct
them in later printings.

This edition published by
Books Are Fun Ltd
1680 Hwy 1
North Fairfield
Iowa 52556
USA

First published by Armadillo Books
an imprint of Bookmart Limited
Registered Number 2372865
Trading as Bookmart Limited Blaby Road
Wigston Leicester LE18 4SE England

ISBN 1-58209-562-0

Produced for Bookmart Limited by Nicola Baxter
P O Box 215 Framingham Earl Norwich Norfolk NR14 7UR

Printed in Singapore

Contents

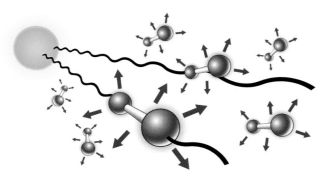

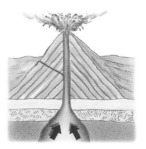

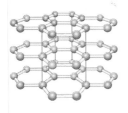

SPACE

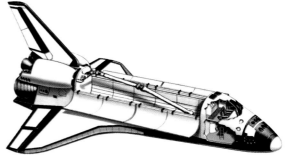

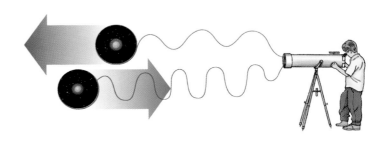

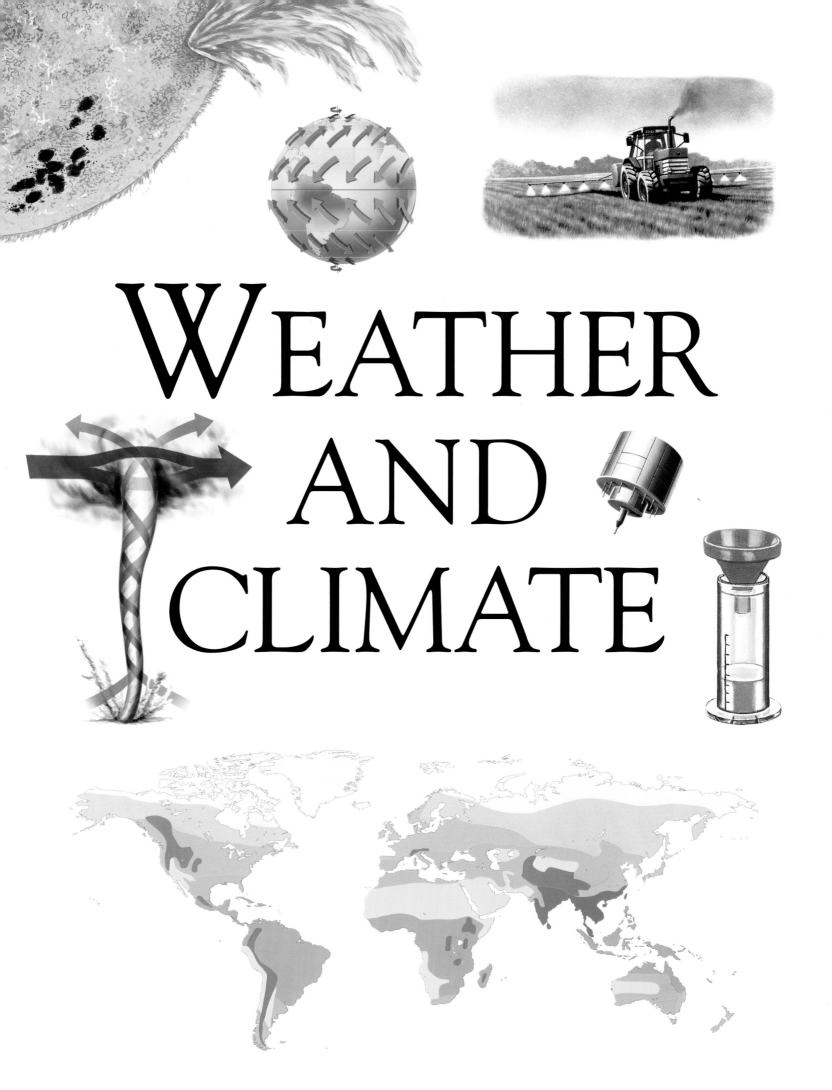

WEATHER AND CLIMATE

DO SUNSPOTS AFFECT THE EARTH'S WEATHER?

SOME SCIENTISTS believe that sunspot activity may have an effect on the Earth's weather. Sunspots seem to occur in cycles of 11 years. Research has shown that major periods of drought have occurred roughly every 22 years, or two sunspot cycles. We have not yet discovered the exact relationship between the two.

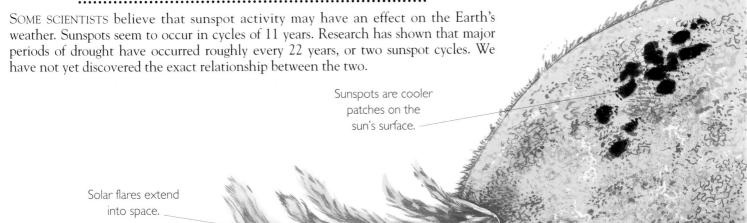

Sunspots are cooler patches on the sun's surface.

Solar flares extend into space.

WHAT IS SOLAR WIND?

SOMETIMES, INTENSE amounts of electromagnetic energy are released from the sun in the form of solar wind, or flares. The Earth is protected from solar wind–essentially an extremely hot gas–by its magnetic field, which stretches out into space. The particles of solar winds are known to affect satellites and even cause power blackouts on Earth. Scientists are still investigating the possible long-term effects of this activity on the Earth's climate.

The glass ball magnifies the sun's heat into a scorching beam.

Hours are marked on a cardboard scale.

HOW IS THE AMOUNT OF SUNSHINE IN A DAY RECORDED?

THE NUMBER of hours of sunshine in a day is recorded on an instrument called a parheliometer. A solid glass ball focuses the sun's rays onto a strip of cardboard. The intensified rays leave scorch marks on the card, moving along as the sun moves through the sky. The longer the marks, the longer the period of sunshine.

HOW DOES A SUNDIAL WORK?

A SUNDIAL SHOWS the time of day by casting a shadow across its face. With the needle–the *gnomon*–of the sundial pointing north–south, the shadow indicates the time as the sun passes through the sky from sunrise to sunset.

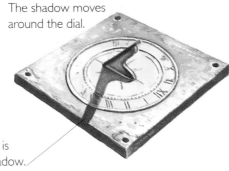

The shadow moves around the dial.

The time of day is indicated by the shadow.

fast facts

WHO WAS RA?

Ra was the sun god worshiped by the ancient Egyptians.

WHAT IS THE MAUNDER MINIMUM?

The British astronomer Edward Maunder noticed that there was no sunspot activity between 1645 and 1715. It was also a time in which Europe's climate was particularly cold. The period is known as the Maunder Minimum.

HOW LONG DOES IT TAKE FOR THE SUN'S LIGHT TO REACH EARTH?

It takes around eight minutes for the sun's light to travel the 150 million km (93 million miles) to Earth.

HOW IS THE SUN USED FOR COOKING?

In some hot countries, people use special curved mirrors to focus the sun's rays to heat a hotplate for cooking their food.

WHY IS IT HOT AT THE EQUATOR?

HOW DOES THE SUN HEAT THE EARTH?

ENERGY FROM the sun arrives on the Earth in the form of radiation. Some of the radiation is absorbed or reflected back into space by the Earth's atmosphere and clouds, but most of it reaches the surface, where it heats up the land and sea. As the Earth heats up, some of this heat is also reflected back into space.

The temperature of an area is largely determined by the way the sun's rays strike that part of the Earth. The way the Earth is tilted and curved means that the sun's rays strike different places at different angles. Generally, temperatures are highest close to the equator, where the sun's rays hit the Earth straight on. At the poles, the rays hit the Earth at an angle, and the area tends to be much cooler.

The sun's rays that hit the Earth are parallel.

Rays hit the poles at an angle and are spread over a large area.

The Earth is heated by radiation from the sun.

The equator feels the maximum effect of the rays–heat is concentrated in this area.

WHAT IS ALBEDO?

THE RELATIVE "shininess" of the Earth's surface in a certain area will affect the local temperature–this is called *albedo*. Icy, snowy areas reflect most of the radiation of the sun and remain cold. Forests and areas of bare soil absorb the radiation and tend to stay warm.

In areas where the land is covered with ice and snow, most of the solar radiation is reflected back into the atmosphere. This helps explain how it can be cold and sunny at the same time.

Forested regions have a low albedo–they tend to absorb the sun's radiation. This helps keep the surface temperature relatively high.

WHAT ARE CONVECTION CURRENTS?

WHERE COOL AIR lies above a warm area of land, the air will be heated. As the air warms up, it expands, becomes less dense (its molecules become less tightly packed), and begins to rise. The surrounding cooler air replaces the rising warm air. As the warm air rises, it cools down and its density increases. These currents of warm and cold air are called convection currents.

Birds and gliders make use of thermals–rising pockets of warm air.

The warm, less dense air rises.

Air sinks as it cools down.

Air is heated close to the ground.

WHAT ARE THERMALS?

RISING CURRENTS of warm air are called thermals. They are useful to glider pilots, who use them to help lift their craft into the air. Thermals can form over "hot spots" on the ground, such as a freshly plowed field. Some large birds make use of thermals to circle in the air.

WHY IS IT COLD AT THE TOP OF A MOUNTAIN?

BECAUSE THE AIR is warmed by heat rising from the ground, the air temperature at the top of a mountain will always be lower than it is at the bottom.

fast facts

WHAT WAS THE HIGHEST RECORDED TEMPERATURE?

A temperature of 136°F (58°C) was recorded near the Sahara Desert in Libya in 1922.

WHAT WAS THE LOWEST RECORDED TEMPERATURE?

In July 1983, a temperature of –129°F (–89°C) was recorded at a meteorological research station in Antarctica.

DO HIGH TEMPERATURES AFFECT PEOPLE?

Studies in the United States have shown that incidences of murder and violent crime increase when the temperature rises above 90°F (32°C).

WHAT IS THE LIQUID IN A THERMOMETER?

Thermometers contain either mercury or colored alcohol–liquids that expand easily in response to air temperature.

WHO INVENTED THE THERMOMETER?

An early thermometer was made by Galileo in the 16th century.

WHAT IS A THERMOSTAT?

A thermostat is a device that regulates heating systems in buildings.

WHY IS TEMPERATURE MEASURED IN THE SHADE?

If the temperature was measured in direct sunlight, it would give a false reading because the thermometer would be heated by both the air and the direct heat of the sun.

Air temperatures at the top of this mountain are generally very low, as illustrated by its snow-capped peaks. The warmer temperatures found at the foot of the mountain result in a lush, green landscape.

WHAT CAUSES THE SEASONS?

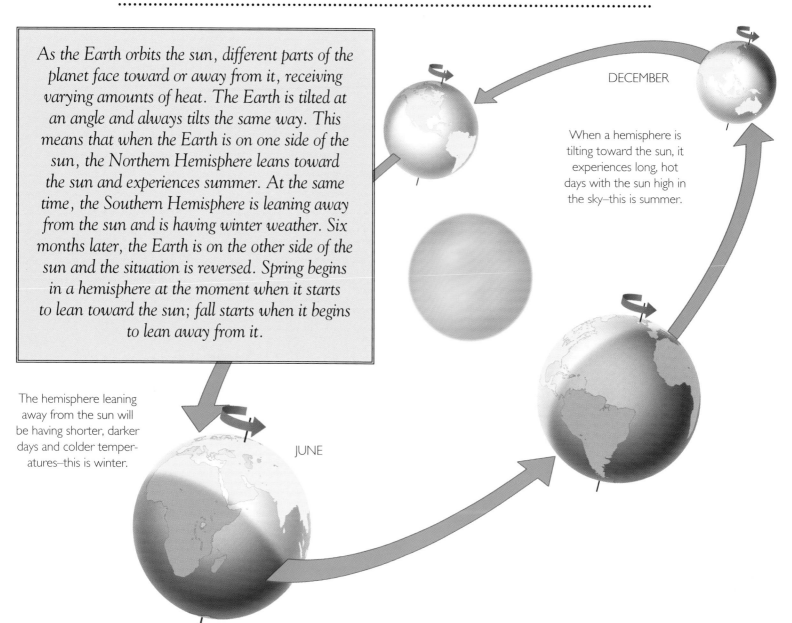

As the Earth orbits the sun, different parts of the planet face toward or away from it, receiving varying amounts of heat. The Earth is tilted at an angle and always tilts the same way. This means that when the Earth is on one side of the sun, the Northern Hemisphere leans toward the sun and experiences summer. At the same time, the Southern Hemisphere is leaning away from the sun and is having winter weather. Six months later, the Earth is on the other side of the sun and the situation is reversed. Spring begins in a hemisphere at the moment when it starts to lean toward the sun; fall starts when it begins to lean away from it.

DECEMBER

When a hemisphere is tilting toward the sun, it experiences long, hot days with the sun high in the sky—this is summer.

The hemisphere leaning away from the sun will be having shorter, darker days and colder temperatures—this is winter.

JUNE

WHAT ARE THE SEASONS IN TEMPERATE ZONES?

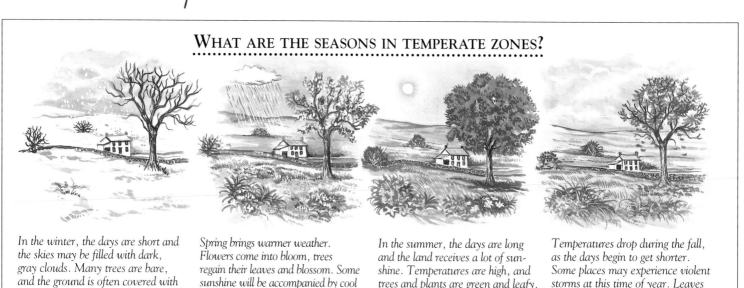

In the winter, the days are short and the skies may be filled with dark, gray clouds. Many trees are bare, and the ground is often covered with frost, snow, or ice.

Spring brings warmer weather. Flowers come into bloom, trees regain their leaves and blossom. Some sunshine will be accompanied by cool breezes and light rain showers.

In the summer, the days are long and the land receives a lot of sunshine. Temperatures are high, and trees and plants are green and leafy. Thunderstorms will bring rain.

Temperatures drop during the fall, as the days begin to get shorter. Some places may experience violent storms at this time of year. Leaves turn brown and fall from the trees.

WHERE CAN YOU SEE THE SUN AT MIDNIGHT?

IN THE PARTS of the world that are close to the poles, the way the Earth tilts means that the summer months in those regions have constant daylight. Parts of Scandinavia, for instance, are known as the "land of the midnight sun." In mid-winter, these areas experience the opposite—total darkness for 24 hours a day.

In places where the sun does not set during the summer, the midnight sky will have a dusklike appearance. It will quickly turn from dusk to dawn, with no real "nighttime."

WHAT IS SEASONAL AFFECTIVE DISORDER?

MANY PEOPLE suffer from the "winter blues." Feeling tired, rundown, and a bit sad is a natural response to the long, dark days, cold weather, and the effects of colds and flu. A few people experience exaggerated symptoms, which doctors have recognized as a medical condition known as Seasonal Affective Disorder, or SAD. Lack of daylight can cause sufferers of SAD to become very depressed and have problems sleeping and eating.

Some sufferers of Seasonal Affective Disorder (SAD) use a light box to simulate daylight during the dark winter months. The additional daylight fools the patient's brain into thinking that the day is longer. The treatment has proved very successful and is especially helpful for sufferers who live in places that experience many hours of winter darkness.

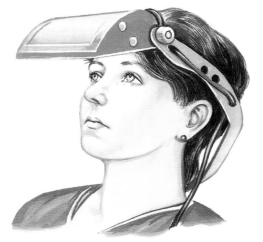

WHAT IS A SOLSTICE?

WHEN THE SUN is directly overhead at its most northern or southern position, it is called the solstice. The Northern Hemisphere's summer solstice occurs when the sun is above the Tropic of Cancer—on June 20, 21, or 22—and marks the beginning of summer. Its winter solstice (the Southern Hemisphere's summer solstice) is on December 21 or 22. The summer solstice is the longest day of the year; the winter equivalent is the shortest.

It is thought that ancient peoples understood the significance of the solstices. Many ancient monuments, such as Stonehenge, England (above), are built in such a way that when the sun rises on a solstice, it is aligned with a particular part of the structure.

WHY ARE THERE DIFFERENT CLIMATES?

A region's climate is the general pattern of weather that it experiences over a long period of time. Climate depends on a number of factors. The position of the area on the Earth's surface, and its height above sea level are two factors. Warmth carried around the world by ocean currents affects the climate on land, and areas far from the ocean will have a different climate from those on the coast. There are eight main types of climate, but there are variations within them.

WHAT IS A TEMPERATE CLIMATE?

THERE ARE two types of temperate climate—cool and warm. Cool temperate areas have rainfall throughout the year, warm summers, and winters with temperatures often below freezing. The warm temperate climate features mild, wet winters where the temperature rarely goes below 39°F (4°C). The summers are hot and dry, with temperatures averaging 68°F to 81°F (20°C to 27°C).

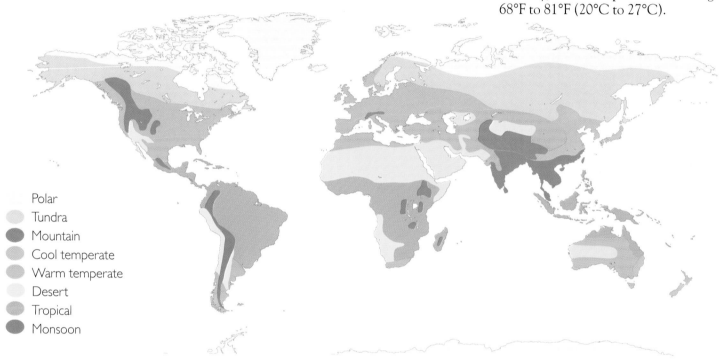

Polar
Tundra
Mountain
Cool temperate
Warm temperate
Desert
Tropical
Monsoon

WHAT IS A TROPICAL CLIMATE?

AREAS WITH A TROPICAL climate have high temperatures (75°F to 81°F [24°C to 27°C]) throughout the year. The atmosphere is very humid (full of moisture) and the levels of rainfall are very high—at least 59 inches (150 cm)—particularly in regions close to the equator.

WHAT IS A MOUNTAIN CLIMATE?

IN THE MOST mountainous regions of the world, the climate is often very different from that of the land that surrounds them. The freezing climate of the Himalayas, for example, is surrounded by desert, warm temperate, and monsoon climates.

WHAT IS A MICROCLIMATE?

SOME RELATIVELY small areas have their own climate, which differs slightly from the climate surrounding it–a microclimate. Cities often have a microclimate, due to the concentration of buildings, people, and vehicles generating heat. This creates a "heat island"–a warm mass of air that sits over the city, making it up to 11°F (6°C) warmer than the surrounding area.

Rising warm air may give rise to clouds and rain.

Tall buildings affect wind direction.

Buildings absorb and generate a lot of heat.

DOES IT EVER GET WARM AT THE POLES?

THE POLAR CLIMATE is very dry and windy, as well as being exceptionally cold. Inland, it is nearly always below freezing, and temperatures often reach –40°F (–40°C). Only near the coasts do temperatures reach about 50°F (10°C) in the summer.

Penguins are found on the coastal areas of Antarctica–the warmest part of that region.

fast facts

DO ISLANDS HAVE A SPECIAL TYPE OF CLIMATE?

Island countries such as New Zealand and Great Britain have a particularly cool, temperate climate because the sea absorbs and stores heat more effectively than the land.

IS THERE SUCH A THING AS A COLD DESERT?

Tundra areas, with very little rainfall and very low temperatures, are sometimes called cold deserts.

WHICH AREAS OF THE WORLD HAVE A TUNDRA CLIMATE?

The tundra climate is found in northern Canada, parts of Scandinavia, and Siberia.

WHERE IS THE WORLD'S DRIEST PLACE?

The Atacama Desert in Chile only has an average of 0.02inches (0.51 mm) of rain in a year.

WHAT IS IT LIKE TO LIVE IN A MONSOON REGION?

PARTS OF INDIA and Southeast Asia have a monsoon climate. In these areas, it changes very suddenly from a wet to a dry season, according to the direction of the prevailing wind. The dry period is extremely hot, and the powerful monsoon winds that blow in from the ocean bring torrential rain, often without warning. Such violent extremes of weather can make daily life very difficult, and heavy flooding, damage to property, and loss of life are commonplace.

In monsoon regions, houses are sometimes built on stilts to avoid being flooded. They also have steep-sided roofs to allow the water to run off easily.

CAN CLIMATES BE SIMULATED?

IT IS POSSIBLE to simulate the conditions of certain climates inside a greenhouse. Glass and other materials can be used to create a space within which the heat and light from the sun is intensified, making it much warmer than it is outside. The temperature, humidity, and air movement can be controlled, re-creating the atmosphere of a particular climate.

The Eden Project in Cornwall, England–the largest botanical garden of its kind –uses the latest technology to re-create different climates from around the world.

DO CLIMATES CHANGE?

The world's climates have been through many changes since the planet was formed over four billion years ago. The Earth has been both hotter and colder than it is now. In the age of the dinosaurs, there were no polar icecaps, and tropical and desert climates were predominant. Since that time, there have been several ice ages, when the polar ice sheets expanded to cover up to one-third of the planet. The planet will continue to experience such dramatic changes, as well as minor fluctuations in the weather. Many people are concerned that the activities of human beings will have a catastrophic effect on our planet's weather patterns.

During the 150 million years that dinosaurs walked the Earth, the climate was warmer than it is today. They probably walked through tropical landscapes, covered with lush vegetation and, later, huge forests. Some scientists believe that a dramatic change in the climate, possibly caused by the impact of an asteroid, led to the extinction of the dinosaurs.

In the last ice age, the world was much colder than it is now. Mammoths roamed the Earth toward the end of this time. Their woolly coats protected them from the extreme cold.

WHAT CAUSES AN ICE AGE?

THE CAUSES of an ice age are not clear. One theory is that the Earth's tilt and its orbit around the sun have changed. An orbit that took our planet farther from the sun would result in a cooler climate.

WHAT IS AN INTERGLACIAL PERIOD?

IT IS THOUGHT that ice ages occur roughly every 100,000 years. The last one ended around 10,000 years ago, so we may experience another one in 90,000 years. Scientists call the time between ice ages an interglacial period.

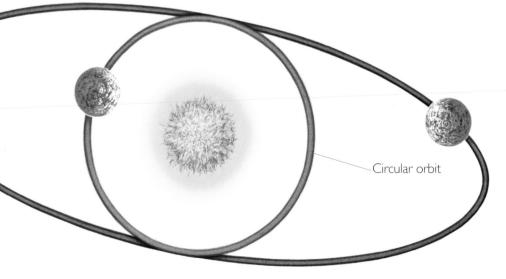

Elliptical orbit

Circular orbit

It is thought that the Earth's orbit has shifted between an elliptical (oval) shape and one that is closer to a circle. In an elliptical orbit, the Earth would have traveled farther from the sun, resulting in less solar energy reaching the planet's surface. Ice ages possibly occur at these times.

HOW CAN TREES TELL US ABOUT PAST CLIMATES?

BY STUDYING the growth rings in ancient trees, scientists can gather information about climates of the past. This science is called dendroclimatology. In each year of a tree's growth, new layers are added to the center of its trunk, producing a growth ring. Warm, wet growing seasons produce several layers, creating a wide growth ring. In a cold, dry period, fewer layers are produced, and the ring will be narrower.

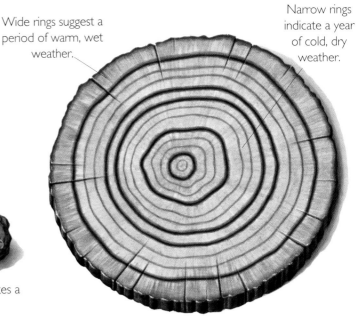

Wide rings suggest a period of warm, wet weather.

Narrow rings indicate a year of cold, dry weather.

HOW CAN ROCKS TELL US ABOUT CLIMATE CHANGE?

FOSSILS CONTAINED in layers of rock can reveal details about the climate millions of years ago. Rock that contains a large variety of fossils was formed during a time when the climate was warm; fewer fossils indicate a cooler climate. Rocks that show signs of glacial erosion were part of the Earth's surface during an ice age. Geologists can figure out the age of the layers, which tells us when the changes took place.

Fossil-rich rock indicates a warm climate.

Ice age rock shows signs of glacial movement.

DO VOLCANOES AFFECT CLIMATES?

LARGE VOLCANIC ERUPTIONS can have an almost immediate effect on the world's weather. The dust that is thrown into the atmosphere creates a kind of screen, which reflects more of the sun's energy back into space. As a result, temperatures around the world can drop slightly, and weather patterns may be affected for several years.

WHAT MAKES SEA LEVELS RISE?

RISING TEMPERATURES cause sea levels to rise in two ways. A warmer sea is less dense, so its volume increases and the level rises as it expands. A warmer climate can also cause glaciers to melt into the sea, raising its level.

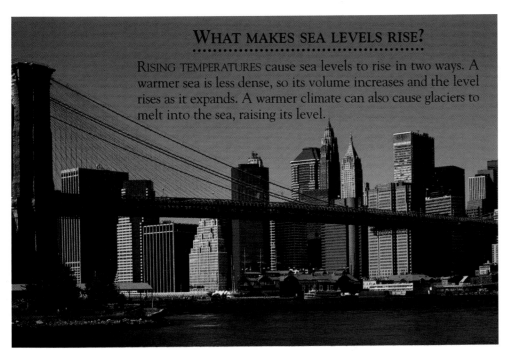

WHAT IS THE ATMOSPHERE?

The Earth's atmosphere is a covering of gases that surrounds the planet to a depth of 600 miles (1,000 km). Without it, no life would exist, and there would be no weather. Scientists divide the atmosphere into five separate layers: the exosphere, thermosphere, mesosphere, stratosphere, and troposphere. The troposphere is the layer nearest the surface and is the only part of the atmosphere where weather happens.

In a view of the Earth from space, weather systems can clearly be seen moving around the atmosphere.

WHAT HAPPENS IN THE TROPOSPHERE?

THE TROPOSPHERE is sometimes called the weather layer. Here, the air is constantly moving as it is heated and cooled in a process known as convection. Clouds form as water in the atmosphere evaporates and then condenses. This movement of air, heat, and water creates the world's weather systems.

HOW FAR UP DOES THE TROPOSPHERE GO?

THE HEIGHT of the troposphere varies between different areas of the Earth. At the equator, for example, it stretches to about (12 miles (20 km) above the surface. At the poles, the layer reaches a height of about 6 miles (10 km).

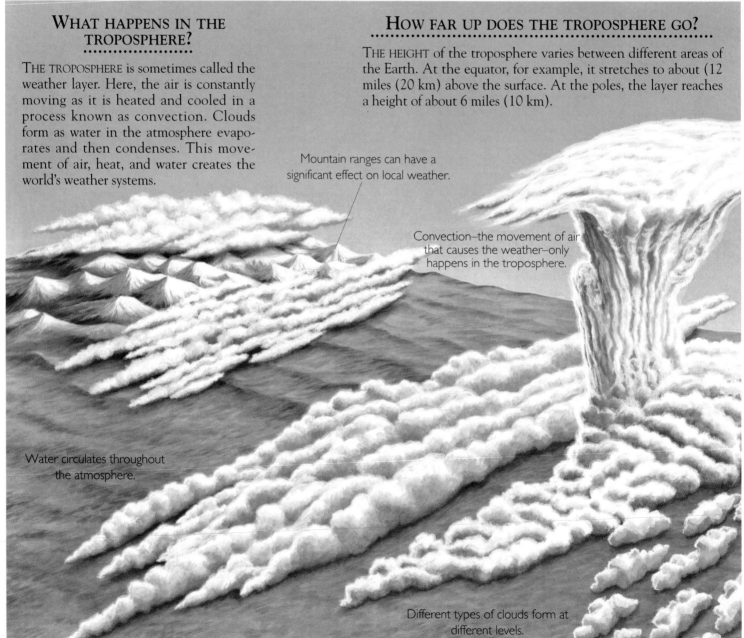

Mountain ranges can have a significant effect on local weather.

Convection–the movement of air that causes the weather–only happens in the troposphere.

Water circulates throughout the atmosphere.

Different types of clouds form at different levels.

WHAT IS ABOVE THE TROPOSPHERE?

THE LAYER directly above the troposphere is called the stratosphere. The stratosphere is warmer than the upper part of the troposphere, and this warm, relatively heavy air acts like a lid, trapping clouds in the troposphere. Going up through the layers, the air gets thinner and thinner–only in the lower parts of the troposphere is there enough air to breathe normally.

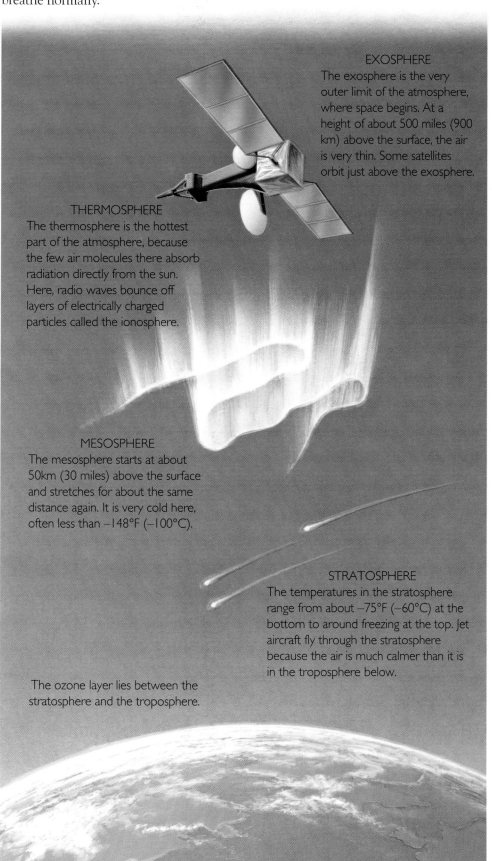

EXOSPHERE
The exosphere is the very outer limit of the atmosphere, where space begins. At a height of about 500 miles (900 km) above the surface, the air is very thin. Some satellites orbit just above the exosphere.

THERMOSPHERE
The thermosphere is the hottest part of the atmosphere, because the few air molecules there absorb radiation directly from the sun. Here, radio waves bounce off layers of electrically charged particles called the ionosphere.

MESOSPHERE
The mesosphere starts at about 50km (30 miles) above the surface and stretches for about the same distance again. It is very cold here, often less than –148°F (–100°C).

STRATOSPHERE
The temperatures in the stratosphere range from about –75°F (–60°C) at the bottom to around freezing at the top. Jet aircraft fly through the stratosphere because the air is much calmer than it is in the troposphere below.

The ozone layer lies between the stratosphere and the troposphere.

WHAT CAUSES AIR PRESSURE?

Air pressure is created by the effect of gravity pulling the atmosphere toward the Earth. It can vary according to temperature, causing different amounts of pressure in different parts of the world. It also changes according to altitude—pressure is greater at sea level because there is more air pushing down than there is at higher altitudes.

HOW DOES A LOW-PRESSURE AREA FORM?

AN AREA of warm air can create low pressure because warm air rises, reducing the level of air pressure. If the warm air evaporates water on the surface, clouds may form, producing the rain and bad weather associated with low pressure.

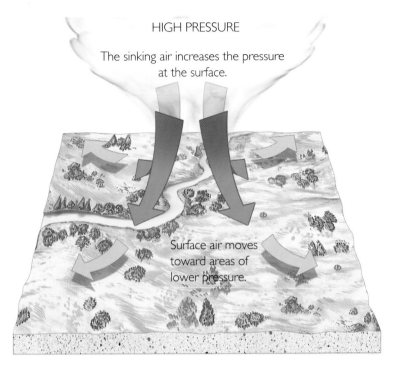

HIGH PRESSURE
The sinking air increases the pressure at the surface.

Surface air moves toward areas of lower pressure.

HOW DOES A HIGH-PRESSURE AREA FORM?

AN AREA of high pressure is created where the air is cold. The cold air sinks, pushing down and creating high pressure. This causes the air molecules to be squashed together, creating heat. As the air warms up, it tends to bring warm and pleasant weather.

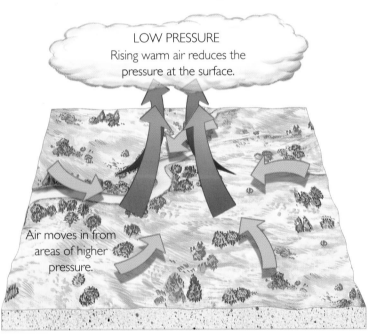

LOW PRESSURE
Rising warm air reduces the pressure at the surface.

Air moves in from areas of higher pressure.

HOW IS AIR PRESSURE MEASURED?

AN INSTRUMENT called a barometer is used to measure air pressure. A mercury barometer consists of a glass tube standing in an open dish of mercury. The air pressure pushes against the mercury and forces it up the tube. The level of the mercury is recorded against a scale. Mercury barometers are clumsy, and mercury is poisonous, so aneroid barometers are used more often. A sealed metal box inside the barometer is connected to the pointer on the clock-like face. The vacuum inside the metal box means that an increase in pressure will squash it; a drop in pressure will make it expand. These changes make the pointer move around the dial.

Aneroid barometer

Mercury barometer

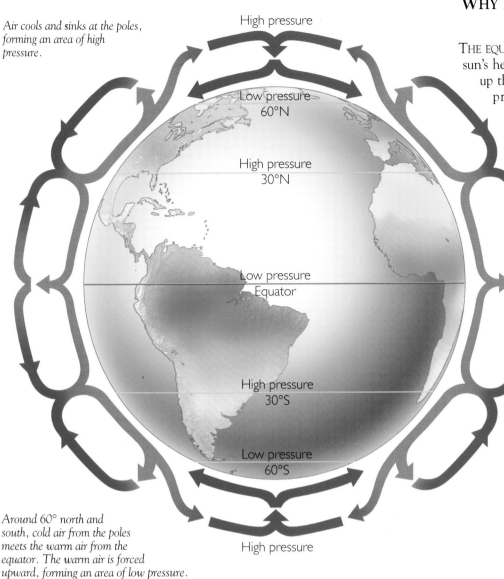

Air cools and sinks at the poles, forming an area of high pressure.

High pressure

Low pressure
60°N

High pressure
30°N

Low pressure
Equator

High pressure
30°S

Low pressure
60°S

High pressure

Around 60° north and south, cold air from the poles meets the warm air from the equator. The warm air is forced upward, forming an area of low pressure.

WHY IS THERE LOW AIR PRESSURE AT THE EQUATOR?

THE EQUATOR receives the greatest amount of the sun's heat, making the land very hot. This heats up the air, creating a large area of mainly low pressure. This area is known as the Intertropical Convergence Zone (ITCZ).

The warm air rising from the equator spreads, cools, and sinks around latitudes 30° north and south of the equator. A band of high pressure forms here.

WHERE ARE THE MAIN AREAS OF HIGH AND LOW PRESSURE?

SEVERAL MAJOR BANDS of high- and low-pressure areas exist in different parts of the world. Air moves from the areas of high pressure to the low-pressure areas. The movements between these areas contribute to the world's winds and weather patterns.

WHY DO SOME AIRCRAFT HAVE PRESSURIZED CABINS?

AT THE ALTITUDE at which many jet aircraft fly, the air pressure is extremely low—less than the pressure inside the human body. This makes it impossible for the body to take in air. There is also very little oxygen, so the air inside the plane has to be pressurized in order to simulate the level of air pressure on the surface.

fast facts

WHAT IS A MILLIBAR?

A millibar is the standard unit that meteorologists use to measure atmospheric pressure.

WHAT IS THE AVERAGE ATMOSPHERIC PRESSURE?

The average pressure of the atmosphere has been set as 1,013 mb (29.91 psi–pounds per square inch).

WHAT IS AN ISOBAR?

An isobar is the curving line on a weather map that links together all the areas of equal pressure.

WHO WAS EVANGELISTA TORRICELLI?

Evangelista Torricelli was the Italian scientist who invented the mercury barometer in 1643.

WHAT IS A WEATHER FRONT?

Swirling masses of high- and low-pressure air are constantly moving around the Earth. When two masses of air with different characteristics meet, they do not mix, and a boundary develops between them. This boundary is called a front. On the ground, the arrival and departure of a front is felt by sharp changes in the weather.

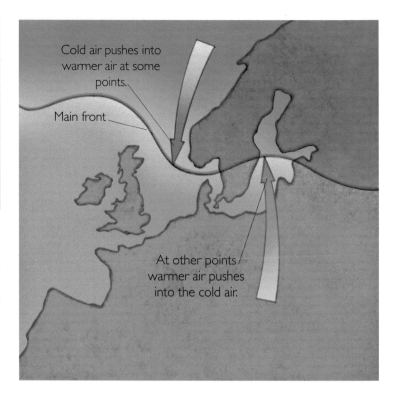

Cold air pushes into warmer air at some points.

Main front

At other points warmer air pushes into the cold air.

WHAT HAPPENS WHEN AIR MASSES MEET?

WHEN DIFFERENT air masses meet, varying pressure differences cause two things to happen. Warm air either bulges into the cold air, or the cold air pushes into the warm air. The collision causes the warm air to rise rapidly over the cold air, creating an area of low pressure called a frontal depression. The weather in this area becomes very unsettled and is worse when the differences in pressure and temperature are greatest. Depressions cover huge areas but tend to pass over in less than a day.

WHICH ARE THE MAIN AIR MASSES?

FOUR MAJOR masses of air lie over different parts of the world. The tropical maritime mass is warm and moist; the tropical continental mass is hot and dry. The polar continental mass is cold and dry, and the polar maritime mass is cold and wet. These air masses are blown around by high-level winds, and their interactions have a major influence on the world's weather. The kind of weather produced depends on the nature of the air mass–tropical masses bring warm, humid weather, and the polar masses tend to bring snow. In places where these masses meet, the weather can be extremely changeable.

TROPICAL CONTINENTAL

TROPICAL MARITIME

POLAR CONTINENTAL

POLAR MARITIME

WHAT HAPPENS UNDER A WARM FRONT?

AS ITS NAME suggests, a warm front has an area of warm, moist air behind it. The warm air rises above the cold air, and clouds are formed along the front. From the ground, the first sign that a warm front is approaching is the appearance of high, wispy cirrus clouds and maybe some light rain. When the warm front has passed, there is usually a short period of dry weather.

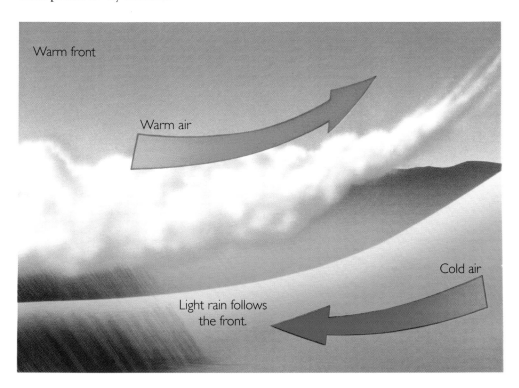

Warm front

Warm air

Cold air

Light rain follows the front.

WHAT HAPPENS UNDER A COLD FRONT?

A COLD FRONT is followed by an area of cold air. Thick, dark clouds, heavy rain, and sometimes violent storms arrive immediately. Viewed from the side, a cold front looks much steeper than a warm front. Cold air pushes beneath the warm air and rising water vapor condenses into clouds and then rain. Rain showers will often follow as the front passes over.

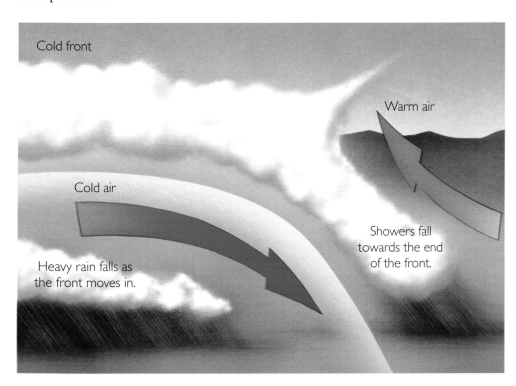

Cold front

Warm air

Cold air

Showers fall towards the end of the front.

Heavy rain falls as the front moves in.

WHAT MAKES THE WIND BLOW?

*The wind is created by differences in air pressure and temperature
—winds blow from areas of high pressure to areas of low pressure.
Rising warm air creates a low-pressure area, and the gap is filled by
high pressure produced by cooler air. The greater the
difference in pressure, the stronger the wind.*

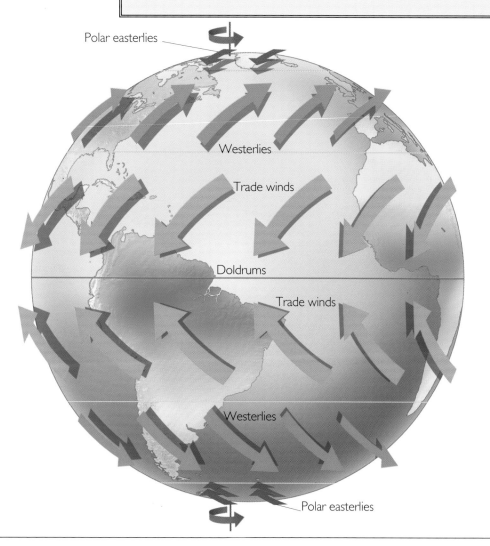

Polar easterlies

Westerlies

Trade winds

Doldrums

Trade winds

Westerlies

Polar easterlies

WHAT IS THE CORIOLIS EFFECT?

THE MOVING AIR that produces the winds tries to take the most direct route possible between the different areas of pressure. However, it is deflected by the rotating movement of the Earth. This is known as the Coriolis effect. In the Northern Hemisphere, the winds are deflected to the right of the direction in which they are headed; in the Southern Hemisphere, they are deflected to the left.

WHAT ARE PREVAILING WINDS?

PREVAILING WINDS are those that blow constantly in certain parts of the world. They are produced by hot air moving north and south from the equator and by cold air moving away from the poles. The prevailing winds are the polar easterlies, found in the extreme north and south; the westerlies, blowing between 30° and 60° north and south of the equator; and the trade winds, which blow northeast and southeast, either side of the equator.

WHAT IS THE WIND-CHILL FACTOR?

THE WIND CAN make the air temperature feel colder than it actually is. A thin layer of warm air normally surrounds your body, creating an insulating "blanket" of air. If the wind is strong, this warm air gets blown away, making you feel a lot colder. This is known as the wind-chill factor. In a breeze blowing at 5.6 mph (9 kmph), an air temperature of 32°F (0°C) will feel like 27°F (–3°C). If the breeze increases to around 9.3 mph (15 kmph), the wind-chill factor will make it feel like 14°F (–10°C).

People who live in freezing conditions wrap themselves in several layers of clothing to insulate themselves from the cold and the wind.

WHAT CREATES A SEA BREEZE?

ON A HOT and sunny day, coastal areas will experience sea breezes. The land and the sea heat up and cool down at different rates, producing moving currents of air. The land heats more quickly than the sea, producing an area of low pressure, into which the cooler sea air moves. This breeze may move in a completely different direction from the prevailing wind and can blow up to (18 miles 30 km) inland.

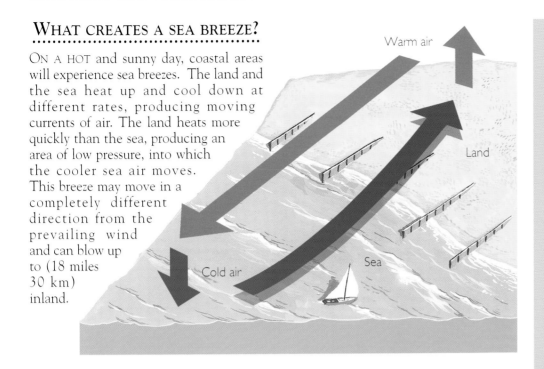

Warm air

Land

Sea

Cold air

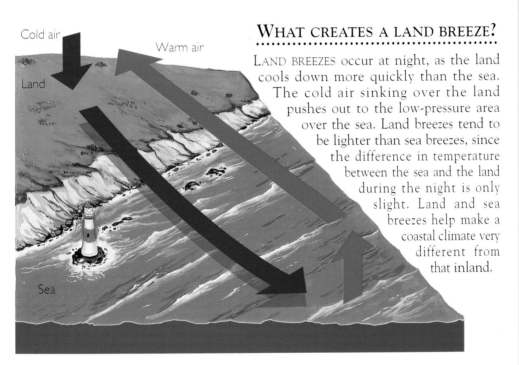

Cold air

Warm air

Land

Sea

WHAT CREATES A LAND BREEZE?

LAND BREEZES occur at night, as the land cools down more quickly than the sea. The cold air sinking over the land pushes out to the low-pressure area over the sea. Land breezes tend to be lighter than sea breezes, since the difference in temperature between the sea and the land during the night is only slight. Land and sea breezes help make a coastal climate very different from that inland.

HOW DO WINDMILLS WORK?

WINDMILLS USUALLY face into the prevailing wind, but they can also be adjusted if the wind direction changes. Some types of windmills can be completely rotated according to the wind direction; in others, the angle of the sails can be adjusted to receive the maximum amount of wind power. Some wooden sails have spring shutters that open and close according to the wind strength. If the wind gusts, the shutters open up; if it drops, they close. In this way, a constant wind force is maintained on the windmill sails.

fast facts

HOW DID THE TRADE WINDS GET THEIR NAME?

The trade winds are so called because they were the winds that powered the merchant ships that once sailed between Europe and the Americas.

WHAT ARE THE DOLDRUMS?

The doldrums are an area along the equator where the trade winds meet. There is very little wind in the doldrums, and sailing ships were often stuck there for long periods of time while they drifted toward the trade winds.

WHAT ARE LOCAL WINDS?

Local winds are those that blow in a relatively small area. Land and sea breezes are local winds, but there are some with specific names. The Mistral is a cold, northerly wind, which sometimes blows along France's Mediterranean coast. The Chinook is a southerly wind that follows the Rockies in North America.

WHAT IS A JET STREAM?

Jet streams are powerful winds that blow at about 6 miles (10 km) above the Earth's surface. Blowing at about 125 mph (200 kmph), they can stretch halfway around the world. They move major air masses and therefore have a considerable effect on the weather.

WHAT IS A WINDSOCK?

Small airports use windsocks—hollow cloth tubes—to show pilots the strength and direction of the wind. In a strong wind, a windsock fills with moving air and billows in the direction the wind is blowing toward. A limp windsock indicates that the wind is very light.

How is wind strength measured?

The strength of the wind varies between gentle breezes and destructive storms. Knowing the strength of the wind and its effects is important for the safety of people and property, particularly for those at sea. In 1805, Sir Francis Beaufort devised a scale for determining the strength of the wind by observing its effects on the environment. This is known as the Beaufort scale.

Why was the Beaufort scale devised?

THE BEAUFORT SCALE was devised for use by sailors. By observing the wind's effect on the ship's rigging and the waves, sailors would know how much sail should be carried or stowed in order for the ship to sail efficiently and safely. The 12 levels of wind strength have since been adapted for use on land.

FORCE 1
Light air. Smoke seen to drift gently in an average wind speed of 1.8 mph (3 kmph).

FORCE 2
Light breeze. Some leaves will rustle. Wind speed: 5.6 mph (9 kmph).

FORCE 3
Gentle breeze. Flags begin to flutter in a wind speed of 9.3 mph (15 kmph).

Why are some bridges closed when it is windy?

DURING HIGH WINDS, some bridges may be closed for safety reasons. The structure of the bridges is rarely in doubt, although there have been cases of bridges collapsing in strong winds. The chief concern is for the safety of the vehicles that cross the bridge, particularly high-sided trucks. Bridges in especially high positions are the most likely to be closed.

FORCE 7
Near gale. Whole trees will sway; litter baskets are blown over in a wind speed of 35 mph (56 kmph).

FORCE 8
Gale. Twigs broken off trees, and walking is difficult. Wind speed: 42 mph (68 kmph).

The Severn Bridge, which links England and Wales, is often closed to traffic when the wind gets above Forces 7 to 8. This is a good example of how the strength of the wind can disrupt everyday life.

When does the wind start to damage buildings?

DAMAGE TO BUILDINGS during a storm obviously varies according to the construction and location of the building, but damage generally occurs above Force 9 or 10. Chimney bricks and roof shingles are the parts of buildings most at risk from storm damage.

HOW DOES A KITE WORK?

KITES USE the strength of the wind to keep them in the air. Held by one or more strings, the kite deflects the force of the wind downward. The wind produces a reaction force that acts in the opposite direction of the pull to the string, supporting the kite in the air. Different designs of kites are suitable for use in different wind strengths.

Flying a kite is a fun way of using the force of a powerful wind.

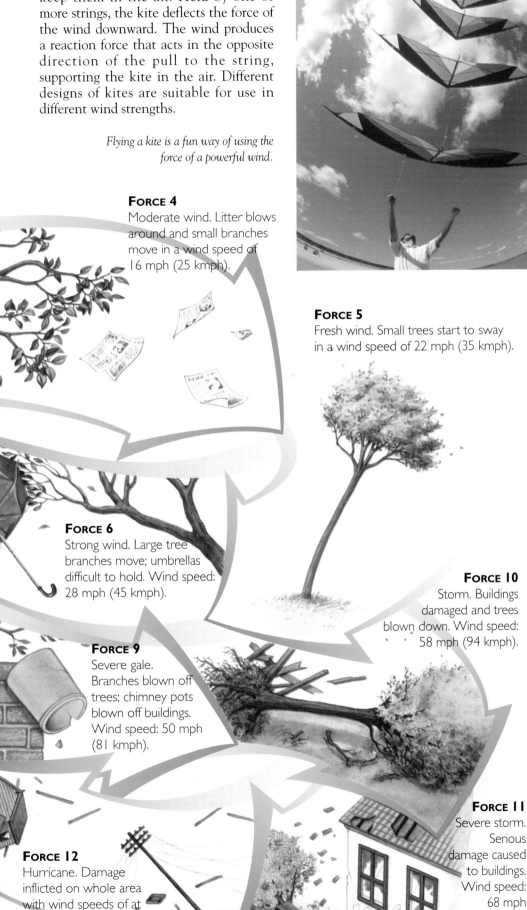

FORCE 4
Moderate wind. Litter blows around and small branches move in a wind speed of 16 mph (25 kmph).

FORCE 5
Fresh wind. Small trees start to sway in a wind speed of 22 mph (35 kmph).

FORCE 6
Strong wind. Large tree branches move; umbrellas difficult to hold. Wind speed: 28 mph (45 kmph).

FORCE 9
Severe gale. Branches blown off trees; chimney pots blown off buildings. Wind speed: 50 mph (81 kmph).

FORCE 10
Storm. Buildings damaged and trees blown down. Wind speed: 58 mph (94 kmph).

FORCE 11
Severe storm. Serious damage caused to buildings. Wind speed: 68 mph (110 kmph).

FORCE 12
Hurricane. Damage inflicted on whole area with wind speeds of at least 73 mph (118 kmph).

WHAT IS AN ANEMOMETER?

ANEMOMETERS ARE instruments that measure the speed of the wind. Some early versions had a ball attached to a swinging arm that traveled up a curved scale according to the strength of the wind. Most anemometers consist of three or more cups mounted on arms that spin around a pole. Inside the pole, a mechanism records the number of rotations in a certain period of time. The speed is usually given in miles or kilometers per hour, although marine anemometers may give the speed in knots.

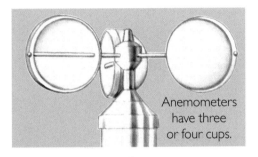

Anemometers have three or four cups.

fast facts

WHO INVENTED KITES?

The Chinese are thought to have invented kites around 500 B.C.

WHEN WERE ANEMOMETERS INVENTED?

The modern type of anemometer was invented in 1846.

WHY IS IT SO WINDY AT SEA?

Winds tend to be strongest at sea because there is nothing to break them up.

WHAT IS DEAD CALM?

No wind at all is dead calm–Force 0 on the Beaufort scale.

WHAT WAS THE STRONGEST RECORDED WIND?

The record wind speed is 231 mph (371 kmph), recorded in New Hampshire in April 1934.

WHAT IS A HURRICANE?

Hurricanes are very powerful, spiraling storms that produce winds of up to 185 mph (300 kmph). A combination of wind and torrential rain causes widespread flooding and damage to buildings. Meteorologists call hurricanes tropical cyclones, due to the nature of their movement and the areas in which they form. They are also known as typhoons and willy-willies.

Hurricanes are powerful enough to uproot trees, overturn cars, and destroy buildings.

HOW DOES A HURRICANE FORM?

HURRICANES FORM when moist air is stirred up by heat over warm oceans. It is thought that areas of very low pressure suck air into the center of the low, producing strong surface winds. The air speeds up and spirals upward, with water vapor condensing to form massive cumulonimbus clouds. Heat is generated, which makes air rise faster and faster and causes the wind speed to increase even more.

WHERE DO HURRICANES OCCUR?

HURRICANES OCCUR only in tropical areas–between latitudes of 5° and 20° north and south of the equator. Extreme temperatures and humidity provide the right conditions for a hurricane to develop. They occur when the sea temperature rises above 80°F (27°C). The southeast coast of the United States and southeast Asia see many hurricanes.

Huge rings of cumulonimbus clouds form around a hurricane's center.

Air rises rapidly at the center, forming a spiraling column.

When a hurricane hits the land, the population will be evacuated, leaving the streets deserted. Those who live in hurricane hotspots have much to fear.

WHAT HAPPENS IN THE EYE OF A HURRICANE?

IN THE CENTER of a hurricane there is a column of air 20–30 miles (30–50 km) wide. This is known as the "eye" of the hurricane. In the eye, the air is sinking slowly, and the wind is relatively light. As the eye passes over an area, the sky will clear, the rain will stop, and there will be a moment of calm. In the area immediately surrounding the eye–the eye wall–winds can reach up to 150 mph (240 kmph). Winds increase as the eye becomes narrower.

HOW ARE HURRICANES TRACKED?

METEOROLOGISTS USE satellite images to determine where and when hurricanes may develop. The movement of a hurricane is determined by a combination of high-level winds and the direction of warm ocean currents. By analyzing data and predicting the potential path of the storm, meteorologists can give people living in danger areas an early warning.

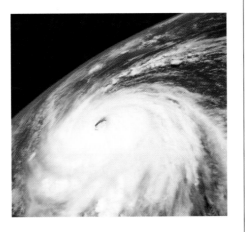

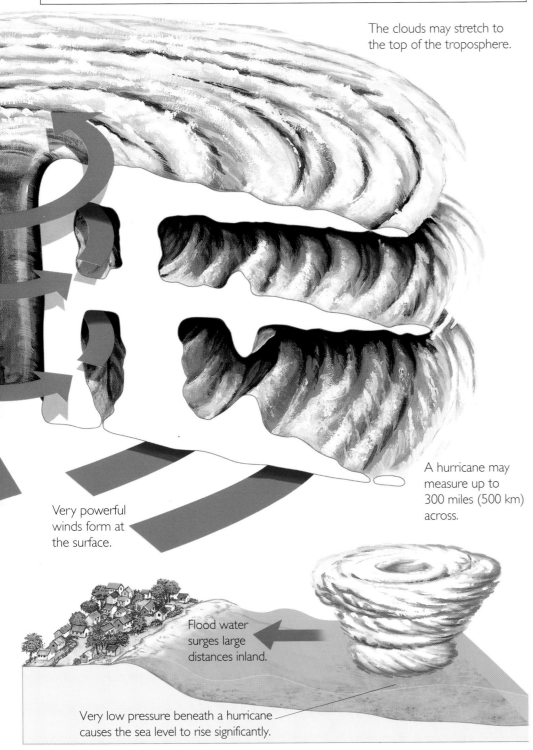

The clouds may stretch to the top of the troposphere.

A hurricane may measure up to 300 miles (500 km) across.

Very powerful winds form at the surface.

Flood water surges large distances inland.

Very low pressure beneath a hurricane causes the sea level to rise significantly.

fast facts

HOW ARE HURRICANES NAMED?

A list of alternating male and female names is produced each year. A new hurricane is simply given the next name on the list.

DO ALL HURRICANES SPIN THE SAME WAY?

Hurricanes spin counterclockwise in the Northern and clockwise in the Southern Hemisphere.

WHAT WAS HURRICANE ANDREW?

In August 1992 Hurricane Andrew caused severe damage in Florida.

WHEN DOES A STORM BECOME A HURRICANE?

A storm becomes a hurricane at a speed of 74 mph (199 kmph).

HOW ARE HURRICANES CATEGORIZED?

Hurricanes are categorized on a scale of 1 to 5 (5 is the strongest).

WHO WAS CLEMENT WRAGGE?

Clement Wragge was the first person to name hurricanes.

WHAT IS A STORM SURGE?

MUCH OF THE destruction caused by a hurricane comes from the ocean. The low pressure in the eye sucks up the ocean beneath, raising it by as much as 20 ft (6 m). At the same time, violent winds whip up waves as tall as houses. The high water level and the freak waves combine to make "storm surges"–towering walls of water that surge inland for many miles, sweeping away buildings, trees, and anything in their path.

WHAT IS A TORNADO?

Violent thunderstorms can often give birth to powerful funnels of wind called tornadoes. The wind in these funnels can reach speeds of over 300 mph (500 kmph). When they come into contact with the ground, tornadoes can pick up vast amounts of dust and debris. Rising air within the funnel sucks objects upward, uprooting trees and destroying houses.

HOW MUCH DAMAGE CAN A TORNADO CAUSE?

SEVEN-TENTHS OF TORNADOES are labeled as "weak" tornadoes because they do not cause much damage. The remaining three-tenths are devastating. At its strongest, a tornado can level a well-built house and suck a fully laden tractor-trailer into the air.

WHEN WAS THE MOST DEVASTATING TORNADO?

IN 1925 A TORNADO carved a path of destruction through the states of Indiana, Missouri, and Illinois, killing 689 people.

WHERE ARE TORNADOES MOST COMMON?

TORNADOES are most common in the United States. Although every state has been hit by a tornado at some time, they occur most frequently in the large, central plains of Missouri, Kansas, and Texas. As a result, this part of the country has been nicknamed "tornado alley."

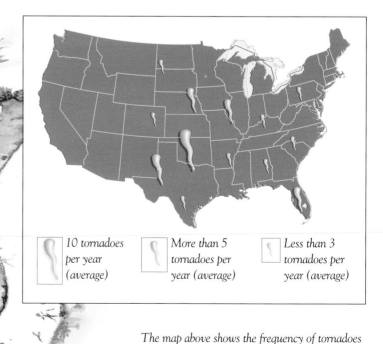

	10 tornadoes per year (average)		More than 5 tornadoes per year (average)		Less than 3 tornadoes per year (average)

The map above shows the frequency of tornadoes in affected areas of the United States.

How are tornadoes graded?

The Fujita Tornado Intensity Scale is used to grade how powerful a tornado is, based on the amount of damage it does. The F (for Fujita) scale uses numbers from 0 to 5. An F0 tornado has winds of less than 72 mph (115 kmph) and does little damage. An F5 tornado has wind speeds greater than 261 mph (418 kmph) and can be devastating to anything nearby.

F1: Minor damage to homes; vehicles overturned.

F2: Large trees are uprooted by the storm.

F3: Major structural damage to buildings.

F5: Total destruction of nearby buildings.

Cold, dry air

A twisting column of air stretches from the ground to the storm clouds above.

Warm, moist air

Do tornadoes just occur over land?

A WATERSPOUT is literally a tornado over water. It may look like a waterfall rising from the water surface as condensed water vapor is pulled into the updraft. Waterspouts are very rarely as powerful as tornadoes, but wind speeds of over 250 mph (400 kmph) can make them a severe hazard to nearby boats.

How does a tornado form?

A TORNADO FORMS in the same way as the funnel created when water drains out of a sink or bathtub. A whirlpool, or vortex, forms when water drains from a sink because of the downdraft created by the hole. Water is pulled downward and begins to rotate. The faster the water rotates, the more powerful the vortex becomes. In a tornado, the same process happens with air. Large thunderstorms are formed by hot air rising from the ground, called an updraft. If an updraft is strong enough, a vortex of air forms beneath the cloud, gradually stretching downward until it touches the ground.

WHAT CAUSES A THUNDERSTORM?

Thunderstorms develop when the weather is very hot and humid. Warm, wet air rises and then cools very quickly to produce thunder-clouds. Inside the clouds, the violent movement of air causes the water droplets and ice to bump against one another, knocking charged electrons from the ice, producing a buildup of static electrical charge. The huge amount of energy is released in the form of thunder and lightning.

Lighter, positively charged particles in the upper part of the cloud

WHAT IS THUNDER?

THE SOUND OF thunder is produced when a strike of lightning produces a huge amount of heat. Heated to a temperature of around 54,000°F (30,000°C), the air around the lightning expands very quickly–faster than the speed of sound. This rapid expansion of air causes the crashing thunder sound.

HOW DOES LIGHTNING STRIKE?

LIGHTNING STRIKES the ground because opposite charges of static build up within the cloud. A positive charge builds up at the top of the cloud, while a negative charge builds up at the bottom. The ground becomes positively charged, and lightning flashes between the cloud and the ground to discharge its electrical charge.

Negatively charged particles at the bottom of the cloud

WHAT DOES A LIGHTNING ROD DO?

THE POWER contained within a stroke of lightning can easily damage buildings and start fires. To avoid this, many tall buildings are fitted with a lightning rod. When lightning strikes the conductor, the electricity travels along the metal strip, which extends from a point above the building all the way to the ground.

The ground is positively charged by the negative charge on the underside of the cloud.

WHAT IS THE DIFFERENCE BETWEEN FORKED AND SHEET LIGHTNING?

ALL FORMS OF LIGHTNING are produced when an electrical charge passes between positively and negatively charged areas. In forked lightning, an initial stroke (known as a leader) travels to the ground at a speed of around 62 miles per second (100 km per second), creating a path of electrically charged air. A return stroke that travels immediately back along the path is what we see. Lightning also flashes between points within the cloud itself and between the cloud and the air, lighting up the sky. If the flash of lightning is hidden by cloud cover, it appears to make the cloud glow. This is called sheet lightning.

Forked lightning takes the quickest path from the underside of the cloud to a point on the ground.

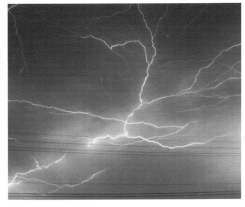

Lightning that discharges within the air and does not reach the ground is sometimes called sheet lightning.

WHERE IS THE SAFEST PLACE TO BE IN A THUNDERSTORM?

BECAUSE LIGHTNING seeks out the quickest route to the ground, you should not take shelter close to an isolated tall point, such as a tree, if you are out in the open during a thunderstorm. The inside of a car is one of the safest places to take shelter, because if the car is struck, the electricity is conducted to the ground over the surface of the car. Of course, a secure building is the safest place to be during a storm.

Zeus was the most powerful of the Greek gods. He is often shown hurling thunderbolts on the world below.

HOW DID EARLY PEOPLE EXPLAIN THE POWER OF THUNDERSTORMS?

LIKE MANY THINGS in the natural world, thunder had a mythological and spiritual significance for some early peoples, who endowed their gods with the power of many natural forces. The Greeks attributed the might of storms to Zeus, the king of the gods. When angry, he would smite the world below with his thunderbolts. In early Scandinavian mythology, the god Thor had some of the same attributes, being the god of the sky and controller of storms, lightning, rain, and thunder. Farmers prayed to Thor for plentiful harvests and good weather.

fast facts

CAN I FIGURE OUT HOW FAR AWAY A THUNDERSTORM IS?

It is possible to calculate how far a thunderstorm is from you by counting the time between seeing the lightning and hearing the thunder. The storm will be around 1 mile away for every 5 seconds, or 1 kilometer away for every 3-second interval.

WHAT ARE THE CHANCES OF BEING STRUCK BY LIGHTNING?

The chance of being struck by lightning has been calculated at around 1 in 700,000.

WHAT ARE FULGURITES?

A fulgurite is an area of soil that has been baked into a shape after being struck by lightning.

HOW BIG IS THE AVERAGE THUNDERSTORM?

Thunderstorms can reach up to 10 miles (16 km) across, and their clouds can stretch for up to 7 miles (11 km) into the atmosphere.

HOW FAST DOES A THUNDERSTORM TRAVEL?

The speed at which they travel will depend on local conditions, but it is estimated that thunderstorms travel at an average speed of 25 mph (40 kmph).

HOW HOT IS LIGHTNING?

Lightning can reach temperatures of around 50,000°F (28,000°C).

HOW LONG IS A LIGHTNING FLASH?

Lightning flashes can measure up to 20 miles (32 km) long. Long flashes occur in very flat areas when the clouds are particularly high.

WHAT DO DIFFERENT TYPES OF CLOUDS INDICATE?

Clouds are named according to their shape, height, and size. They are usually associated with rain, snow, sleet, or hail, but not all clouds mean that bad weather is on the way. Dark, angry-looking clouds usually bring wet and windy weather, but a sky full of fluffy white clouds on a warm and sunny day usually means that the weather will stay that way.

Cirrus clouds

Cirrus clouds that form into an almost transparent layer high in the sky are called cirrostratus clouds. Wet weather often follows.

A combination of cirrus and cumulus are called cirrocumulus clouds. They are rows of icy particles and indicate a period of unsettled weather.

WHAT ARE CIRRUS CLOUDS?

CIRRUS CLOUDS form at heights above 20,000 feet (6,000 m). At this altitude, it is so cold that the water inside the clouds is frozen into crystals of ice. They have a feathery, wispy appearance and are sometimes called "mares'-tails." A large number of cirrus clouds will occasionally form a complete layer of white cloud.

A thin, watery sheet of gray cloud is called altostratus cloud. Rain often follows its appearance.

Cumulonimbus clouds are huge, flat-topped clouds that often bring heavy storms, rain, and thunder. Because of their shape, they are sometimes called anvil clouds and may stretch to great heights.

Altocumulus clouds are small, flattened cumulus clouds, gray or white in color. They may appear after a long period of hot weather, before a thunderstorm.

Cumulus clouds

Stratocumulus clouds are formed from a sheet of cumulus clouds that almost join together. They are probably the most common type of cloud.

WHAT ARE STRATUS CLOUDS?

STRATUS CLOUDS form at the lowest levels of the cloud layer–around 1,600 feet (500 m). They form in layers that can build up across the whole sky. Stratus clouds produce light rain and drizzle and, in hilly areas, often produce wet fog and mist over the ground.

WHAT ARE CUMULUS CLOUDS?

CUMULUS CLOUDS form at different heights, although they are most often seen in the middle of the cloud layer. Fluffy in appearance, cumulus clouds are often gray on the bottom and a very bright white at the top. Sometimes known as cauliflower clouds, they are usually seen on dry, sunny days.

Nimbostratus clouds are very thick and gray. They bring rain or snow and block out the sun completely.

Stratus clouds

HOW DO CLOUDS FORM?

THE AIR CONTAINS millions of microscopic dust particles, which absorb water from rivers, lakes, and oceans. This happens when the water is heated. The heat turns the water into an invisible gas called vapor–a process called evaporation. When the warm, moist air cools down, it condenses (turns back into a liquid) on the surface of the dust particles. When the tiny droplets of water group together, a cloud forms. Clouds can be formed in several different ways, such as by warm air rising up through thermals, or when warm air is forced over hills and mountains. They can also be formed when two air masses meet and the cold air pushes under the warm air, forcing it up.

Warm air cools and water vapor condenses to form convective clouds.

As air at the surface is heated, it expands and rises.

Clouds form when warm air rises above a heated part of the Earth's surface.

Clouds form over the hills.

Warm air cools down as it is forced over hills and mountains.

Clouds form when warm air is forced over high areas.

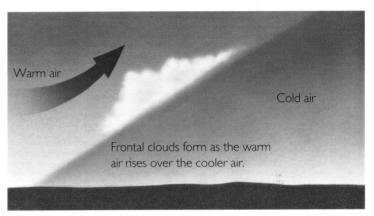

Warm air

Cold air

Frontal clouds form as the warm air rises over the cooler air.

Clouds form when two air masses meet.

HOW IS CLOUD COVER MEASURED?

METEOROLOGISTS MEASURE cloud cover in oktas–the number of oktas indicates how much of the sky is covered with cloud. On a scale of 0 to 8, 0 oktas means that there are no clouds; 8 oktas means the sky is completely covered.

This scene shows a cloud cover of about 4 oktas, meaning that four-eighths (half) of the sky is covered.

A sky almost completely covered in cloud measures about 7 on the okta scale.

WHAT ARE CONTRAILS?

AIRCRAFT FLYING at high altitudes leave a white trail behind them when the air is very cold. These trails are caused by the exhaust gases that are expelled by the aircraft's engines. The gases contain a large amount of water vapor, which condenses and freezes in the cold, high-altitude air, leaving behind cloudlike trails called contrails.

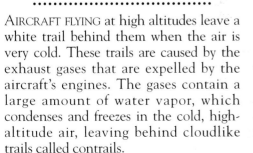

fast facts

WHO CLASSIFIED CLOUDS?

Amateur meteorologist Luke Howard classified clouds in 1803.

HOW MANY TYPES OF CLOUD ARE THERE?

There are many different clouds, but only ten are officially classified.

WHAT DO THE NAMES MEAN?

Cumulus means "heaped," cirrus means "feathered," and stratus means "layered." Nimbus is Latin for "rain."

HOW IS A CLOUD'S HEIGHT MEASURED?

By reflecting a laser beam off the underside of the cloud to a receiver on the ground, it is possible to calculate the cloud's height.

HOW DOES RAIN FORM?

Rain can form in two ways. In tropical areas, where temperatures are warm, tiny water droplets in the clouds join together to form raindrops that are heavy enough to fall from the clouds. Elsewhere, rain starts life as snow in the freezing temperatures of the high clouds. As the snow falls and gets closer to the ground, it will turn to rain if the temperature is above freezing.

Melting snowflakes form rain.

Raindrops are made up of millions of tiny particles of water vapor.

Tiny water droplets join together, or coalesce, to form raindrops.

WHEN WAS THE UMBRELLA INVENTED?

UMBRELLAS HAVE been used for over 1,000 years, and it is thought that they probably originated in China. Early umbrellas were made of paper and bamboo and waterproofed with varnish.

WHEN DOES "LIGHT" RAIN BECOME "HEAVY" RAIN?

IF LESS THAN 1/48 inch (0.5 mm) of rain falls in an hour, meteorologists describe it as light. When over 1/6 inch (4 mm) falls, the rain is described as heavy. The heaviest rainfall occurs in the tropical and monsoon regions of the world. In other areas, periods of heavy rain rarely last longer than an hour.

HOW DOES RAINFALL VARY AROUND THE WORLD?

TROPICAL AREAS experience a lot of rain because high temperatures cause a large amount of water to evaporate from the sea to make clouds. Coastal areas of the world tend to experience more rainfall than those inland. One side of a mountain range may be drier than the other, because the mountains block the winds that bring the rain. These and other factors account for the varying amounts of rainfall around the world.

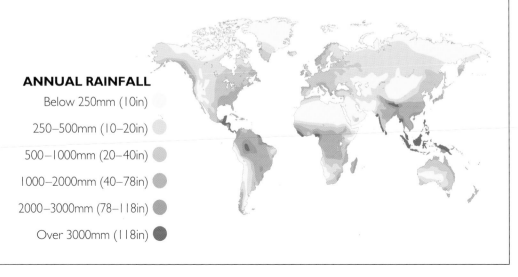

ANNUAL RAINFALL

Below 250mm (10in)

250–500mm (10–20in)

500–1000mm (20–40in)

1000–2000mm (40–78in)

2000–3000mm (78–118in)

Over 3000mm (118in)

WHAT CAUSES A DROUGHT?

A DROUGHT occurs when there is less than 1/100 inch (0.2 mm) of rainfall in an area over a period of about two weeks. Droughts are usually caused by an area of high pressure that stays in one place for a long period of time. This is called a blocking high. The blocking high prevents the movement of low-pressure systems into an area, meaning that hot, dry weather will dominate that area, leading to a drought. Parts of Africa, Asia, and Central America often experience periods of drought.

This pink flower is growing in Death Valley, California—one of the hottest and driest areas of the world.

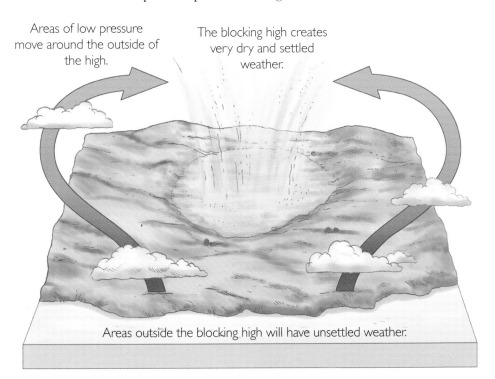

Areas of low pressure move around the outside of the high.

The blocking high creates very dry and settled weather.

Areas outside the blocking high will have unsettled weather.

HOW DO FLOWERS GROW IN A DESERT?

DESERT REGIONS experience very little rainfall, but flowers may still bloom after the rains come. Some flower seeds survive in the desert soil for years, suddenly coming into bloom at the first sign of rain. These flowers will grow long enough to produce seeds, so that the cycle can continue.

WHY DO FLOODS OFTEN FOLLOW A DROUGHT?

AN AREA that has experienced a very long period of hot, dry weather or drought may suffer a flood if heavy rain follows. This is because the soil will have become baked so hard and dry that the water produced by very heavy rainfall will not be able to drain away. This is sometimes called a flash flood.

Flash floods can occur when heavy rainfall immediately follows a prolonged dry period.

HOW IS RAINFALL MEASURED?

RAINFALL IS usually measured in millimeters or inches. Rainwater is collected in a metal drum about 20 inches (50 cm) tall called a rain gauge. The rain gauge is placed on the ground, just high enough to avoid splashes. The rainwater collects in a funnel at the top and passes into the drum.

Rain gauges are used by weather stations to measure rainfall. They are placed in clear, open spaces.

fast facts

WHY IS IT SAID TO RAIN "CATS AND DOGS"?

The old English saying "raining cats and dogs" may be based on the ancient Chinese spirits of wind and rain—a cat and a dog.

WHAT WAS THE DUST BOWL?

The Dust Bowl was a large area of farmland in North America that suffered severe drought in the 1930s.

WHAT SHAPE ARE RAINDROPS?

Raindrops are shaped like a flattened ball, rather than a teardrop.

CAN YOU "SMELL" RAIN?

After a dry period, moisture in the air can release oils trapped in the soil. These give off smells that are associated with rain.

HOW DOES SNOW FORM?

Snow forms in clouds when the temperature is within the range −4°F to −40°F (−20°C to −40°C). Ice crystals in the clouds begin to melt and join together with supercooled water droplets. They then freeze together and form snowflakes, which, provided the air temperature is low enough, fall from the clouds. The process of forming snowflakes is called accretion.

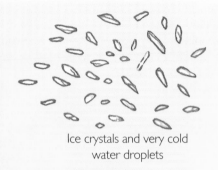

Ice crystals and very cold water droplets

WHAT IS SLEET?

SLEET IS usually snow that has half-melted, or it can be formed from raindrops that have partly evaporated and then cooled down as they fall to the ground. It often feels like very cold, wet rain when it falls on you.

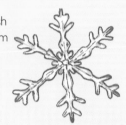

Ice crystals crash together to form snowflakes.

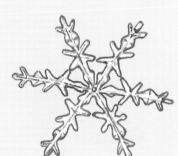

All snowflakes have a six-sided pattern.

ARE ALL SNOWFLAKES THE SAME SHAPE?

THERE ARE thought to be about 80 different varieties of snowflakes, which form into shapes ranging from needles and columns to stars, prisms, plates, and hexagons. All snowflakes have a symmetrical, six-sided pattern, but no two snowflakes have been found with exactly the same shape. Scientists think the shape of a snowflake depends on the height and temperature at which it was formed.

Stars

Plates

Needles

IS ALL SNOW THE SAME?

SNOW IS OFTEN described as being "dry" or "wet." The snowflakes that make wet snow are relatively large and form when the temperature is at or around freezing. Wet snow packs together easily when it falls and is the best snow for making snowmen and snowballs. Dry snow is formed at lower temperatures, and the snowflakes are smaller than those that make wet snow. It is referred to as "powder" by skiers and snowboarders and is the best kind of snow for winter sports enthusiasts. It is lighter and much easier to clear away.

Wet snow is the easiest type to form into shapes and is ideal for making snowmen.

Dry snow is much better for skiing.

HOW DOES HAIL FORM?

HAILSTONES ARE essentially frozen raindrops. They are made inside very tall cumulonimbus clouds that have great differences in temperature between the top and bottom. Freezing temperatures at the top and warmer temperatures at the bottom of the cloud create very strong upward and downward currents of air. Ice crystals and supercooled water droplets are thrown around by these currents and collide with each other. As they do so, they are coated with more and more layers of ice. The layers of ice build up until the hailstones are heavy enough to fall to the ground.

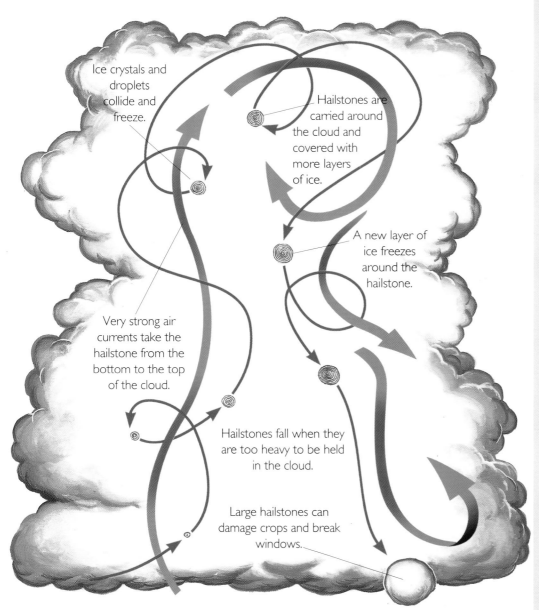

Ice crystals and droplets collide and freeze.

Hailstones are carried around the cloud and covered with more layers of ice.

A new layer of ice freezes around the hailstone.

Very strong air currents take the hailstone from the bottom to the top of the cloud.

Hailstones fall when they are too heavy to be held in the cloud.

Large hailstones can damage crops and break windows.

WHAT DOES THE INSIDE OF A HAILSTONE LOOK LIKE?

IF YOU were to cut through a hailstone, you would see that it is made up of several layers of ice and frost. Each layer is produced by one journey up and down the height of the cloud. The greater the amount of turbulence inside the cloud, the greater the number of layers and the bigger the hailstones.

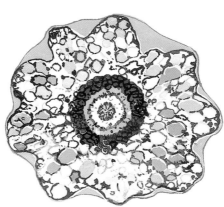

A cross-section of a hailstone shows that it is made up of layers, much like an onion.

WHEN DOES FROST FORM?

Frost most often forms over the land when the air remains clear after a cold winter day. The ground loses its heat more quickly than the air above it, and if the temperature falls below freezing, any moisture in the air freezes, covering almost any surface with frost. Different conditions can produce different types of frost.

WHAT IS HOARFROST?

HOARFROST is the most common type of frost. It covers every exposed surface with layers of crunchy ice crystals. In certain conditions, the ground may be covered with a very thick layer of white hoarfrost, which looks like snow.

If there is not enough moisture in the air, the ground may freeze without a white covering.

Frost will cover any freezing-cold surface.

WHY IS IT DANGEROUS TO WALK OR SKATE ON FROZEN WATER?

RIVERS AND LAKES can become frozen over if the temperatures get very low. This will usually depend on the depth of the water–the shallower it is, the more likely it is to freeze over. A layer of ice forms on the surface that is strongest and thickest nearest the banks. There will be weaker spots further out, making it very dangerous to walk or skate on the ice–anyone falling in could easily become trapped in the freezing water.

Before skating or walking on a frozen lake or river, make certain the ice is thick enough to be safe.

HOW DO ICICLES FORM?

ICICLES USUALLY form when the water from thawed ice and snow freezes again. This happens during a bright winter day when sunny areas are warm, but shaded areas remain below freezing, or when a cold night follows a warmer day. When the melt-water drips over the edge of a surface, the drops freeze to form an icicle.

Icicles get longer as more water runs over them and turns to ice.

WHAT IS RIME?

RIME FROST forms on leaves, branches, and other solid objects when an icy wind freezes water droplets over them. It forms a solid white crust on the windward side of objects and can damage buildings and other structures if it is allowed to build up. Rime is usually found in very cold, exposed areas.

CAN ICICLES FORM UPSIDE DOWN?

IT IS POSSIBLE for a type of icicle to form upside down. This happens in small, shallow pools of water–ornamental bird baths, for example. When the water freezes, it expands and forms a dome of ice in the center. A crack in the dome will allow water out, which then freezes. As this happens over time, an "ice spike" will form.

Water freezes and forms into a dome shape.

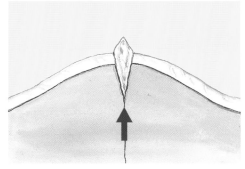

A crack forms in the dome and water expands through it.

As water continues to flow through the gap, it freezes and forms "upside-down" icicles.

WHAT IS FERN FROST?

FROST CAN sometimes create beautiful patterns on the inside of windows. The delicate shapes, called fern frost because they resemble fern plants, form when water vapor condenses into tiny droplets on the windowpane. Ice crystals form, making water freeze on the sharp points of the ice crystals, creating a chain reaction that creates the patterns.

WHAT IS DEW?

DEW IS condensed water vapor, which forms when air comes into contact with a cold surface. It forms on clear, still nights, but it is especially noticeable after a night of fog, when there is a lot of water vapor in the air close to the ground. Dew will appear as water droplets on any cold surface.

Dew drops form on the petals and leaves of outdoor plants and flowers.

Tiny droplets of morning dew clinging to spider's webs are a common sight.

WHAT IS HUMIDITY?

The air absorbs water from oceans, rivers, and lakes, and also from trees and plants. Humidity describes the amount of water vapor the air contains. The warmer the weather, the more moisture the air can hold. The air can reach a point of saturation, where it is no longer able to absorb any more water—this is 100% humidity. In such conditions, water vapor condenses to form mist, clouds, and rain.

In very high humidity, there is a lot of water in the atmosphere.

Rainforests are very high in humidity—this is why so many plants and animals thrive in them.

WHICH PARTS OF THE WORLD HAVE HIGH HUMIDITY?

HUMIDITY IS highest in tropical areas, where the climate is warm. A continuous cycle of water movement exists, where water evaporates from the ocean into the air and falls again in heavy rainfall. The conditions are ideal for plants and other forms of life—the plants themselves put more moisture into the atmosphere.

WHY IS EXERCISE SO DIFFICULT IN HIGH HUMIDITY?

PHYSICAL EXERCISE is difficult in a humid atmosphere if you are not used to it. This is because sweat cannot evaporate into the air properly, making it very difficult for the body to cool down. Athletes and other sports players sometimes train in humid conditions to prepare themselves for competition in such an environment.

Strenuous exercise is very difficult in humid conditions.

WHICH PARTS OF THE WORLD HAVE LOW HUMIDITY?

DESERT REGIONS have very low levels of humidity–often less than 10%. The low levels of water vapor in the air, and the overall scarcity of water, make conditions for life very difficult. Agriculture is practically impossible in such areas and is only really successful in places where humidity levels are generally moderate.

Levels of humidity are very low in desert regions, making conditions for life very harsh.

WHAT IS RELATIVE HUMIDITY?

TO MEASURE HUMIDITY accurately, meteorologists look at relative humidity. This is the amount of water in the air, relative to the maximum amount of water it can hold at that temperature. To measure relative humidity, a wet and a dry thermometer is used. The wet bulb is covered with wet muslin. The water in the muslin evaporates, making the temperature around the wet bulb cooler than that around the dry bulb. The amount of water that evaporates increases along with the dryness of the air–the greater the difference in temperature, the lower the humidity. A smaller difference means higher humidity. The thermometers are housed in a Stevenson screen, to shade them from the sun.

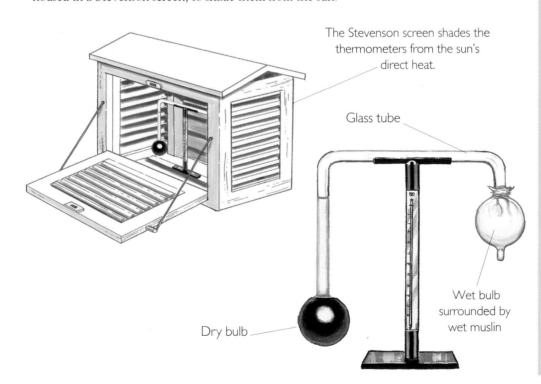

The Stevenson screen shades the thermometers from the sun's direct heat.

Glass tube

Dry bulb

Wet bulb surrounded by wet muslin

WHAT IS A HAIR HYGROMETER?

ONE OF THE simplest ways to measure humidity is to use a hair hygrometer. This uses a piece of human hair, which stretches or contracts according to the amount of water in the air. In a weather house–a type of hair hygrometer–a hair attached to a turntable stretches and contracts, making the man appear in humid conditions and the woman appear when it is drier.

The man is outside the house when humidity is high.

The woman is outside the house when humidity is low.

HOW DOES FOG FORM?

Fog is cloud that forms close to the ground. It appears when the wind is light, the air is damp, and the sky is relatively clear. It often forms when moisture in the air close to the ground condenses and spreads upward—this is called radiation fog. It is most common at the beginning or end of the day, when the ground cools down quickly.

Water vapor condenses to form fog

Cooler surfaces

Warmer air

Cooler surfaces

WHAT IS THE DIFFERENCE BETWEEN FOG AND MIST?

THE DIFFERENCE between fog and mist is defined according to the density of the cloud. If the visibility through the cloud is less than 0.6 miles (1 km), it is described as fog. If it is between 0.6 and 1.25 miles (1–2 km), it is called mist.

The city of San Francisco regularly experiences summer fog, as shown in this picture of its most famous landmark, the Golden Gate Bridge. The fog is created when a cold-water current in the Pacific meets the warm air of the land. It often takes a long time to clear.

WHAT IS ADVECTION FOG?

ADVECTION FOG forms when warm, moist air blows over a cold expanse of water, such as a river or ocean. The fog forms a layer just above the water and is held in place by warm air above the fog. The fog will only blow inland if the land is low-lying, and when it does, it usually evaporates quickly.

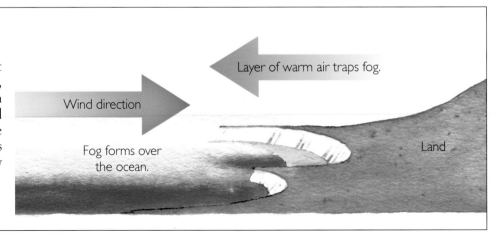

Layer of warm air traps fog.

Wind direction

Fog forms over the ocean.

Land

WHY IS DRIVING IN FOG SO DANGEROUS?

THE LOW VISIBILITY that dense fog brings makes driving very hazardous. Low speeds and greater distances between vehicles need to be maintained, while headlights should be on low beam at all times. Using them on high beam makes the light reflect off the fog, dazzling both the driver and other road users.

Headlights must be on low beam in fog.

Rear fog lights shine through the fog.

WHAT IS SPECIAL ABOUT FOG LIGHTS?

REAR FOG lights use high-intensity bulbs filled with a special gas such as halogen. The light they produce is more intense than that of ordinary headlights.

HOW DO SHIPS NAVIGATE IN FOG?

LIGHTHOUSES AND LIGHTSHIPS are used to warn sailors of hazards at sea, but their effectiveness is reduced during dense fog. The beams will be less visible, and it is difficult to judge the actual position of the hazard. In fog, audible warnings–foghorns–are sounded, and most modern ships use sophisticated radar systems to detect hazards and other shipping in the area nearby.

WHAT IS ICEBERG FOG?

FOG OFTEN forms around icebergs when the air surrounding them is very cold but the water is fairly warm. As the water evaporates, it condenses when it meets the cold air. It is thought that the ocean liner *Titanic*, which sank on its maiden voyage when it struck an iceberg in 1912, may have been in an area where icebergs were hidden from view by the dense fog surrounding them.

fast facts

WHAT IS A "PEA-SOUPER"?

During the late 19th and early 20th centuries, London, England, used to experience lots of heavy smogs caused by the burning of coal in homes and industries. The yellow-colored smog caused respiratory problems, cut down visibility, and was often described as being as "thick as pea soup," hence the nickname "pea-souper."

WHAT IS FOG STRATUS?

Sometimes, a layer of fog can be seen with clear air above and below it. This occurs when the sun's rays pass through the fog, heat the ground, and make the bottom of the fog evaporate. The layer that remains is called fog stratus.

HOW DOES A FOG MACHINE WORK?

Fog is produced artificially for special effects in theaters and sometimes in nightclubs. It is made using machines that heat a mixture of an oil-based substance and water, which is then blown into the air. A similar effect is achieved using "dry ice"–made by dissolving frozen carbon dioxide in hot water.

WHY DOES MIST OFTEN FORM IN VALLEYS?

Mist often forms early in the morning in wooded valley areas. Higher up the valley slopes, the temperatures tend to be higher, making moisture on the trees condense to form low-lying mist. The mist gradually evaporates as the sun warms the ground.

WHAT IS FREEZING FOG?

When fog forms and the temperature drops dramatically soon afterward, the droplets of water vapor become larger, producing "freezing fog." Visibility is greatly reduced in freezing fog.

WHEN DOES A RAINBOW APPEAR?

A rainbow appears when sunlight shines through raindrops. When the light passes through the raindrops at certain angles, the "white" light is split, or refracted into the seven colors of the light spectrum. The best time to see a rainbow is early morning or late evening, when the sun is low in the sky. You will see a rainbow only when the sun is shining behind you and it is raining in front of you.

The colors are always seen
in the same order.

The colors red, orange, yellow,
green, blue, indigo, and violet
are seen in a rainbow.

*From an aircraft, you may
see a rainbow as a full circle.*

HOW DOES A RAINDROP SPLIT LIGHT?

RAINDROPS ACT like tiny prisms–splitting white light into all the colors of the spectrum. As light rays pass through the raindrop, they are refracted, causing them to split into different colors. The rays bounce off the back of the raindrop and pass out, divided into all the colors seen in the rainbow.

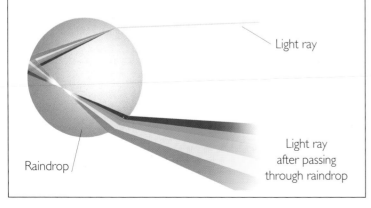

Light ray

Raindrop

Light ray
after passing
through raindrop

WHAT MAKES A SECOND RAINBOW APPEAR?

A SECOND, fainter rainbow can sometimes be seen a little higher than the main rainbow. It is made by light being reflected twice on the surface of each raindrop. The colors are seen in reverse order, with red at the bottom of the bow. A slight loss of sunlight with each reflection makes the second bow appear fainter.

CAN AURORAS BE SEEN FROM SPACE?

THE SPECTACULAR LIGHT shows known as auroras are seen in the skies above Arctic and Antarctic regions. They are caused by electrically charged particles from the sun colliding with the Earth's magnetic field and atmosphere. The green, pink, and blue lights produce a dazzling display when seen from space. From such a view, the aurora is seen from the beginning of its formation–from the point the particles first make contact with the atmosphere.

Seen from the window of a Space Shuttle, an aurora seems to radiate from the Earth. Of course, the opposite is true–the source of the aurora is the sun.

HOW DO HALOS FORM AROUND THE MOON?

IN CERTAIN conditions, a bright moon may appear to be surrounded by glowing "halos" of light. This happens when moonlight (sunlight reflected by the moon) passes through ice crystals high in the atmosphere. The light is reflected at certain angles to produce one or two halos. They are usually incomplete, and they are most often seen when the moon is at its fullest.

IS THERE EVER A BLUE MOON?

"ONCE IN A BLUE MOON" is a phrase that suggests a rare or unlikely occurrence. However, certain atmospheric conditions can cause the moon to appear to change color. A blue moon has been reported in periods following massive volcanic eruptions. The dust in the atmosphere makes the moon look blue.

During a lunar eclipse, when the Earth casts a shadow on the moon, it may appear red, as the sun's rays are bent around the Earth.

fast facts

WHAT IS A BROCKEN BOW?

In mountain areas, the sun sometimes casts an eerie shadow called a "Brocken bow" or "Brocken specter" onto mist and clouds.

WHAT IS ST. ELMO'S FIRE?

Sailors used to report seeing a glowing electrical discharge on the masts of ships during storms. It was known as St. Elmo's fire.

WHAT IS A MOONBOW?

Occasionally, raindrops refract bright moonlight, creating a moonbow.

WHAT IS AN ICEBOW?

An icebow is a rainbow produced by ice particles in very cold air.

WHAT IS A SUNDOG?

Ice crystals can sometimes bend the sun's light, creating the illusion of a second sun, called a "sundog."

WHAT COLOR IS A SUNDOG?

Sundogs can appear in any color from white to red.

WHAT IS EL NIÑO?

El Niño is a Pacific Ocean current that causes freak weather occurrences around the world. Scientists have noticed that every five to seven years, prevailing winds in the Pacific occasionally change direction, driving warm water east toward South America. This tends to start in January–during the Southern Hemisphere's summer. The effect has been known to occur for centuries, but it is only since the 1970s that scientists have understood El Niño and the way it upsets the world's climate.

WHAT DOES EL NIÑO MEAN?

EL NIÑO is Spanish for "boy child"–a reference to Jesus. It was named in the 17th century by Spanish-speaking fishermen who lived in Peru, South America. It was given this name because the unusual weather associated with El Niño began around Christmas.

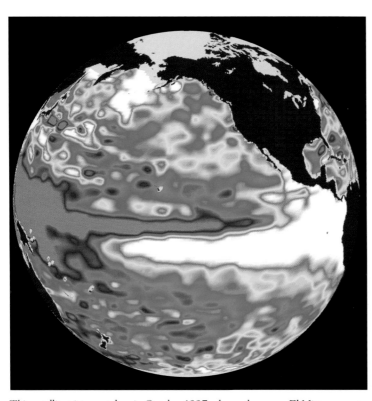

This satellite picture, taken in October 1997, shows the warm El Niño current as a white/red gash extending across the Pacific to the coast of South America.

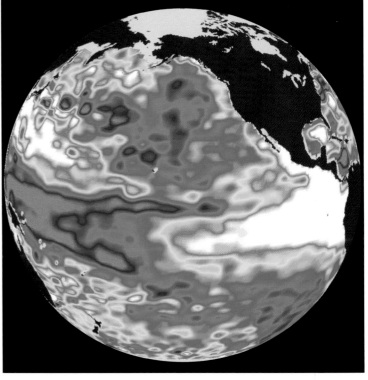

By January of the following year, this picture shows that El Niño had retreated slightly. However, the Pacific waters remained unusually warm.

WHAT ARE THE EFFECTS OF EL NIÑO?

IN AN EL NIÑO year, weather systems around the world become very unpredictable. This is most noticeable in the Pacific region. In the El Niño of 1997–98, massive floods caused widespread devastation in many parts of South America, making many thousands of people homeless. It also triggered a hurricane, bringing torrential rain to the deserts of California and Nevada. In the west of the region, El Niño brings hot, dry weather in what ought to be a rainy season. In the past, this has caused forest fires in Australia and Indonesia.

During an El Niño year, the waters off the coast of California are much warmer than usual, causing massive storms. Some have produced giant waves that have washed away entire beaches.

The El Niño of 1982 caused some of the most widespread and devastating drought conditions for hundreds of years. In South Africa, the drought virtually wiped out that year's grain crop.

HOW CAN IT RAIN FROGS AND FISH?

THERE HAVE been numerous reports of frogs, fish, and other animals falling from the sky during heavy thunderstorms. One possible explanation for this unusual phenomenon is that the unfortunate creatures are sucked into the air by tornadoes, carried a long distance by the moving weather system, and then dropped to the ground along with the rain.

Few weather forecasts predict a heavy shower of fish and frogs!

ARE CROP CIRCLES CAUSED BY WEIRD WEATHER?

THERE ARE MANY theories about the origin of mysterious patterns that appear in grain fields around the world—commonly known as crop circles. While some people believe they are the work of alien spacecraft, many of them are known to be man-made. Unusual weather, such as small tornadoes or electrical storms, is thought to be the cause of some of the patterns.

Some experts believe that many crop circles are formed by tornadoes.

fast facts

WHY IS EL NIÑO GETTING MORE POWERFUL?

Some scientists think that global warming has made El Niño more powerful in recent years.

WHAT IS LA NIÑA?

La Niña–"the little girl"–is a current that has the opposite effect to that of El Niño. The result is an exaggerated version of normal weather conditions.

HOW DOES EL NIÑO AFFECT SEA LIFE?

El Niño stops currents from bringing nutrients from the ocean floor to the surface, affecting the food supply of marine animals.

WHAT IS ENSO?

ENSO stands for "El Niño Southern Oscillation"–the name scientists use for what is often called El Niño.

WHAT IS BALL LIGHTNING?

Ball lightning is a rare phenomenon that is as yet unexplained. These mysterious globes of electrical energy have been reported during thunderstorms, usually appearing for only a few seconds.

CAN WEIRD WEATHER HELP EXPLAIN UFOS?

Strange, saucer-shaped clouds, ball lightning, mirages, and auroras are often reported as unidentified flying objects.

HAS IT EVER RAINED BLOOD?

Reports of "raining blood" may be explained by dust carried into the atmosphere by sandstorms or volcanoes falling as red or brown (blood-colored) rainfall.

WHO FORECASTS THE WEATHER?

Meteorologists and weather forecasters are employed by national and regional weather centers, and by organizations such as the military and by airports. They make forecasts based on their knowledge of weather patterns and information received from local, national, and global sources. The forecasts are delivered to the public through television, radio, newspapers, and the Internet.

HOW ARE WEATHER FORECASTS SHOWN ON TELEVISION?

TELEVISION WEATHER forecasts are the most easily understood and widely seen source of weather information for the general public. The weather forecasters may be trained meteorologists who work at a weather center, or television presenters may read out forecasts provided for them. A detailed forecast is presented as a sequence of weather maps generated on a computer. They usually show temperatures and wind speed and direction, and give some indication of the expected weather conditions for different parts of the country. Local television stations will present a more detailed forecast for their region.

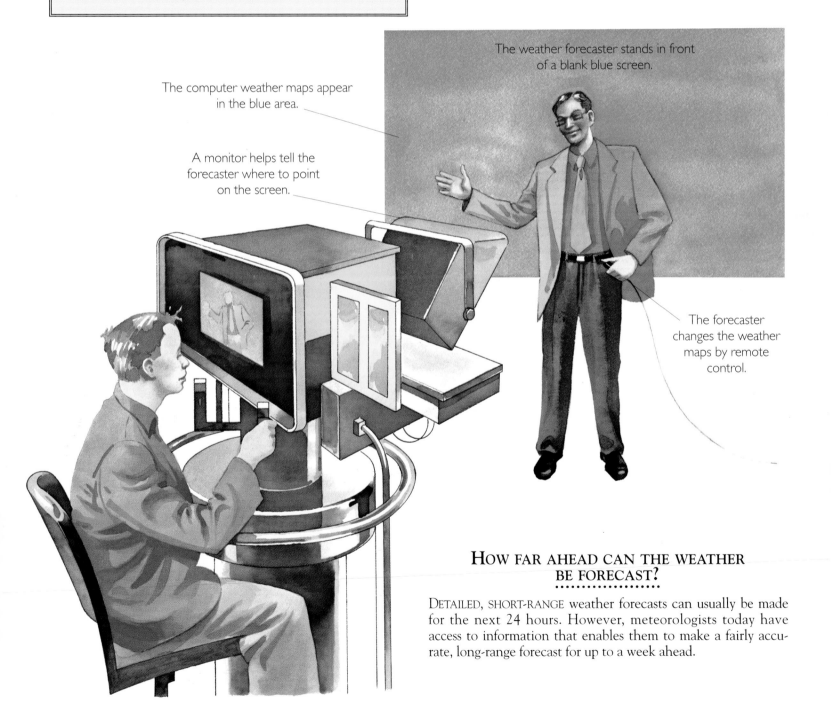

The weather forecaster stands in front of a blank blue screen.

The computer weather maps appear in the blue area.

A monitor helps tell the forecaster where to point on the screen.

The forecaster changes the weather maps by remote control.

HOW FAR AHEAD CAN THE WEATHER BE FORECAST?

DETAILED, SHORT-RANGE weather forecasts can usually be made for the next 24 hours. However, meteorologists today have access to information that enables them to make a fairly accurate, long-range forecast for up to a week ahead.

WHAT DOES A SATELLITE IMAGE SHOW?

WEATHER SATELLITES produce images by interpreting different levels of heat and light. When an area is lit by sunlight, different features–clouds, land, sea, ice, and so on–reflect different amounts of light, which are recorded by the satellite as varying shades of gray. When an area is in darkness, heat emissions are recorded by infrared equipment to produce a similar picture. The information is transmitted to a base station, where it is converted into images. Television forecasts often put a series of satellite images together to produce a "movie" of a moving weather system.

This computer-enhanced satellite picture shows Hurricane Fran approaching the coast of Florida in September 1996.

WHAT IS A SYNOPTIC CHART?

METEOROLOGISTS DRAW up special weather maps called synoptic charts to show a forecast. The long curved lines–isobars–show areas of equal pressure. Black circles mark the center of low- and high-pressure areas. Lines of red semicircles indicate a warm front, and a cold front is shown by a line of blue triangles. A combination of triangles and semicircles indicates an occluded front. Ideally, all the observations shown on a synoptic chart should be made at the same time ("synoptic" means "seen together"), but this is rarely possible, so slight variations must be taken into account when interpreting a chart.

The synoptic chart illustrated below shows a weather system over northwest Europe.

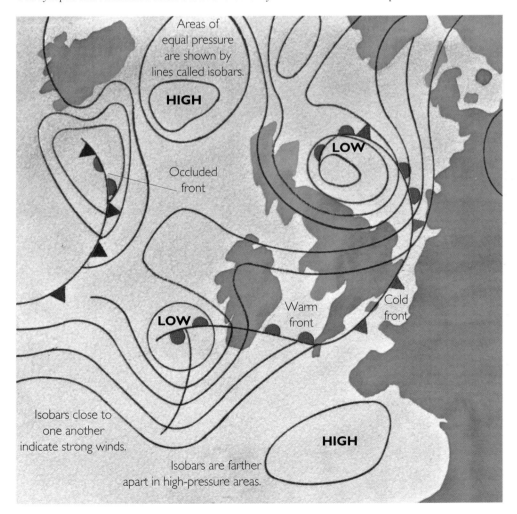

Areas of equal pressure are shown by lines called isobars.

HIGH

LOW

Occluded front

LOW

Warm front

Cold front

Isobars close to one another indicate strong winds.

Isobars are farther apart in high-pressure areas.

HIGH

HOW DOES THE INTERNET HELP US FIND OUT ABOUT THE WEATHER?

Global weather information is available via the Internet 24 hours a day–ideal if you are planning a vacation and want to know what clothes to take!

HOW ACCURATE IS A WEATHER FORECAST?

Modern technology helps meteorologists make increasingly accurate forecasts, but they are not always correct. Forecasts are judged to be "accurate" if the actual wind speed is within 5 mph (8 kmph) and the actual temperature is within 4°F (2°C) of what was predicted.

HOW OFTEN ARE FORECASTS ACCURATE?

Weather forecasts are thought to be accurate about 9 times out of 10.

WHO WERE THE FIRST METEOROLOGISTS?

In Renaissance Italy in the 17th century, scientists such as Galileo and Torricelli invented a number of instruments to monitor the atmosphere. Their work laid the foundations for modern meteorology.

WHEN WAS THE FIRST WEATHER FORECAST MADE?

The first weather forecasts were made in 1869 in the United States.

HOW WERE WEATHER FORECASTS FIRST TRANSMITTED?

The first weather forecasts were passed on by telegraph.

WHAT IS A BAROGRAPH?

A barograph is an instrument that makes a continuous record of the changes in air pressure.

HOW IS WEATHER INFORMATION GATHERED?

Meteorologists forecast the weather based on information gathered from a huge variety of sources. To get the clearest picture about the weather, both people and technology are employed around the world to continuously take weather measurements. Instruments on land, at sea, in the air, and in space feed the information into a global network, where it is accessed and analyzed by the world's weather experts.

The helium-filled balloons burst when they reach a certain altitude.

WHAT IS A WEATHER BALLOON?

WEATHER BALLOONS are used to take measurements of humidity, pressure and temperature at altitudes of up to 12 miles (20 km). The readings are taken by instruments called radiosondes carried beneath the balloon. These transmit the information to processing stations on the ground. Wind strength and direction is monitored by tracking the movement of the balloon.

The radiosondes return to Earth on a small parachute–they are not always retrieved.

Instruments in the long nose of this aircraft record temperature and humidity.

HOW ARE AIRCRAFT USED TO COLLECT WEATHER DATA?

RESEARCH AIRCRAFT are used to obtain detailed information about the atmosphere. They carry very sophisticated radar and laser equipment that records a three-dimensional picture of clouds at various levels in the atmosphere. Some planes are dedicated to monitoring hurricanes, often flying into the center of the storm itself. The information collected by aircraft is much more detailed than that collected by weather balloons.

HOW IS THE WEATHER MONITORED ON LAND?

WEATHER DATA in remote areas is collected by automated weather stations. Equipped with a wide range of instruments and computers, the stations record and transmit information via satellite every hour. Individual observers with a small number of simple instruments also play an important part in all levels of weather forecasting.

Automated weather stations are located in places such as Antarctica.

HOW ARE COMPUTERS USED TO PREDICT THE WEATHER?

COMPUTERS ARE used to collect weather information and also to help meteorologists predict the weather. Special software uses the data to develop a "model" of the expected weather.

HOW DO SATELLITES HELP FORECAST THE WEATHER?

SATELLITES SERVE two purposes in weather forecasting. Communications satellites are used to send weather data around the world, while dedicated weather satellites monitor the movement of weather systems and the patterns of cloud cover. There are two types of weather satellite. Geostationary satellites are fixed in one position, observing a certain area from their orbit high above the equator. Polar-orbiting satellites circle the Earth from pole to pole. The planet's rotation means that each orbit takes in a different part of the Earth.

There are around five geostationary weather satellites in orbit around the Earth.

The information from weather satellites is beamed back to weather stations on Earth.

Meteorologists may carry out long-term research on board ships.

HOW IS THE WEATHER MONITORED AT SEA?

AT SEA, weather conditions are monitored by ships, which take measurements of pressure and sea and air temperatures. Ships may be used to launch weather balloons. Free-floating buoys are also used to collect weather data. They drift with ocean currents, transmitting sea-level weather details to satellites. They are much less expensive to maintain than specialized weather ships.

A transmitter on the buoy notifies satellites of its position.

fast facts

WHEN ARE WEATHER BALLOONS RELEASED?

Weather balloons are released around the world twice a day–at noon and midnight, Greenwich Mean Time.

WHAT WAS THE FIRST WEATHER SATELLITE?

The first weather satellite, TIROS, was launched by the United States in 1960. It beamed back the first images from space of clouds moving around the Earth.

WHAT DID LEWIS FRY RICHARDSON DEVISE?

In the 1920s, British mathematician Lewis Fry Richardson devised a way of using mathematics to predict the weather. The calculations involved were so enormous that the system only became practical with the invention of the electronic computer around twenty years after his work was published.

WHAT DOES WEATHER RADAR SHOW?

Weather radar shows where rain, hail, or snow is falling and how heavy it is. It works by sending out radiation waves, which bounce off the raindrops or snowflakes and are reflected back to a receiver. The intensity and location of the precipitation is shown in color on the radar screen.

WHAT IS THE WORLD METEOROLOGICAL ORGANIZATION?

The World Meteorological Organization analyzes the data collected from weather satellites, balloons, ships, and land stations operated in 150 countries around the world. The information is shared to produce accurate, up-to-date forecasts.

HOW CAN NATURE TELL US ABOUT THE WEATHER?

People have been forecasting the weather for thousands of years, based on changes seen in the world around them. Many such observations are little more than folklore and superstition, but it is true that certain plants and animals can detect variations in the air that people cannot, providing us with natural signs of changes in the weather.

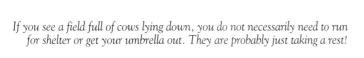

Seaweed is a good indicator of whether it will rain or stay dry.

WHAT DO RED SKIES AT DAWN AND DUSK MEAN?

THE SAYING "red sky at night, sailor's delight; red sky in morning, sailor take warning" probably originated in Europe. There, prevailing winds bring weather systems from the west, so a clear red sky at sunset is thought to indicate the arrival of good weather. A similar sight in the eastern skies at dawn could suggest that the good weather is passing away.

HOW DOES A PIECE OF SEAWEED WARN OF RAIN?

A PIECE OF SEAWEED is an excellent indicator of humidity. Any moisture in the seaweed evaporates when the air is dry, making it brittle and hard to the touch. When humidity levels increase, the seaweed absorbs moisture again, making it expand and become soft. A high level of moisture in the air is a sure sign that rain will follow soon. Pieces of seaweed are often seen hanging outside houses in towns on the British seashore.

WILL IT RAIN WHEN COWS LIE DOWN?

IT IS OFTEN said that when cows lie down in a field, rain is on the way. This piece of folklore is based on the idea that the cows can sense dampness in the air, so they lie down to make sure they'll have a dry space. As well known as this saying is, it is rarely accurate. Cows lie down when they are tired, not just when they think it might rain, so they are probably not the best weather forecasters!

If you see a field full of cows lying down, you do not necessarily need to run for shelter or get your umbrella out. They are probably just taking a rest!

WHAT CAN PINECONES TELL US ABOUT THE WEATHER?

PINECONES make one of the best natural weather indicators. The scales of a pinecone open out when the weather is dry and close up when the air is humid–a good sign that rain is coming. The natural state of the cone is closed–the scales are shriveling up when it is dry. When the air is moist, the cone becomes flexible again and returns to its regular shape.

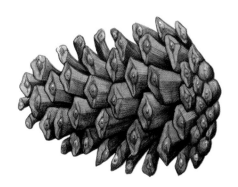

The opened-out scales of the pinecone above indicate dry air and pleasant weather.

When a pinecone closes up, you can be sure that colder, wetter weather is on the way.

HOW DO BLOSSOMS TELL US ABOUT THE WEATHER?

THE APPEARANCE of blossoms on trees is traditionally said to mark the beginning of spring and the end of winter. Trees do only come into bloom in mild weather, but as anyone who lives in a temperate part of the world knows, cold weather often returns after the blossoms appear! The dates on which blossoms appear have been recorded in some weather records for many years, which helps show what the weather was like in the past.

The Japanese tradition of noting the date on which cherry blossoms (left) appear has been carried out for hundreds of years.

WHAT IS THE ORIGIN OF GROUNDHOG DAY?

IN THE United States, February 2 is an important date for traditional weather forecasting. On this day, it is said that a groundhog emerges from hibernation to check on the weather. If it is sunny on that day, the groundhog will see its shadow and return to its burrow in the belief that the weather will be cold for the next six weeks. A cloudy

day (and no shadow) will keep the groundhog aboveground in anticipation of good weather. The tradition originates in Europe, where February 2, known as Candlemas, marks the point halfway between the winter solstice and the spring equinox.

Weather records show that the groundhog is not an especially accurate weather forecaster. In fact, a sunny February 2 is more likely to herald six weeks of better weather!

fast facts

WHO WAS ST. SWITHIN?

In the United Kingdom, it is said that if it rains on St. Swithin's day (July 15), it will rain for forty days and forty nights. St. Swithin was a 9th-century bishop of Winchester, England. It is said that it rained heavily on the day that he was buried in the city's cathedral.

CAN PEOPLE FEEL THE WEATHER IN THEIR BONES?

People who suffer from rheumatism (a disease that affects the joints) tend to feel more pain when the weather is cold and damp because it makes their joints less flexible.

HOW DOES WOOL REACT TO HUMIDITY?

A piece of wool shrinks and becomes curly when the air is dry. When there is a lot of moisture in the air, the wool expands and straightens.

WHY DO SOME FLOWERS CLOSE THEIR PETALS BEFORE IT RAINS?

Many flowers whose petals are wide open during sunny weather close up when rain is approaching. It is thought that this response is designed to stop rain washing pollen away.

WHY DO BIRDS GO TO ROOST WHEN A STORM IS APPROACHING?

Birds going to roost during the day is often taken as a sign of an approaching storm. This may be because they find it harder to fly in the low-pressure air that brings the stormy weather. There are also likely to be fewer thermals, which many birds rely on to gain height.

HOW DO FROGS ACT AS BAROMETERS?

It is thought that frogs croak when the air pressure drops–a natural barometer?

HOW CAN I INVESTIGATE THE WEATHER?

The experiments on these pages will help you make your own weather record and understand how some weather conditions occur. These experiments are perfect for school projects or just for fun! You may need help with some of them. Remember to record your results.

CAN I MAKE A CLOUD?

YOU CAN create your very own cloud in a bottle with this simple experiment. Be very careful when handling the hot water–ask an adult to help you.

YOU WILL NEED:

Glass bottle   Hot water   Black paper

Ice cube

WHAT TO DO:

1 Fill the bottle with hot water and leave it to stand for about five minutes.

2 Pour about three-quarters of the water away and then place the ice cube on top of the bottle.

3 Put the black paper behind the bottle and watch what happens.

WHAT IS HAPPENING?

The warm air makes some of the water turn into water vapor. When the water vapor rises and meets the cold air below the ice cube, it condenses, forming a cloud at the top of the bottle.

HOW DO I MAKE A RAIN GAUGE?

THIS RAIN GAUGE is similar to those used in real weather stations. Record the depth (in millimeters) every morning. An amount too small to register is called a "trace" measurement.

YOU WILL NEED:

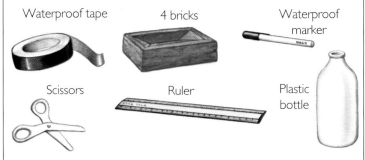

Waterproof tape   4 bricks   Waterproof marker

Scissors   Ruler   Plastic bottle

WHAT TO DO:

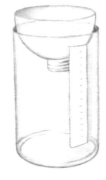

1 Ask an adult to cut the top off the bottle.

2 Mark a scale on a piece of waterproof tape as shown and stick it to the bottle's base.

3 Fit the upturned top of the bottle into the base as shown –this acts as a funnel.

4 Place the gauge in an open space, supported by the four bricks.

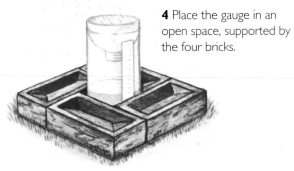

IS IT POSSIBLE TO MAKE RAIN?

THIS EXPERIMENT shows you how rain is created inside a cloud. First, put a large metal spoon in the freezer for about half an hour. Boil some water in a kettle and put a saucer under its spout. Using an oven mitt, hold the cold spoon in the steam coming from the boiling kettle. "Rain" forms when the steam (water vapor) from the kettle hits the cold spoon. The vapor condenses and forms water droplets, which fall from the spoon.

HOW DO I MAKE A RAINBOW?

THE TWO EXPERIMENTS below show you how to create your own rainbow—outdoors and indoors! Choose a sunny day. All you need to do is to provide a source of water through which the sun's light can be split into the spectrum. The second experiment works well with a small plant-sprayer if you do not have a garden hose—always ask before you borrow them!

Place a glass of water on a sunny windowsill. Put a piece of white paper on a table just beneath the windowsill. Adjust the position of the paper until you can see rainbow colors.

This works best when the sun is low in the sky—early morning or evening. Stand with your back to the sun and spray the water into a fine mist. Face a dark background to see the colors clearly.

HOW DO I MAKE AN ANEMOMETER?

REAL ANEMOMETERS are very expensive. Follow the steps below to make your own version of this essential weather instrument. All the things needed to make it are easily available in hardware or craft stores.

YOU WILL NEED:

wooden post

1 red plastic cup

3 large beads

2 12-in (30-cm) pieces of balsa wood

nail

3 white plastic cups

WHAT TO DO:

1 Glue the pieces of balsa wood together at right angles to one another to form an × shape.
2 When the glue has set, ask an adult to use the nail to make a hole through the center. Remove the nail.
3 Glue the bases of the cups to the ends of the balsa-wood arms. Make sure the cups all face the same way!
4 Thread one bead onto the nail, then push it through the hole in the wooden × and thread on the two remaining beads.
5 Ask someone to help you hammer the nail into the top of the wooden post.

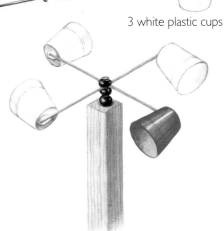

Hold your anemometer in the wind. Keep your eye on the red cup and count how many times it turns in a minute. Record your observations in your weather record.

fast facts

HOW OFTEN SHOULD I MAKE OBSERVATIONS?

To make your weather record accurate, take measurements as often as possible and at the same times each day.

WHAT IS A WEATHER SCRAPBOOK?

You can keep a record of significant weather events in your area in a scrapbook. Fill it with articles and photographs from newspapers, along with that day's weather map.

WHERE CAN I FIND OUT MORE?

Your school will be able to help you discover more about investigating the weather. A trip to the library or a search on the Internet will lead you to sources of relevant information, groups, and organizations.

WHAT IS CLOUD SEEDING?

Cloud seeding is a scientific process that makes clouds produce rain and snow. It works by sending tiny particles of silver iodide, or other substances such as dry ice or liquid propane, into rain-bearing clouds, usually by aircraft. These substances stimulate rain production by providing something for water droplets to freeze onto–scientists call them ice nuclei. Once enough of the droplets take hold, they become heavy enough to fall to the ground. Cloud seeding cannot produce clouds–it can only make existing clouds produce rain.

Cloud seeding is used in some parts of the world to help farmers in areas of low rainfall. In the future, it may be possible actually to create rain-bearing clouds and help solve the problems of drought.

The crystals stimulate the production of ice, bringing about rain or snow.

IS IT POSSIBLE TO REDUCE A HURRICANE'S POWER?

HURRICANES ARE probably the most destructive of all extreme weather events–a category 5 hurricane is thought to contain the same amount of energy as all the world's power plants combined. The ability to reduce this power would be a huge benefit. American scientists are looking at ways of cutting off a hurricane's energy source by using cooking oil. The theory is that aircraft would be used to spray a thin layer of oil over the surface of the ocean. This would help prevent water from evaporating into the atmosphere–the process that provides a hurricane with its heat and energy. This would work with any kind of oil, but vegetable oil is considered the most environmentally friendly substance. It is thought that using a process similar to cloud seeding could also be used to tame a hurricane by "cooling it down."

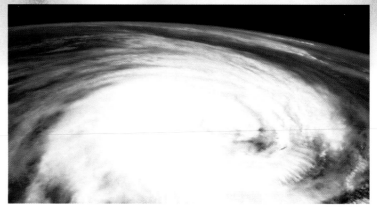

Being able to control the power of a hurricane would help reduce the loss of life and damage to property that the most powerful hurricanes bring. The technology involved in controlling hurricanes is only at an experimental stage.

HOW DO SCIENTISTS PLAN TO TAME TORNADOES?

SCIENTISTS BELIEVE that it may be possible to "kill" a tornado. Space satellites could be used to fire beams of microwave energy toward the base of a thunderstorm. The theory is that this would heat up the cool downdraft of air that helps create the tornado, effectively knocking it out. This sounds a lot like science fiction, and many scientists claim that it could never work.

The satellite sends a beam of microwave energy towards the tornado.

The beam heats the downdraft of the tornado, weakening it.

IS IT POSSIBLE TO CONTROL LIGHTNING?

THE NEXT generation of lightning rod could be a type of laser gun. A laser beam fired from the ground into a storm cloud could charge the air molecules along the way, creating a path for the lightning bolt to follow. Once the lightning is set on a direct path, its charge can be neutralized. It is thought that such a device could be used to steer lightning away from exposed structures such as power lines.

HAS ANYONE ATTEMPTED TO STOP HAILSTONES?

THE DAMAGE that large hailstones cause to crops has prompted many attempts to prevent hail from forming. Techniques similar to those used in cloud seeding have been tried, aiming to turn hailstones into rain, but this does not seem to work. In the early 20th century, people tried using "anti-hail guns." These fired huge amounts of debris into the clouds in an attempt to break up the hailstones. They were tried many times, unsuccessfully, in the vineyards of France.

The use of anti-hail guns was largely unsuccessful. More often than not, they caused injury to people on the ground–and the hailstones still fell.

fast facts

DOES WEATHER CONTROL HAVE MILITARY USES?

The use of weather control is a very controversial issue. It is claimed that the United States used cloud seeding during the war in Vietnam to flood areas and make them impassable. The use of weather modification for military purposes is now banned by the United Nations.

WHEN WAS CLOUD SEEDING INVENTED?

The General Electric Company discovered the principle of cloud seeding in its research laboratory in 1947.

HOW DID ANCIENT PEOPLE TRY TO INFLUENCE THE WEATHER?

In many ancient cultures, rituals would be performed asking the gods to bring certain weather conditions, usually rain or sunshine.

HOW HAS THE WEATHER AFFECTED HISTORY?

Throughout history, the weather has had a major influence on the outcome of certain events. Adverse weather conditions have helped decide the outcome of battles and military campaigns, while over longer periods of time, climate change is thought to have brought about the end of some civilizations and the beginning of others.

HOW DID THE WEATHER DEFEAT NAPOLEON IN RUSSIA?

NAPOLEON BONAPARTE was one of the finest military leaders in history. His clever tactics brought a series of victories that allowed him to rule large parts of Europe more than 200 years ago. However, it was the weather that proved instrumental in his downfall. He invaded Russia in the summer of 1812 and captured Moscow, following the Russians deeper into the country. By November, a lack of supplies forced Napoleon and his army to retreat, and the extremely harsh winter killed many thousands of troops as they returned to France.

WHAT HAPPENED AT THE BATTLE OF WATERLOO?

THREE YEARS after his retreat from Russia, Napoleon faced the allied forces of Britain and Prussia at Waterloo. Again, the weather played its part. Very heavy rain in the region made the ground muddy, which delayed Napoleon's attack. The delay meant that the allies, under the leadership of the Duke of Wellington, were able to send in additional troops and supplies, which ultimately helped them to victory.

Thousands of French troops died as they returned from Russia. They had been made cold, hungry, and demoralized by the severe cold of the winter. The retreat from Moscow proved to be the beginning of the end of Napoleon's domination of Europe.

DID DROUGHT BRING ABOUT THE END OF THE MAYAN CIVILIZATION?

1,200 YEARS AGO, the Mayan civilization thrived in what are now southern Mexico, Belize, and Guatemala. The Mayans were brilliant astronomers and mathematicians, and their society was very stable and established. However, at some point during the 9th century, their civilization suffered a sudden and devastating collapse. Archeologists have struggled to find an explanation for the Mayans' fate, but recent studies suggest that a massive drought was responsible. Analysis of mud samples from the bottom of Lake Chichancanab in the Yucatan area of Mexico has found that the region's climate in the 9th century was the driest it had been for 7,000 years.

The ruins of spectacular Mayan temples can be found scattered throughout the rainforests of southern Mexico and northern South America. It is difficult to imagine how a drought could affect such a lush, tropical region, but it is thought that a sudden change in climate–possibly caused by El Niño–was responsible for the collapse of one of history's great civilizations.

WHY WERE FLOODS IMPORTANT TO THE STABILITY OF ANCIENT EGYPT?

THE RIVER NILE was the source of life and prosperity in Egypt. The ancient Egyptians relied on the annual floods of the Nile to irrigate their crops, but studies have shown that the way in which the river floods varies considerably. Working together, historians and climatologists have found links between years of low flooding and periods of instability in Egyptian society. Records show that the famines that followed low floods led to disease and civil unrest–possibly causing the collapse of the Old Kingdom.

The Nile remains an important part of life in Egypt to this day. Did its failure to flood in the past lead to the collapse of the Old Kingdom of Egypt?

DID THE GREAT FLOOD DESCRIBED IN THE OLD TESTAMENT ACTUALLY HAPPEN?

SOME EXPERTS believe that when glaciers melted 7,000 years ago, this caused the Mediterranean to overflow into the Black Sea, then a small freshwater lake. This may form the basis of Middle Eastern tales, such as the one recorded in the Old Testament, of a hugely destructive flood.

fast facts

HOW DID EL NIÑO AFFECT THE INCAS?

The Incas of Peru offered up human sacrifices to persuade their gods to send fair weather. The bad weather was probably caused by El Niño.

DID THE RUSSIAN WINTER AFFECT WORLD WAR II?

In 1942, heavy cloud cover prevented German air forces from bombing Russian positions, allowing the Russians to fight back.

DID EL NIÑO HELP PEOPLE REACH EASTER ISLAND?

The reverse currents caused by El Niño probably helped the Polynesians sail 1,000 miles south to Easter Island.

WHY WAS CHRISTOPHER COLUMBUS LUCKY?

Christopher Columbus was lucky to avoid disaster, since he was in the Caribbean in the hurricane season.

WHEN WAS THE "YEAR WITHOUT A SUMMER"?

In the United States, the very cold 1817 was known as "the year without a summer."

WHO USES WEATHER FORECASTS?

Weather forecasts are used by everybody, but some people pay closer attention to them than others. Severe weather conditions can endanger lives on the roads, at sea, and in the air, so transportation and safety organizations are regularly updated on the weather situation. Many businesses, from farming and fishing to hotels and restaurants, can be affected by the weather, so a forecast can help with business planning.

It is useful to know in advance if it is going to rain—we can prepare ourselves by wearing waterproof clothes or taking an umbrella. Weather forecasts are even more important for people whose lives or livelihood depends on the weather conditions.

WHY ARE WEATHER FORECASTS IMPORTANT FOR PEOPLE AT SEA?

PEOPLE WHO work at sea depend heavily on detailed, specialized weather forecasts because their lives can be at risk when stormy conditions bring high winds and rough seas. Fishermen may decide where to fish according to weather conditions, while sport sailors pay close attention to wind details to plan their racing tactics. All mariners listen to radio stations and coast guard broadcasts for advance warnings of weather conditions, which focus on the speed and direction of the wind, visibility, and barometer readings.

Oil rig workers and sailors listen for gale warnings because their lives may depend on knowing where and when gales will occur.

The nature of farming means that accurate weather forecasts are essential for business.

HOW DO FARMERS USE WEATHER FORECASTS?

FARMERS NEED to pay special attention to the weather in order to tend their crops or feed their animals. Knowledge of a severe frost or rain will influence when they sow seeds or harvest crops. Accurate weather forecasts also help farmers decide when to treat crops with chemicals. For example, if it rains shortly after pesticides are applied, they will be washed away and have little effect—a waste of time and money for the farmer. Forecasts for farmers provide as much information as possible about the weather for the next week or so.

HOW ARE SPORTS AFFECTED BY THE WEATHER?

MOST OUTDOOR SPORTS events can be affected by adverse weather conditions in one way or another. "Rain stopped play" is a familiar phrase to cricket fans in England, where the often unpredictable summer weather regularly interrupts games. Tennis is similarly affected when heavy rain makes play impossible on open-air grass courts. Some sports can be played in almost all kinds of weather (only severe snow and freezing temperatures will stop a soccer or rugby game), but the conditions can influence tactics and the outcome of the game.

Cricket demands excellent light, so an overcast, gloomy day will often cause the game to be stopped because the players cannot see the ball clearly. Some special evening games are played under floodlights, using a fluorescent ball and with the players in colored uniforms.

Golfers pay particular attention to the strength and direction of the wind, selecting their clubs and playing their shots accordingly.

Humidity can influence a game of tennis. A tennis ball moves faster and farther in dry air than it does in air that is full of moisture.

Rain is an important factor in horseracing. Some horses run better on firm ground and some on softer ground, so gamblers often consider this before placing a bet.

GLOSSARY

Atmosphere The mixture of gases that surrounds the Earth. They are held in place by the pull of gravity.

Atom The smallest amount of a particle of matter that cannot be split up.

Climate The general pattern of weather conditions that occur in a place over a long period of time.

Climatology The science of climates and climate change.

Condensation A process in which vapor cools and turns back into liquid.

Convection The transfer of heat through the movement of gas or liquid. This is how heat moves through the atmosphere.

Drought An unusually long period of time without rainfall.

Equator An imaginary line that stretches around the Earth, exactly halfway between the two poles.

Evaporation A process in which liquids turn into gases.

Forecast A prediction of weather conditions for a period of up to a week in advance.

Hemisphere One half of the Earth. This usually refers to the Northern and Southern Hemispheres, which are divided by the equator.

Hurricane A violent tropical storm with winds that spiral inward toward a center of low pressure called the eye.

Ice ages These occur when the Earth's climate becomes much cooler, and the amount of ice increases.

Meteorology The science that studies the atmosphere, enabling us to forecast the weather accurately. Weather forecasters are also called meteorologists.

Molecule The smallest amount of a non-elementary substance that can exist while still having the basic chemical structure of that substance.

Monsoon Seasonal winds that affect large areas of the tropics and subtropics.

Precipitation Water that falls to the ground in the form of rain, sleet, snow, or hail.

Radiation The transmission of heat in waves of energy. The sun's heat reaches the Earth by radiation.

Refraction The bending of light when it passes through an object or matter. Rainbows are seen when the viewer sees the sun's light refracted through raindrops.

Seasons These are caused by different regions of the Earth being tilted toward the sun at different times of the year. For example, spring begins at a particular place on Earth at the moment when it begins to lean toward the sun.

Synoptic chart Type of chart that shows the weather expected in a certain area for a particular time.

Temperate climate A climate that does not generally have extreme weather conditions.

Thermometer Instrument used to measure temperature.

Tropical climate A hot climate in the areas roughly between 23° north and south of the equator.

Vapor A gas that would usually be found in a liquid or solid form, such as water vapor.

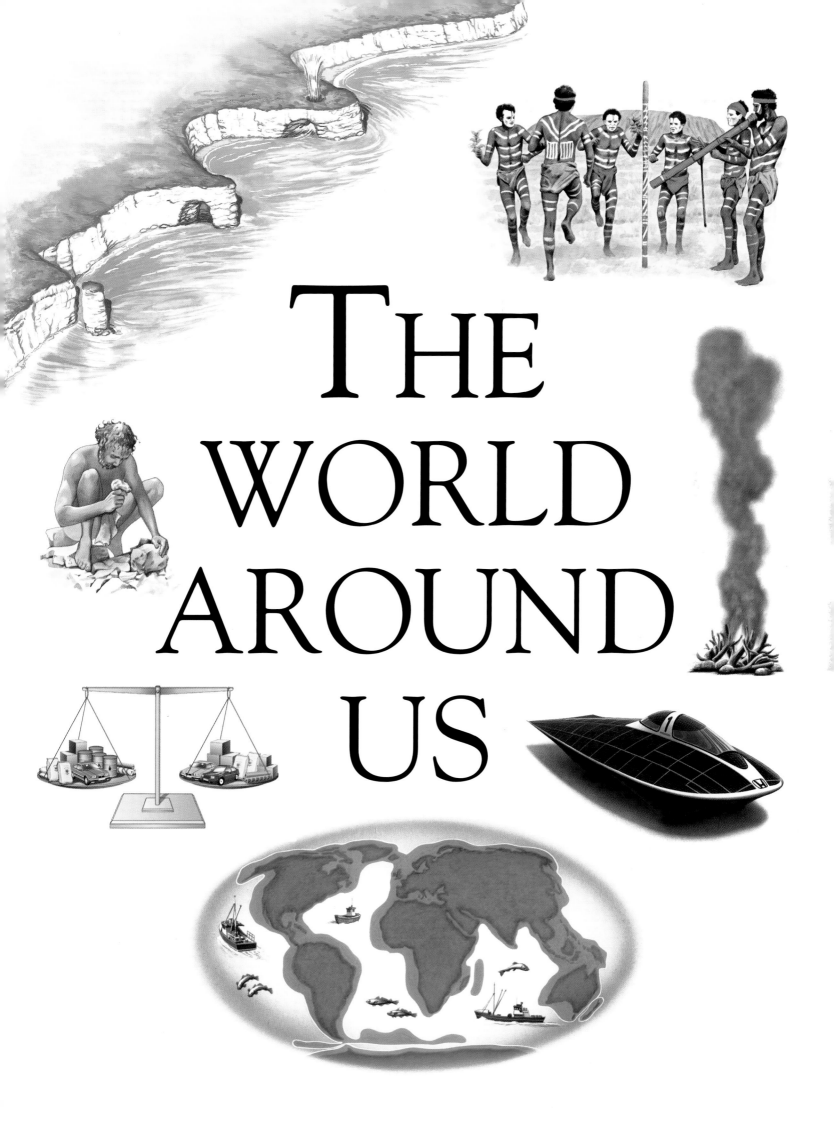

THE WORLD AROUND US

HOW OLD IS THE EARTH?

The amount of time that the Earth has been in existence is immense, and it is impossible to give it an exact age. However, around five billion years ago, our planet was nothing more than part of a cloud of dust and gas, spinning around in space. Around this time, something caused the material in this enormous cloud to contract, forming the sun, the Earth and the other planets in our Solar System.

HOW WAS THE EARTH FORMED?

1 The Earth and the other planets in the Solar System formed from solid lumps of ice and rock in a massive cloud.

2 The newly formed Earth became a sphere of molten rock as iron and nickel sank to create the Earth's core.

3 The Earth's crust began to form around four billion years ago. Small plates of crust floated on oceans of molten rock.

4 As the crust developed, volcanoes erupted, water vapor condensed to form the oceans, and the continents began to form.

WHAT IS THE EARTH'S TILT?

THE AXIS of the Earth (the imaginary line along which it spins) is set at a slight angle. This tilt affects the Earth's climate, because it causes the poles to point toward and away from the sun at different times of the year. We divide these times into the seasons.

The Earth bulges at the equator.

The Earth rotates on its axis, tilted at about 23°.

HOW LONG DOES THE EARTH TAKE TO ORBIT THE SUN?

IT TAKES the Earth one whole year to make one full orbit of the sun.

HOW BIG IS THE EARTH?

THE SIZE of the Earth depends upon how you measure it. If you were to circumnavigate the world (on land and sea) following the equator, you would travel 24,902 miles (40,075 km). Starting at one pole and visiting the other, you would travel 42 miles (67 km) less. The Earth's diameter, pole to pole, is 7,900 miles (12,714 km), while the distance through the Earth at the Equator is another 27 miles (43 km).

WHAT MAKES THE EARTH SPIN?

THE EARTH spins as a result of things colliding with each other when the Solar System was formed. Some scientists believe that the Earth started spinning after a direct collision with the moon. Kept moving by the force of momentum, the Earth takes one day to make one full rotation.

IS THE EARTH A PERFECT SPHERE?

THE ROTATION of the Earth causes it to bulge slightly in the middle. Centrifugal force makes the Earth's material move away from the center–the faster the spin, the greater the force. Since places at the equator are moving faster than places at the poles, the center of the Earth pushes out slightly more than the rest.

Like all the planets in our Solar System, the Earth is a sphere that orbits the sun. The atmosphere and the oceans give our planet its distinctive blue color.

fast facts

IS EARTH SLOWING DOWN?

Scientists think that days were shorter 400 million years ago. Maybe the Earth was spinning more slowly.

WHAT MAKES THE EARTH SLOW DOWN?

It is thought that the friction created by the movement of tides has slowed down the Earth's spin.

IF THE EARTH IS SPINNING, WHY DON'T WE GET THROWN OFF?

All objects in the Universe produce the force of gravity–the larger the object, the stronger the force. It is gravity that keeps us on our planet.

HOW FAST DOES THE EARTH SPIN?

The Earth rotates at a speed of 1,000 mph (1,609 kmph).

DOES THE EARTH WOBBLE ON ITS AXIS?

Research has shown that as the Earth spins, it wobbles slightly on its axis. This very slight movement (a few feet) has been named the Chandler Wobble.

WHAT IS THE EARTH MADE OF?

The surface of the Earth, the crust, makes up a very small part of the whole planet. While it is relatively simple to find out about the Earth's surface, investigating deep within the Earth is part science, part guesswork. What is known is that there are three main layers: the crust, the mantle, and the core, and that these consist of rocks and metals in various states and forms.

WHAT IS THE EARTH'S CRUST?

THE CRUST is the hard, outer layer of the Earth that forms the land and the ocean floor. The continental crust (the land masses) is the oldest and thickest part and made up mostly of silica and aluminum. The oceanic crust, made up mostly of silica and magnesium, is around 200 million years old.

HOW FAR IS IT TO THE EARTH'S CORE?

THE OUTER CORE begins 1,822 miles (2,935 km) below the Earth's surface. It is another 2,134 miles (3,432 km) before reaching the very center of the Earth.

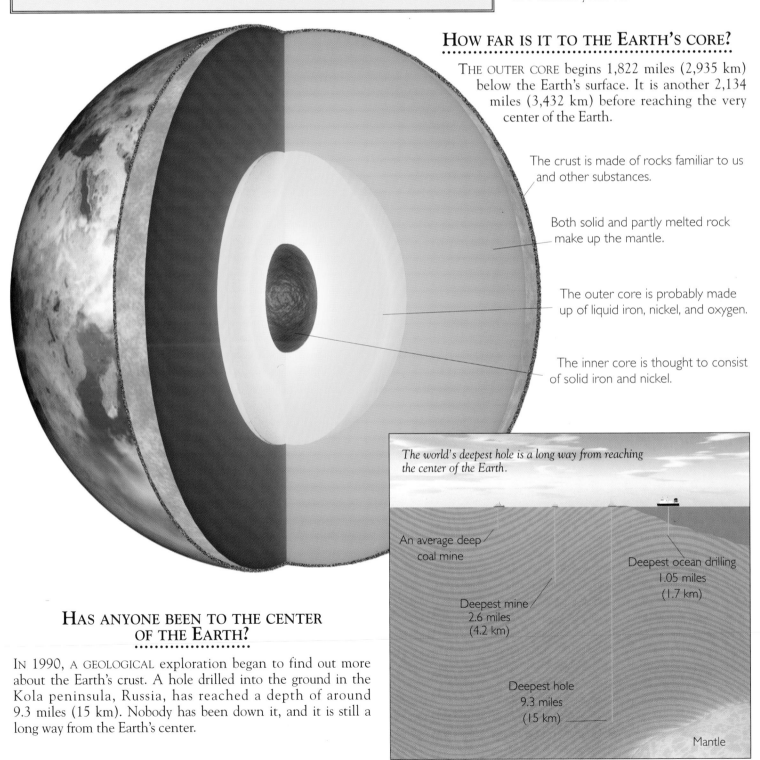

The crust is made of rocks familiar to us and other substances.

Both solid and partly melted rock make up the mantle.

The outer core is probably made up of liquid iron, nickel, and oxygen.

The inner core is thought to consist of solid iron and nickel.

The world's deepest hole is a long way from reaching the center of the Earth.

An average deep coal mine

Deepest mine 2.6 miles (4.2 km)

Deepest ocean drilling 1.05 miles (1.7 km)

Deepest hole 9.3 miles (15 km)

Mantle

HAS ANYONE BEEN TO THE CENTER OF THE EARTH?

IN 1990, A GEOLOGICAL exploration began to find out more about the Earth's crust. A hole drilled into the ground in the Kola peninsula, Russia, has reached a depth of around 9.3 miles (15 km). Nobody has been down it, and it is still a long way from the Earth's center.

WHAT MAKES THE EARTH MAGNETIC?

THE MOLTEN IRON that partly makes up the Earth's core flows around continually. As this happens, it generates powerful electric currents that create the Earth's magnetic field. This is similar to the way magnetic currents are generated by an electric motor.

The Earth's magnetic field reaches out to about 37,000 miles (60,000 km).

WHAT IS THE MAGNETIC FIELD?

THE EARTH is something like an enormous magnet. Otherwise known as the magnetosphere, the Earth's magnetic field stretches out into space, helping protect the Earth from the sun's radiation. The magnetic poles are close to the geographic North and South Poles.

The alignment of the Earth's magnetic field is shown on a compass.

WHAT MAKES SOME ROCKS MAGNETIC?

THE MAGNETIC FIELD of the Earth at any given time is preserved in the magnetic minerals within rocks that solidified during that period. Geologists are thus able to study the magnetic field of rocks thousands of years old, such as those used to build the pyramids at Giza, Egypt.

In industry, iron and steel need to be heated to around 3,500°F (1,900°C) for them to melt. These are the kinds of temperatures that are found at the Earth's core.

HOW DO WE KNOW WHAT THE EARTH IS MADE OF?

Drilling beneath the Earth's surface is very difficult and expensive, so most of what we know about the Earth's structure comes from a science called seismology. Vibrations caused by earthquakes, called seismic waves, tell scientists about the Earth's interior by the way they behave as they pass through the Earth.

WHAT IS THE MOHO?

A Croatian scientist called Andrija Mohorovicic was one of the first people to observe the behavior of seismic waves. The area between the mantle and the crust is named the Mohorovicic discontinuity, or Moho.

HOW DOES A COMPASS SHOW DIRECTION?

A compass is a magnet carefully balanced on a pivot or in a fluid. The Earth's magnetic field will align the magnet in a north–south direction.

DOES THE EARTH'S MAGNETIC FIELD EVER CHANGE?

The Earth's magnetic field is always changing. Sometimes, the change is so powerful that the magnetic poles switch positions; this is known as polar reversal. Nobody knows why this occurs, but it last happened around 30,000 years ago.

IS THE EARTH COMPLETELY SOLID?

MOST OF THE EARTH is made of various solid rocks. The 1,240-mile-thick (2,000 km) outer core is the only part of the Earth that exists in an entirely liquid form. Iron, nickel, and other materials are liquefied by the extremely high temperatures. Molten rock is found in parts of the mantle, some of which comes to the surface as lava.

WHAT IS CONTINENTAL DRIFT?

It may not be apparent to us, but the major land masses of the Earth, the seven continents, are not in fixed positions. They are constantly shifted around by forces deep within the Earth. Around 250 million years ago, the land on Earth formed one huge continent known today as Pangaea. Over time, this broke up into the continents we know today. This continual movement of the land is known as continental drift.

WHAT ARE TECTONIC PLATES?

THE EARTH'S CRUST is divided into enormous slabs of rock called tectonic plates. There are about 15 major plates, covering both the land masses and the ocean floor. They fit together like a huge jigsaw puzzle, and, because of continental drift, their boundaries are either colliding with or pulling away from each other.

This map shows (in red) the boundaries of the world's tectonic plates.

WHAT MAKES THE LAND MOVE?

THERE ARE A NUMBER of theories about the causes of continental drift. One puts forward the idea that hot rocks rise through ocean ridges, cool down, and then drag the plates downward. Another theory suggests that the heat from inside the Earth creates movement in the mantle. The resulting currents then shift the plates around. The third idea is the simplest. At the ocean ridges, the plates are higher than elsewhere, resulting in the force of gravity pulling the plates downward.

Mountain ranges are formed where continental plates collide. This is called convergence.

The subduction zone is where two plates collide and one is forced over the other.

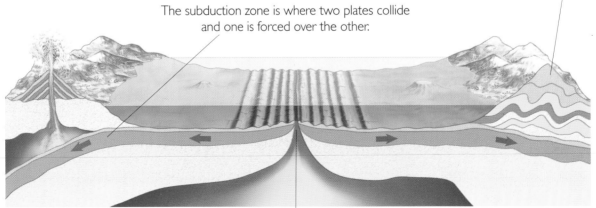

Mid-ocean ridges occur where two plates are pulling apart. Where this occurs on land, they produce steep-sided valleys.

WHAT GIVES THE CONTINENTS THEIR SHAPE?

A GLANCE AT a modern map of the world makes it easy to see that all the continents were once joined together. Perhaps the clearest example is the east coast of South America and the west coast of Africa. Their shapes suggest that they would fit closely if brought together.

Present-day map:
the shapes of the continents suggest that
they were once joined together.

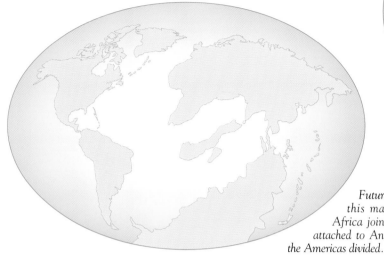

Future map:
this map shows Europe and
Africa joined together, Australia
attached to Antarctica, and Asia and
the Americas divided.

WILL THE CONTINENTS EVER BE PUSHED TOGETHER AGAIN?

CONTINENTAL DRIFT is still happening, and the continents will continue to move in the future. They are unlikely to return to the shape of Pangaea, but a map of the world 150 million years from now could look significantly different from today's.

IS THERE EVIDENCE THAT THE LAND HAS MOVED?

FOSSILIZED REMAINS found in different parts of the world are good evidence that the continents were once joined together. Remains of the same animal have been found in both South America and Africa, which means it must have lived at a time when the continents were part of the same landmass. Plant fossils of the same type and age have been found all over the world, and geologists have identified parts of the same mountain range in different continents.

IS THE BOTTOM OF THE OCEAN MOVING?

THE EARTH'S entire crust is subject to continental drift, including the ocean floor. Most of the tectonic plates are both continental (part of the land) and oceanic (part of the ocean floor). Evidence of movement on the seabed is found in different magnetic alignments in the rock and volcanic activity on the ocean floor.

Volcanic activity on the ocean floor is evidence of
continental drift beneath the oceans.

fast facts

WHICH CONTINENT IS THE LARGEST?

Asia is the world's largest continent. It covers an area of 17,176,090 sq miles (44,485,900 sq km) and has 30% of the world's total land area.

WHICH CONTINENT IS THE SMALLEST?

Australasia is the smallest continent. It covers an area of 3,445,610 sq miles (8,924,100 sq km).

WHAT IS THE ASTHENOSPHERE?

The asthenosphere is a fairly soft layer of the Earth's mantle. It helps lubricate the movement of the plates above it.

HOW QUICKLY IS THE LAND MOVING?

The land is moving extremely slowly. Although some of the plates move faster than others, the average rate of movement is no more than 1 inch (2.5 cm) a year.

WHAT IS THE LITHOSPHERE?

The crust and top part of the mantle are known as the lithosphere.

WHY ARE EARTHQUAKES SO DESTRUCTIVE?

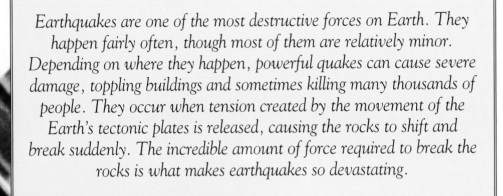

Earthquakes are one of the most destructive forces on Earth. They happen fairly often, though most of them are relatively minor. Depending on where they happen, powerful quakes can cause severe damage, toppling buildings and sometimes killing many thousands of people. They occur when tension created by the movement of the Earth's tectonic plates is released, causing the rocks to shift and break suddenly. The incredible amount of force required to break the rocks is what makes earthquakes so devastating.

The side effects of an earthquake can be almost as destructive as the quake itself. Here, a bridge has been demolished by a landslide triggered by a powerful earthquake.

WHERE ARE EARTHQUAKES MOST LIKELY TO HAPPEN?

EARTHQUAKES CAN HAPPEN anywhere, but they occur most frequently above the boundaries of the Earth's tectonic plates. The most powerful earthquakes occur where the plates are moving deep below the surface. These boundaries are known as transform faults or fault lines.

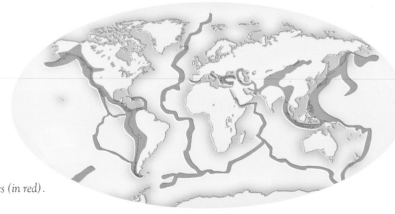

This map shows the world's earthquake zones (in red).

HOW ARE EARTHQUAKES RECORDED?

THE SIZE, or magnitude, of an earthquake is recorded using an instrument called a seismometer. Using very heavy weights that remain still while the room around it is shaking, the machine records the amount of movement on a rotating drum of paper. This type of record is measured on the Richter scale. The physical and visible effects of a quake are measured using the modified Mercalli scale (see below).

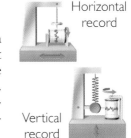

Horizontal record

Vertical record

The modified Mercalli scale:

1   Only detected by instruments. Doors may begin to swing.
2   Some people inside high buildings may feel a tremor.
3   Rapid vibrations possibly felt indoors.
4   Stationary cars rock; windows shake; people indoors feel something.
5   Effects felt outdoors; small objects fall; some buildings shake.
6   Trees begin to shake; dishes broken; everyone in the area feels it.
7   People alarmed; chimneys begin to crack; windows break.
8   Cars crash; buildings and trees damaged.
9   Many people panic; cracks in the ground; buildings fall down.
10   Buildings destroyed; landslides happen; rivers affected.
11   Bridges collapse; railroads affected; underground services disrupted.
12   Widespread devastation; landscape changed.

WHAT HAPPENS AT THE FOCUS OF AN EARTHQUAKE?

DEEP BENEATH the Earth's surface, the place where the earthquake actually occurs is called the focus. This is where the greatest amount of rock movement is to be found. The ground directly above the focus is known as the epicenter. This is where the most damage occurs.

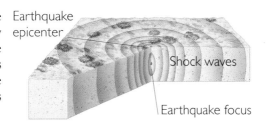

Earthquake epicenter

Shock waves

Earthquake focus

DO EARTHQUAKES HAVE ANY SIDE EFFECTS?

THE SHOCK WAVE of a powerful earthquake can easily destroy buildings and other structures, but there are some side effects of the quake itself. Underground gas pipes may rupture, leading to serious fires and explosions. The health of survivors is put at risk by damaged sewage systems that allow disease to spread. In mountainous areas, landslides or avalanches can be triggered, and an undersea earthquake can generate a huge wave called a tsunami.

WHAT IS THE SAN ANDREAS FAULT?

PERHAPS THE WORLD'S best known fault line is the San Andreas Fault. Situated in California, it is an area of the world where earthquakes and tremors occur frequently. The citizens of San Francisco know that a very powerful quake (often referred to as "The Big One") could occur at any time.

IS IT POSSIBLE TO BUILD EARTHQUAKE-PROOF BUILDINGS?

MODERN BUILDING technologies mean that homes, offices, and other buildings can be designed to withstand the effect of an earthquake. Tall buildings are built with a strong central column from which the structure "hangs". Conical or triangular designs are able to absorb shocks more easily, while the use of new materials allows buildings to be constructed in earthquake zones at a relatively low cost.

The TransAmerica building is one of San Francisco's landmarks. Known as "the Pyramid," its distinctive shape comes from being designed to resist the effects of an earthquake.

fast facts

HOW LONG DOES AN EARTHQUAKE LAST?

Earthquakes generally last for less than a minute. However, some of the most destructive have lasted for up to four minutes.

CAN ANIMALS DETECT EARTHQUAKES?

It is thought that some animals can sense that an earthquake is about to happen. Dogs are known to become uneasy and start to howl in the moments before a quake.

WHAT WAS THE STRONGEST RECORDED EARTHQUAKE?

An earthquake in Chile in May 1960 measured 9.5 on the Richter scale.

WHAT WAS THE MOST DESTRUCTIVE EARTHQUAKE?

An earthquake in China in 1566 killed almost one million people, while a 1923 earthquake in Japan destroyed around 575,000 homes.

WHO DEVISED THE RICHTER SCALE?

American seismologist Charles Richter devised the method of measuring earthquakes in 1935.

WHAT HAPPENS WHEN A VOLCANO ERUPTS?

Volcanoes erupt when molten rock, known as magma, is forced to the Earth's surface by the movement of the Earth's tectonic plates. Sometimes a volcano explodes, sending thick clouds of ash high into the atmosphere. Other volcanic eruptions produce rivers of red-hot lava that flow over the landscape, covering everything in their path. Whichever way a volcano erupts, it is one of the natural world's most powerful and destructive forces.

ARE THERE DIFFERENT TYPES OF VOLCANO?

STEEP-SIDED, cone-shaped andesitic volcanoes are formed by melted plates exploding to the surface. These types of volcano are extremely violent, and their eruptions are very destructive. Basaltic volcanoes form where molten rock rises slowly to the surface from the mantle. They are broad and low, and when they break the surface they can spray their lava into the air, producing blobs of lava known as volcanic bombs.

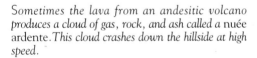

Andesitic volcano

Volcanic bomb

Magma chamber

Sometimes the lava from an andesitic volcano produces a cloud of gas, rock, and ash called a nuée ardente. *This cloud crashes down the hillside at high speed.*

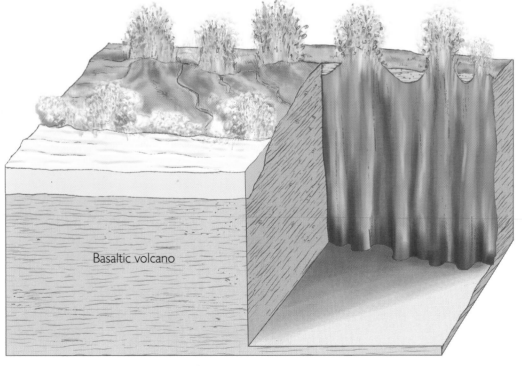

Basaltic volcano

WHAT IS A VOLCANIC HOT SPOT?

AREAS OF VOLCANIC activity in the Earth's mantle are known as hot spots. As plates move over these areas, basaltic volcanoes are formed above, often resulting in a chain of several volcanoes.

CAN VOLCANOES ERUPT UNDERWATER?

BASALTIC VOLCANOES are found mainly beneath the ocean. The lava that erupts cools very quickly, forming round lumps of rock called pillow lava.

IS ALL LAVA THE SAME?

VOLCANIC LAVA differs according to the type of rock it is made from, the gases it contains, and where it erupts. Pahoehoe lava moves quickly and looks something like coils of rope when it cools. The thicker, lumpier aa lava cools into chunky rocks.

Pahoehoe lava moving across a road.

Hot lava flowing from a volcano.

HOW DOES VOLCANIC ACTIVITY AFFECT THE LANDSCAPE?

WHEN WATER is heated by volcanic activity, strange and spectacular landscapes are created. Known as hydrothermal areas, they can feature steaming hot springs, gurgling pools of mud, and jets of water spouting hundreds of feet into the air.

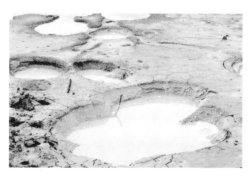

Water heated underground by hot volcanic rock rises to the surface to form a hot spring.

Foul-smelling jets of volcanic gas and steam are released from vents in the ground known as fumaroles.

Where corrosive volcanic gases dissolve mineral particles around pools of hot water, pools of hot mud are formed.

Ancient volcanic activity can leave unusual rock formations, such as this "Fairy Chimney" in Turkey.

fast facts

CAN VOLCANIC ERUPTIONS BE PREDICTED?

Volcanic eruptions are very difficult to predict. They do not occur at regular intervals, and dormant volcanoes (those that have been "sleeping" for years) can erupt without warning.

WHAT WAS THE BIGGEST VOLCANIC ERUPTION?

The biggest volcanic eruption on record occurred in Indonesia in 1815. One on the island of Sumbawa sent over 24 cubic miles (100 cubic km) of ash into the air. Around 100,000 people were killed, and the island sank by 4,100 feet (1,250 m).

WHAT IS THE LARGEST ACTIVE VOLCANO?

With a diameter of 62 miles (100 km), Mauna Loa in Hawaii is the world's largest active volcano.

WHAT ARE PYROCLASTS?

All volcanic eruptions produce solid products known as pyroclasts, consisting of dust, ash, lapilli (stone fragments), and bombs or blocks.

ARE THERE VOLCANOES ON OTHER PLANETS?

Scientists have found evidence of volcanoes elsewhere in the Solar System. It is thought that Venus has many active volcanoes, while huge volcanic eruptions have been recorded on Io, one of Jupiter's moons.

WHAT HAPPENED AT POMPEII?

The Roman city of Pompeii was completely buried under hot ash when Vesuvius erupted in A.D. 79.

Geysers burst out from underground chambers of heated water. The now-extinct Waimangu Geyser in New Zealand reached 1,500 feet (445 m).

WHAT ARE ROCKS MADE OF?

All rocks are made of various natural substances called minerals. Each mineral has its own chemical makeup, and the different minerals combine together in various ways. Most rocks contain around six different minerals that grow together in a crystal structure.

Scientists called petrologists study rocks close-up. A very thin slice of rock is examined under a microscope that uses polarized light. Each mineral produces its own color and texture, and this helps identify the type of rock. This picture shows a sample of marble under a petrologist's microscope.

ARE THERE DIFFERENT TYPES OF ROCK?

THE EARTH'S ROCKS are divided into three main types. Igneous rock is the original material that makes up the Earth, formed when magma rises to the surface and cools. The planet's oldest rocks are all of the igneous type. Sedimentary rock is made up of particles of other rock that has been affected by contact with the atmosphere. Erosion caused by water, wind, and ice breaks the rock down into tiny particles that are carried away and settle in rivers, lakes, and other areas. Over time, the particles compress to form sedimentary rock. Metamorphic rock is formed by the natural effects of heat and pressure changing igneous and sedimentary rock.

Igneous rock tends to be very hard. When broken up, it makes a good material for building roads. Granite is one of the most common types of igneous rock.

Sandstone and limestone are good examples of sedimentary rock. Though relatively hard, they are easy to cut and are often used in construction.

Marble is found in layers of metamorphic rock. It can be used to create attractive and impressive surfaces in important buildings.

WHAT IS THE ROCK CYCLE?

THE ROCK CYCLE is the process through which all the Earth's rock is continually changing.

Particles of eroded rock are washed away to the ocean and riverbeds, where they form sedimentary rock.

Igneous rocks are worn down by atmospheric conditions.

Where molten rock rises to the surface, it cools to form various types of igneous rock.

Pressure from mountain-building and heat from under the Earth transform igneous and sedimentary rock into metamorphic rock.

WHAT SHAPES DO CRYSTALS FORM?

CRYSTALS are formed from minerals that melt or are dissolved in liquids. Crystals in different types of rocks and minerals form one of six different geometric shapes. These shapes were discovered in the 18th century by Abbé René Haüy.

CRYSTAL SHAPES

CUBIC — Diamond is an example of a mineral with a cubic structure.
HEXAGONAL — Beryl has a hexagonal crystal shape.
TETRAGONAL — Zircon has a tetragonal crystal structure.
MONOCLINIC — Gypsum has a monoclinic design.
ORTHORHOMBIC — Sulfur has an orthorhombic crystal structure.
TRICLINIC — Turquoise has crystals in a triclinic shape.

Cubic   Hexagonal   Tetragonal

Monoclinic   Orthorhombic   Triclinic

WHY ARE GEMSTONES VALUABLE?

SOME MINERALS are very precious. Diamonds, rubies, emeralds, and sapphires are examples of gemstones that are valued for their rarity and beauty. They are difficult to find and expensive to extract from the Earth. Some of them also have special uses in science and industry that can increase their value.

fast facts

WHAT IS GEOLOGY?

Geology is the science of studying rocks.

WHAT DOES A GEOLOGIST DO?

Geologists are scientists who take specimens of rocks and study them in the laboratory.

WHAT ARE ORGANIC GEMSTONES?

Organic gemstones are those that are formed from plant or animal materials. Pearls and amber are examples of these.

WHAT IS THE WORLD'S LARGEST PEARL?

The Pearl of Lao-tze was found inside a giant clam. Weighing 14 lb 1 oz (6.37 kg), it was found in the Philippines in 1934.

HOW ARE DIAMONDS CUT?

The only way to cut the hardest mineral is by using tools tipped with diamond. Diamond-tipped tools are also used extensively in industry to cut materials finely.

WHY ARE SOME MINERALS HARDER THAN OTHERS?

THE HARDNESS OF MINERALS varies according to the structure of their atoms. A mineral's hardness is measured using the Mohs scale. Diamond is the hardest mineral, and thus has a rating of 10 Mohs.

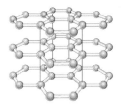

Diamond atoms are strongly bonded to each other, making them very hard.

The atoms of graphite are layered apart, giving it a fairly soft structure.

HOW IS A PEARL FORMED?

PEARLS ARE PRECIOUS STONES formed inside shellfish such as oysters, mussels, and clams. They form when a piece of grit enters the creature's shell. The most valuable pearls are from oysters.

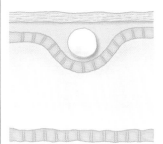

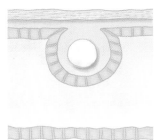

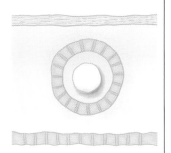

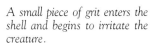

A small piece of grit enters the shell and begins to irritate the creature.

Mother-of-pearl is secreted from within the creature around the grit.

As the grit becomes surrounded by mother-of-pearl, it separates, forming the precious stone.

WHAT IS GLACIATION?

Glaciation occurs when layers of snow build up in areas over a long period of time. The layers become compressed and form a mass of ice. Where this happens in the valley areas of mountain ranges, the layers form into glaciers that, over time, move slowly down the mountainside. In the polar regions, vast frozen areas known as icecaps are formed.

Glaciers begin high in a mountain range.

HOW QUICKLY DO GLACIERS MOVE?

THE SPEED AT WHICH glaciers move depends on the steepness of the slope, though they average a speed of around 2m (7ft) a day. It generally takes ice several thousand years to move from one end of a glacier to the other.

The front of the glacier is called the snout.

The glacier scours out rocks as it slowly tumbles down the valley.

Cracks in the glacier are called crevasses.

Meltwater forms at the lower areas of the glacier.

WHAT HAPPENS WHEN GLACIERS MELT?

AFTER THOUSANDS of years, the climate may warm and the glacier melts. During glaciation, the valley's shape will have changed from a V- to a U-shape. Water can fill the area to form fjords and lakes.

Before glaciation

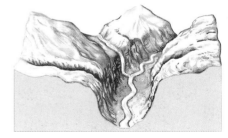

After glaciation

HOW DOES AN ICECAP FORM?

In the far north and south, glaciation causes vast sheets of ice to form over the land. The temperature never rises enough for the ice to melt completely.

Icecaps move outward toward the sea. Snow in the center of the cap becomes ice at the edges.

The two largest icecaps are in Greenland and Antarctica. With the global climate warming up, the Antarctic icecap is beginning to melt.

HOW ARE ICEBERGS FORMED?

ICEBERGS ARE FORMED from freshwater ice brought to the ocean by glaciers, or when chunks are broken off an icecap due to the effect of the tide and waves. This effect is known as calving. Icebergs contain large amounts of rock fragments that make them heavy, and they sit low in the ocean. Once an iceberg has broken off, its movement depends upon the wind and sea currents.

Around 88% of an iceberg lies below the surface of the water. It is estimated that around 10,000 icebergs break off the icecaps of Greenland each year.

DOES THE SEA EVER FREEZE?

WHEN THE TEMPERATURE of the sea dips below 28°F (−1.9°C), it can freeze. This happens off the Antarctic coast and other glaciated regions. The entire North Pole is in fact frozen sea that is never more than several yards thick. Sea ice is often referred to as pack ice.

Specially designed ships known as icebreakers can penetrate areas of sea ice in the polar regions. Their hulls are strengthened to enable them to batter their way through the ice and also to withstand the force of the ice when the sea freezes around the ship.

WHAT CAN SCIENTISTS DISCOVER IN THE POLAR REGIONS?

SCIENTISTS WHO STUDY glaciers and polar ice are called glaciologists. There are permanent research stations based in polar regions, manned by glaciologists who can discover a great deal about the Earth. Working in laboratories dug out of the ice, they investigate layers of ice that contain gases and substances from climatic conditions of the past. Ice cores are also drilled from the ice and taken back to laboratories for detailed testing.

fast facts

WILL THERE BE ANOTHER ICE AGE?

There are times when the Earth's climate grows so cold that the icecaps become huge. These periods are called ice ages. Scientists think that there have been around five ice ages in the last million years, the last one ending around 10,000 years ago. If ice ages happen in cycles, then another one could be a distinct possibility.

HOW BIG WAS THE LARGEST ICEBERG?

One iceberg was measured at 208 miles (335 km) long and 60 miles (97 km) wide.

WHERE IS THE THICKEST ICE IN THE WORLD?

Ice in Antarctica has been measured at 3 miles (5 km) deep.

HOW OLD ARE ICEBERGS?

It is thought that the ice in icebergs is about 5,000 years old.

WHAT CAUSES AN AVALANCHE?

AVALANCHES are huge masses of snow that suddenly crash down a mountainside. They are caused by a combination of heavy snow and a sudden rise in temperature. Avalanches can be up to 0.6 miles (1 km) across and generate winds of up to 185 mph (300 kmph). Their effects on towns and local populations can be devastating.

Sometimes a skier can accidentally trigger an avalanche.

HOW ARE MOUNTAINS FORMED?

Mountain ranges make up some of the world's most impressive landscapes. Like earthquakes and volcanoes, they are formed as a consequence of the activity of the Earth's tectonic plates. Where the plates push up against one another, the Earth's crust buckles and folds, resulting in ranges of rocky mountains. Volcanoes also make up some of the world's greatest mountains.

WHAT ARE THE DIFFERENT TYPES OF MOUNTAIN?

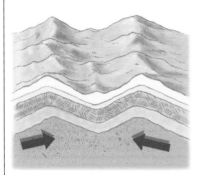
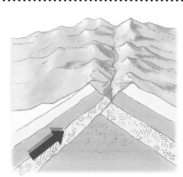
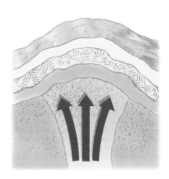
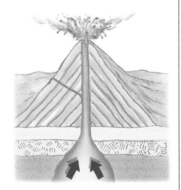

Fold mountains
Fold mountains form where tectonic plates collide, and the crust bends and buckles.

Fault-block mountains
When layers of rock crack or snap to form faults, slabs of rock may be forced upward to form block mountains. Some of these are flat-topped.

Dome mountains
Dome mountains form above a rising layer of molten rock. Where the rock moves outward, a dome shape is formed.

Volcanoes
Volcanoes form mountains as layers of solidified lava pile up into a cone shape.

WHERE ARE THE WORLD'S HIGHEST MOUNTAINS?

NO FEWER THAN ten of the highest mountains in the world are in the Himalayas. Highest of all is Everest, which lies on the border of Nepal and China. At a height of 29,028 feet (8,848 m), it is almost 6,562 feet (2,000 m) higher than the highest mountain outside the Himalayas–Aconcagua in Argentina, South America.

The highest peak in the Himalayas, Everest, has long represented a challenge to adventurous mountaineers. It was first climbed in 1953.

Ancient mountain ranges such as the Scottish Highlands are evidence of continents colliding millions of years ago. Once massive, they have eroded over time.

ARE SOME MOUNTAINS OLDER THAN OTHERS?

MOUNTAINS FORM OVER many millions of years, and due to the continual movement of the Earth's plates, they are still being formed. Young mountain ranges are those that have formed in the last 50 million years or so, such as the Himalayas in Asia. Older mountain ranges, such as the Urals in Russia or the Scottish Highlands, were formed many more millions of years ago and have eroded significantly.

HOW IS A RIVER VALLEY FORMED?

OVER TIME, rainfall erodes the land to form valleys and other features. At mountain peaks, the rainwater flows quickly to form narrow gullies. Slowing down as it moves further downhill, the water forms a wide valley.

Narrow valley in higher area

Valley widens in the lower reaches.

WHAT ARE RIFTS AND CANYONS?

RIVER WATER does not always carve out wide valleys. In some areas, for instance, where there are fairly soft rocks, very deep, narrow valleys with vertical sides called canyons are formed. In places where continents are drifting apart, very wide rift valleys and flat areas known as plateaus can appear. The Great Rift Valley in Africa is the biggest example of these.

The Grand Canyon in Arizona was formed by the Colorado River which runs along its base. Reaching depths of over 1 mile (1.5 km) and running for 217 miles (350 km), the surrounding cliffs are made of a striking, multicolored rock.

HOW DO CAVES FORM?

CAVES can form in different ways, depending on the type of landscape in which they are situated. Limestone is a very soft rock, and caves are fairly common in limestone areas because it dissolves in rainwater. Caves can be formed out of coastal cliff faces by waves crashing against them, and ice caves may appear where streams of meltwater run beneath a glacier. The hardened lava of a volcanic eruption may also leave a hollow beneath, producing a lava cave.

fast facts

WHAT IS THE WORLD'S LONGEST MOUNTAIN RANGE?

The Andes in South America is the world's longest mountain range. It stretches for 4,500 miles (7,200 km).

WHAT IS THE HARDEST MOUNTAIN TO CLIMB?

K2, the second highest mountain in the Himalayas, is notoriously difficult to climb because of its acutely angled rock faces. Many people have died trying to reach its summit.

WHAT IS THE WORLD'S DEEPEST CANYON?

Contenders for the deepest canyon include Hell's Canyon in the United States, Colco Canyon in Peru, and the Yalung Zambo in the Himalayas.

WHO CLIMBED MOUNT EVEREST FIRST?

Sir Edmund Hillary and Sherpa Norgay Tenzing climbed Mount Everest in 1953.

WHY DO SOME CAVES HAVE STALACTITES AND STALAGMITES?

STALACTITES AND STALAGMITES can be found in limestone caves. As water drips down through limestone, it dissolves it and leaves behind deposits of a mineral called calcite. This produces distinctive stalactites that hang from the roof of the cave. When the calcite forms in pools of water on the cave floor, deposits grow upward, forming stalagmites. Where the two features meet, they form columns.

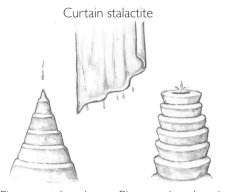

Curtain stalactite

Fir-cone stalagmite   Plate-stack stalagmite

HOW MUCH OF THE EARTH IS COVERED BY WATER?

Though the bulk of our planet is made of rock, around 70% of its surface is covered with water. The Earth's seas and oceans account for most of this coverage–the Pacific Ocean alone covers more than a third of the Earth.

HOW ARE WAVES MADE?

WIND BLOWING ACROSS the surface of the sea creates ripples of energy in the water. Although it appears that the water is moving straight ahead, it is actually moving in a circle. At the shore, the circular movement is broken, and the crest of a wave topples over as it meets the land. Powerful waves create a tremendous force when they crash against the shore–in storms they can cause severe damage. The height and power of a wave depends on the power of the wind.

WHAT CAUSES OCEAN CURRENTS?

CURRENTS OF WATER in the world's oceans and seas are generated by wind and the movement of warm and cold water. Warm currents created by wind flow near the surface of the water and move away from the equator. Cold water from the poles sinks below the warm water and moves into its place. Warm and cold currents often flow in the same area in different directions. The rotation of the Earth affects some currents by turning them into twisting movements called gyres.

Surf is produced where large waves pass over a beach that becomes shallow slowly. The wave breaks over a relatively long period, creating large crests. A surfer uses a surfboard to travel along the "tube" that the circular motion of the wave creates.

Cold current

Warm current

Arctic Ocean: 3.65% of total sea area

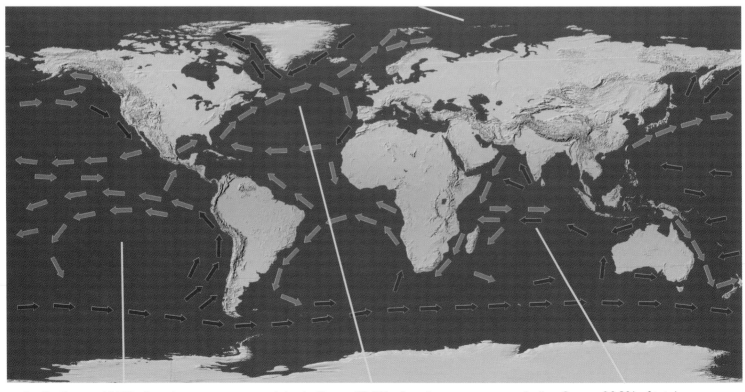

Pacific Ocean: 45.7% of total sea area   Atlantic Ocean: 22.7% of total sea area   Indian Ocean: 20.3% of total sea area

WHAT CAUSES A WHIRLPOOL?

WHIRLPOOLS ARE CAUSED where ocean currents, tidal flows, winds, and irregularities in the coastline and ocean floor combine to form a swirling mass of water. Whirlpools powerful enough to produce a twisting vortex capable of sucking boats down beneath the surface are rare and only found near coasts, not in open seas. The Charybdis whirlpool, which is found between Sicily and mainland Italy, is a well-known example.

HOW WERE THE OCEANS FORMED?

THE OCEANS were formed many millions of years ago. Water vapor thrown into the atmosphere by volcanoes condensed, resulting in rainfall. Hollow areas of the crust filled with water to form the oceans.

Water vapor forms in the atmosphere.

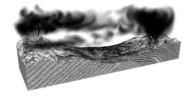

Rainfall fills hollows.

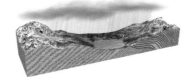

Oceans are formed.

HOW DO SCIENTISTS STUDY THE OCEAN?

OCEANOGRAPHY IS THE SCIENCE concerned with the study of oceans and seas. Because of the vastness and depths of the oceans, there is a great deal to study, and many things are not yet understood. Modern technology has helped oceanographers immensely. Computer analysis of water and sediment samples can give an accurate picture of the content of oceans, and currents can be electronically monitored and predicted. Robotic submersibles and sonar imaging help in the study of the sea floor.

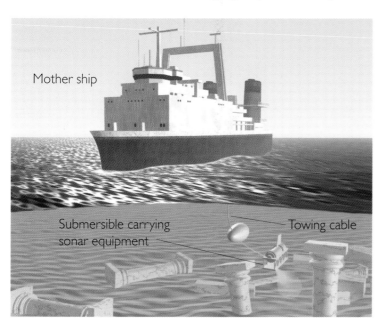

Mother ship

Submersible carrying sonar equipment

Towing cable

Sonar imaging helps oceanographers build up a picture of the ocean floor. Sound waves are beamed onto the seabed, from which they bounce back to a receiver. A computer then translates the information into a sonic "image" called a sonograph.

HOW ARE ISLANDS FORMED?

ISLANDS VARY in size and type. They can be formed by volcanoes erupting beneath the ocean, depositing lava that eventually builds up to the surface. Some volcanic islands form long chains, known as arcs. Islands in tropical areas may form when tiny marine organisms called coral build up in shallow water. Sometimes, the sea may rise to such an extent that it cuts off an area of land to form an island.

The Whitsunday Islands on the coast of Queensland, Australia, form part of the Great Barrier Reef—the world's largest group of coral islands.

fast facts

IS THE OCEAN FLOOR FLAT?

The ocean floor is far from flat. It is almost as varied as the continental landscape, with mountainous areas, plains, and ridges.

WHICH OCEAN IS THE BIGGEST?

The Pacific is the biggest ocean with a total surface area of 63,855,000 sq miles (165,384,000 sq km).

ARE THE WORLD'S OCEANS CONNECTED?

None of the world's five oceans is completely surrounded by land; they flow into one another through open water.

WHAT IS AN ATOLL?

A ring of coral around a sunken island is called an atoll.

WHERE DOES A RIVER BEGIN AND END?

Rivers begin in places where water collects and eventually trickles over the land. The water in all rivers comes from rain or snow. Sometimes rain falls onto a mountainside and flows directly into gullies that flow into small streams and eventually into a river. Mountain springs form when rainwater soaks into the ground through permeable rocks and then bubbles up again, usually at the foot of a mountain. The water from the spring then forms a river flow. Other rivers begin where glaciers melt, and some rivers, such as the Nile, have a lake as their source. All rivers flow into the sea through an estuary.

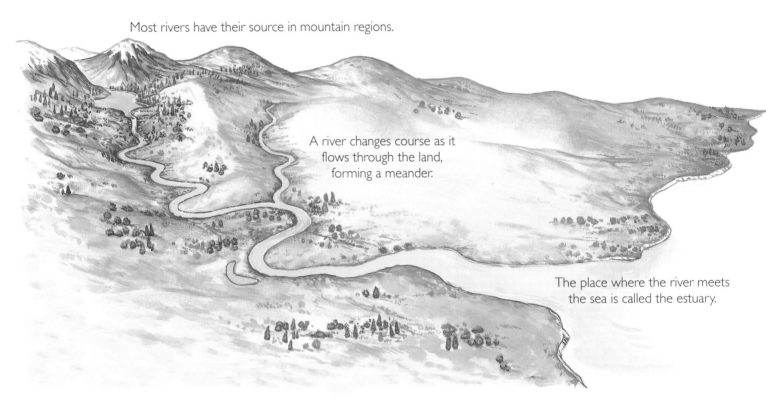

Most rivers have their source in mountain regions.

A river changes course as it flows through the land, forming a meander.

The place where the river meets the sea is called the estuary.

HOW ARE WATERFALLS FORMED?

WATERFALLS ARE GENERALLY found near the source of a river, where it is flowing fastest. They form where a layer of soft rock lies below a layer of hard rock. Because the soft rock wears away faster than the hard rock above it, a ledge forms, and the water crashes over it. The water will continue to erode the soft rock, moving the waterfall's position gradually backward.

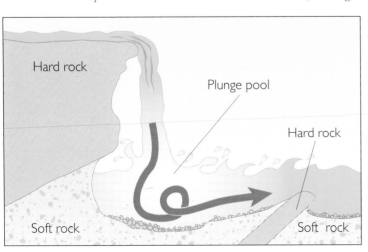

Hard rock

Plunge pool

Hard rock

Soft rock

Soft rock

This waterfall is in Yellowstone National Park in Wyoming.

WHAT MAKES A RIVER FLOOD?

THERE ARE A NUMBER of reasons for rivers flooding. Heavy rainfall, such as that in tropical regions during the monsoon season, may produce more water than a river can hold, making it burst its banks. A flood can also happen if a river is blocked by something, such as a landslide. Tidal rivers can flood when very high tides and strong winds combine to force more water upstream. In cold countries, melting snow has the same effect as heavy rainfall, while ice melting upstream before it does further downstream can cause ice blockages in the channel, resulting in a flood.

Some kinds of flooding can be prevented by building dams or water barrages. The Thames Barrier in London, England, is one such example. If a flood is expected, the Barrier's gates can be raised to help prevent serious flooding in the city.

ARE THERE DIFFERENT TYPES OF LAKES?

LAKES ARE AREAS of water surrounded by land. They occur where water collects in hollows in the Earth's surface. The type of lake depends on how the hollow was formed.

Artificial lake

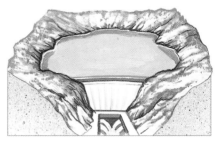

Glacial lake

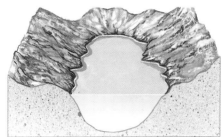

Lakes can form in abandoned gravel pits, quarries, or open-cast mines. Dammed rivers may also flood areas to make artificial lakes.

Lakes can form in areas where ice sheets and glaciers have carved out hollows in hard rock. Finland has many lakes that formed this way.

Rift-valley lake

Crater lake

Where the Earth's crust slips down to form a rift valley, water may collect to form a lake. Lake Nyasa in East Africa is an example of a rift-valley lake.

Water may collect in the hollow of a long-extinct volcano, such as the one at Crater Lake in Oregon. Some meteorite craters may also form lakes.

ARE THERE ANY RIVERS WITHOUT WATER?

Ephemeral rivers are found in many desert areas. They are completely dry, except during periods of freak rainfall.

WHAT IS THE WORLD'S LONGEST RIVER?

The river Nile, which stretches for 4,160 miles (6,695 km) through Africa, is the world's longest river.

WHERE IS THE WORLD'S DEEPEST LAKE?

Lake Baikal, in Siberia, is the world's deepest lake at 5,315 feet (1,620 m).

WHAT IS THE HIGHEST WATERFALL IN THE WORLD?

The Angel Falls in Venezuela drop 3,212 feet (979 m), making them the highest in the world.

WHAT IS IRRIGATION?

When water is diverted from a river or lake to farmland, it is known as irrigation.

WHICH LAKE IS THE BIGGEST?

The Caspian Sea is, despite its name, the world's largest lake.

DO LAKES LAST FOREVER?

LAKES may eventually disappear. This happens as they drain away through man-made barriers, fill up with sediment from rivers, or evaporate as the climate changes.

WHY ARE COASTLINES SO VARIED?

The world's coastlines show more varied features than any other kind of landscape. The type and appearance of a coastline depends on the kind of rock present where the land meets the sea, as well as the strength and direction of the prevailing winds, tides, and currents.

The distinctive white cliffs found along the south coast of England are this color because the rocks in the area are made mainly of chalk.

HOW ARE COASTLINES ERODED?

THE SEA is so strong that many coastlines are easily eroded. Caves and arches are created as the waves attack a headland from all sides. These features then continue to be eroded in two ways. Stones thrown up by the sea scrape away at the rocks, wearing the cliffs into the sea. Cracks in the rock are then made bigger as air forced into them by the water expands when the waves retreat.

Headlands are made of hard rocks, that resist the force of the sea.

The air in a sea cave may be forced through the roof, creating a blowhole.

Cracks in the head-land erode to make sea caves.

Arch

Stack

This natural arch has formed in the coastline at Durdle Door, Dorset, England.

WHAT ARE ARCHES AND STACKS?

SOME OF THE MOST DRAMATIC coastlines are seen where rocky headlands have been eroded into arches and stacks. As the sea erodes the rocky coastline, only the toughest rocks remain, sometimes forming arch-shaped head-lands. Eventually, the roofs of these arches may fall, leaving tall, rocky columns known as sea stacks.

These stacks are found in the Magdalen Islands, Canada.

HOW ARE BEACHES FORMED?

BEACHES ARE MADE as rocks, worn away from headlands, are ground down into shingle and sand. The sea then deposits these particles in a sheltered place, forming a beach.

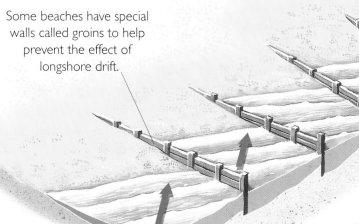

Sand may be carried away from the beach to form a spit.

Some beaches have special walls called groins to help prevent the effect of longshore drift.

You can see how the sand and gravel is moved around by the way it piles up against groins and sea walls.

DO BEACHES ALWAYS REMAIN THE SAME?

BEACHES ARE changing all the time. Gravel and sand on beaches is constantly shifted around by the action of the wind and waves–a process known as longshore drift. The same beach may be made of pebbles at one time of the year, yet be sandy a few months later.

CAN COASTLINES BE PROTECTED FROM THE SEA?

IT IS POSSIBLE to prevent, or at least slow down, the erosion of some coastlines. Groins help to prevent longshore drift, while trees and grasses can be planted especially to stop sand dunes from being blown away. Sea walls help prevent coastal erosion and protect low-lying areas from flooding.

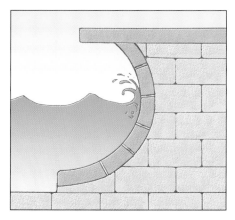

Sea walls can be designed to repel waves, protecting the coast.

Concrete barriers, or breakwaters, extend into the sea to break up waves.

WHAT IS SPECIAL ABOUT CORAL REEFS?

CORAL REEFS are special areas of coastline made from living things. They grow in areas where the water is particularly warm, clear, and shallow. Tiny sea animals cling to the coastline. When they die, they create limestone skeletons to which more creatures attach themselves. As these die, more creatures take hold, and the process continues. Coral reefs are among the strongest structures on Earth, and they make up some of the world's most beautiful coastlines.

Coral reefs are most commonly found near the shoreline. The reef above is known as a fringing reef–it is connected directly to the land. Barrier reefs create a lagoon of calm water between the reef and the land.

fast facts

WHICH BEACH IS THE WORLD'S LONGEST?

At 75 miles (121 km), Cox's Bazar, Bangladesh, is the longest beach.

WHAT IS A RIA?

A ria is an inlet on a coastline that appears when the land sinks or the sea level rises.

WHY DOES THE SEA CHANGE COLOR?

The color of the sea depends on two things: what the weather is like and what the seabed is made up of. For example, stormy weather stirs up sediment from the seabed, making it a brown color. The sea also reflects the color of the sky, so a sunny day will mean blue seas; cloudy skies make the water look murky.

DO INLAND LAKES HAVE BEACHES?

Some inland lakes have beaches, although they do not change as dramatically as those on the coast.

WHAT IS A SAND SPIT?

Longshore drift can carry sand away out to sea to form a sand spit.

WHERE DO FORESTS GROW?

Forests will grow in areas where the temperature rises above 50°F (10°C) in the summer and the annual rainfall is more than 8 inches (200 mm). The type of forest depends on the local climate, the soil, and the altitude. Forests that grow in the extreme north of the Northern Hemisphere are called boreal forests; temperate forests grow in areas of moderate climate in both the Northern and Southern Hemispheres. Tropical regions are best known for their vast, dense areas of rainforest.

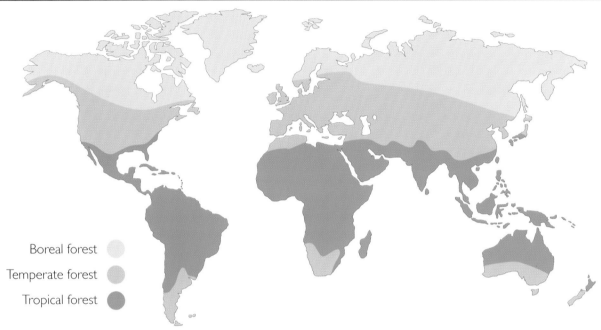

Boreal forest

Temperate forest

Tropical forest

HOW DO THE WORLD'S FORESTS DIFFER?

Rainforest

Coniferous forest

Deciduous forest

Rainforests feature an extremely wide variety of broad-leaved trees, characterized by long, slim trunks. Most of the greenery is at the top of the tree and is known as the canopy. Temperate rainforests grow in parts of North America. They are home to some of the oldest and largest trees on Earth.

All boreal forests are of the coniferous type. The harsh climate (very cold winters, hot summers, and little rainfall) means that only hardy conifers, such as spruce, fir, and pine trees, can grow in these areas. These "evergreen" trees usually have needle-shaped leaves.

Deciduous forests grow in the world's temperate regions. The trees in these areas shed their leaves during winter or the dry season. High rainfall and a relatively mild climate mean that broad-leaved trees such as oak and beech thrive in these areas.

WHAT IS IT LIKE ON THE FOREST FLOOR?

THE FLOOR of a forest is teeming with wildlife. Decaying vegetation provides food for insects and allows many kinds of fungi to grow. The warm, humid atmosphere of a tropical rainforest is the perfect environment for plants and mosses that thrive in shady areas. Palm trees will grow here among other young trees growing toward the forest canopy. Climbing plants such as liana twist and curl around the trunks of the trees.

WHY ARE FORESTS DESTROYED?

THE WORLD'S FORESTS provide many resources for human beings. Trees are cut down for timber, which is used for many different purposes, from building materials and fuel to making paper and chemicals. Forest areas are also cleared to create land for farming and other uses. There is a great deal of concern about the rate at which rainforests in particular are being destroyed. It is thought that an area of rainforest the size of a football field disappears every second. Such devastation has a dramatic effect on plant and animal species, as well as on the land itself.

Deforestation–the destruction of forests–is happening at an alarming rate. Some forests are carefully managed, and trees are replanted to create sustainable forests for the future. However, many tropical rainforests are destroyed for economic reasons, without any replanting. Half of the world's rainforests were cut down during the twentieth century.

HOW CAN RAINFORESTS BE REGENERATED?

WITH CAREFUL PLANNING, areas of rainforest can be re-established, although it takes over a hundred years for the forest to return to its original state. However, if the land is damaged, only scrubby vegetation will grow again.

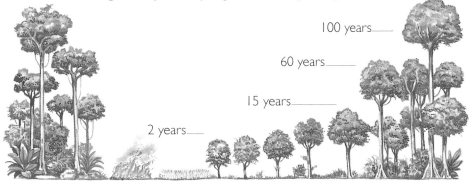

100 years

60 years

15 years

2 years

| Original forest grows undisturbed. | Forest is cut down and land is used for farming. | Special species of tree are planted. | Original species become established. | Forest returns to its original state. |

WHICH ANIMALS LIVE IN RAINFORESTS?

TROPICAL RAINFORESTS ARE home to an incredible range of animal life. Colorful birds, such as toucans, parrots, and macaws, live alongside gorillas or other primates, while tigers, pumas, and wolves may roam among poisonous snakes and insects. Over half of the world's known species exist in the Amazon rainforest alone.

fast facts

HOW MUCH OF THE WORLD IS COVERED BY FOREST?

Around one-third of the Earth's surface is covered by forest, although the number of trees is decreasing steadily.

WHERE IS THE WORLD'S LARGEST FOREST?

The world's largest forest is in Siberia. It covers around 4.2 million sq miles (11 million sq km).

WHICH IS THE WORLD'S LARGEST RAINFOREST?

Covering an area of 2.7 million sq miles (7 million sq km), the Amazon rainforest is the largest of its kind.

WHAT IS COPPICING?

Cutting down areas of woodland to promote the growth of new wood is known as coppicing.

WHAT IS THE UNDERSTORY?

The layer just above the floor of a rainforest is called the understory.

WHAT ARE THE MAIN FEATURES OF A DESERT?

Deserts are hot, dry areas formed by the constant weathering and erosion of the land by fierce winds, extreme temperatures, and occasional flows of water. They can contain barren mountain ranges, vast canyons cut into the Earth, and huge plains covered with rocks or sand dunes. Many deserts have unusual rock formations, produced by certain kinds of erosion caused by wind and sand.

Strange rock formations are a common sight in many of the world's deserts. Winds stir up sand that wears away softer rocks, leaving only the hard layers visible. These red rocks in the Painted Desert, in Arizona, are one such example.

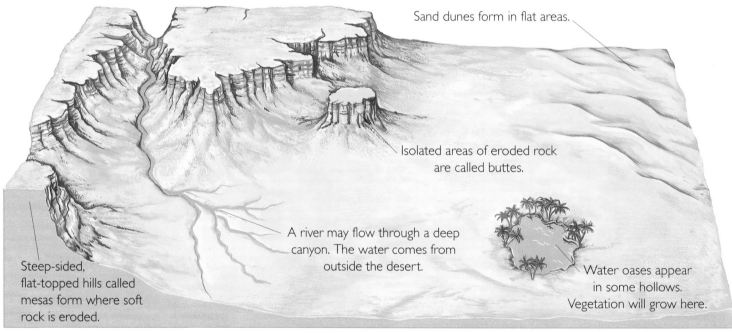

Sand dunes form in flat areas.

Isolated areas of eroded rock are called buttes.

A river may flow through a deep canyon. The water comes from outside the desert.

Water oases appear in some hollows. Vegetation will grow here.

Steep-sided, flat-topped hills called mesas form where soft rock is eroded.

HOW ARE SAND DUNES FORMED?

SAND DUNES FORM when sand is heaped up by the desert winds. They do not remain still, but are being constantly shifted around by the wind. Dunes form in several different ways, producing various shapes.

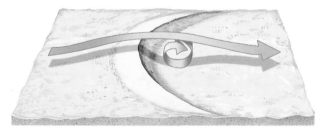

Barchan sand dune
The most familiar types of sand dunes are the crescent-shaped barchan dunes. The sand at either end of the crescent is being blown faster than that in the middle.

Seif sand dunes
In areas where there is little sand and a powerful wind, seif sand dunes can form. Long ridges of sand are heaped up in lines, parallel to the wind's direction. The wind slows down at the edges of the ridges, producing eddies of sand.

ARE THERE DIFFERENT TYPES OF DESERT?

ALL DESERTS FORM in areas where there is very little rainfall–less than 10 inches (250 mm) a year. While they share many features, deserts around the world form because of varying climatic conditions. Tropical deserts form when dry air drops all its rain at the equator. Continental deserts are found in areas so far inland that there is no moisture in the air–the Gobi Desert in central Asia is one example. Rain-shadow deserts exist near mountain ranges where all the rain in the region falls, while cold ocean currents can force dry air downward, creating coastal deserts.

The Sahara is a continental desert. Too far inland to receive any moisture, vast, shifting sand seas known as ergs make up a typical Saharan landscape.

Monument Valley in Arizona is a typical rain-shadow desert. These types of desert often have a mainly rocky landscape.

CAN PEOPLE LIVE IN DESERTS?

DESPITE THE HARSH CONDITIONS of deserts, people have lived in these areas for thousands of years. The nomadic people of the Middle East and Africa–the Bedouin–move herds of camels through the desert, settling near oases and river valleys.

The Bushmen of the Kalahari in Africa live off the native wildlife and have developed special skills for finding water.

The Bedouin have traveled through the desert for centuries. In the modern age, there are more people than ever living in deserts. The desert locations of valuable mineral resources such as oil have led to the growth of permanent settlements in areas that were previously seen as uninhabitable. Modern engineering means that water can now easily be supplied to these areas.

WHAT IS A MIRAGE?

HOT DESERT AIR can distort light in a way that makes objects in the distance appear in the wrong place. Light travels more quickly through warm air close to the ground than it does through the cooler air above it. This causes light from an object to bend, making it appear upside down and closer to the viewer. The shimmering effect can look a little like a lake–an effect that is also often seen on hot roads.

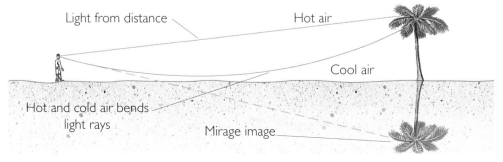

Light from distance

Hot air

Cool air

Hot and cold air bends light rays

Mirage image

---

fast facts

HOW DOES A SANDSTORM HAPPEN?

Strong desert winds whip up the sand and transport it many miles to produce a sandstorm.

WHERE IS THE HOTTEST PLACE IN THE WORLD?

The hottest place in the world is Death Valley, California, where temperatures can reach 134°F (57°C).

HOW LONG CAN A HUMAN BEING SURVIVE IN THE DESERT?

With adequate water, shade, food, and clothing, people could survive happily in the desert. Without these, at temperatures in excess of 115°F (46°C), the average person would be dead within a day.

WHY ARE SOME DESERTS COLD AT NIGHT?

Clear skies in desert areas mean that the heat escapes during the night, often making them very cold.

WHICH IS THE LARGEST DESERT?

The Sahara is by far the world's largest desert. Covering an area of 3,320,000 sq miles (8,600,000 sq km), it is almost four times bigger than the next largest, the Arabian Desert.

WHAT IS DESERTIFICATION?

Intensive farming methods and the destruction of forests are two ways in which humans have increased the size of deserts. Such activity damages soil. When deserts grow because of this, it is known as desertification.

WHAT IS A DREIKANTER?

A pebble that has been eroded flat by desert wind and sand is called a dreikanter.

WHERE DOES COAL COME FROM?

Coal is the fossilized remains of plants that have been put under high pressure beneath the ground for millions of years. Ancient trees and plants became buried in swampy areas, where the process of decay was very slow. The first level of decay produced a soft, earthy material called peat. As the material became covered with more and more sediment, the pressure gradually transformed it into coal. The type of coal varies according to the amount of water and carbon it contains. The more deeply coal is buried, the more carbon and the less water it contains, forming a drier, better-quality coal. Coal is found in layers called seams. The lower a seam is found, the narrower it tends to be.

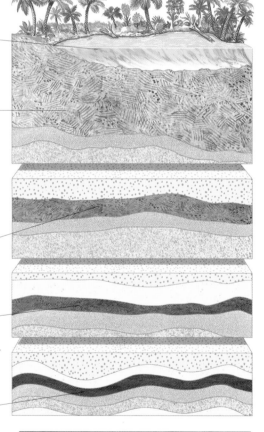

Trees and plants become buried in swamps.

First layer of decay produces peat.

Brown coal, or lignite, is fairly soft, as it still contains a lot of water. It is about 70% carbon.

Bituminous coal is slightly harder, with an 85% carbon content.

The hardest type of coal, with a carbon content of 90%, is called anthracite.

ARE THERE DIFFERENT WAYS OF MINING COAL?

DIFFERENT MINING techniques need to be used depending on the depth at which the coal is found. Where coal is found deep underground, a mineshaft is drilled to reach it. Shaft-mining is the most expensive and potentially dangerous form of mining. Drift mines can be used in hilly areas, where a coal seam can be accessed through a horizontal tunnel. Open-cast or strip-mining is the simplest method; layers of ground are stripped away to get at the coal found close to the surface.

Strip or open-cast mining has dramatically changed landscapes in the past. Modern methods involve refilling areas that have been dug out. The reclaimed land can then be put to other uses. Around two-thirds of modern coal extraction is carried out this way.

Coal is an efficient source of energy and is widely used in power stations. Burning coal releases carbon dioxide into the atmosphere, which is harmful to the environment. The cooling towers of this power station (right) are actually releasing steam, not smoke.

WHAT IS COAL USED FOR?

THE PRIMARY USE of coal is as fuel. Although it is now used less as a domestic heating fuel, many power stations around the world use coal to drive their generators. Coal is also used to produce other products. Coke is a form of processed coal used in blast furnaces to make metals. It is made by heating coal without air, a process that removes ammonia and coal tar. These two products can then be processed into other chemicals to make products such as pesticides, paints, and medicines.

This diagram shows the kind of rock formations that may contain oil and gas reservoirs.

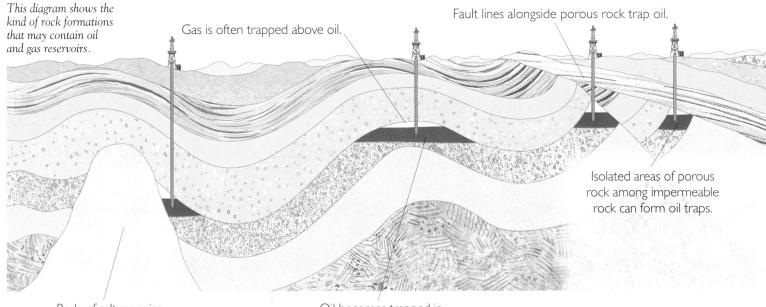

Gas is often trapped above oil.

Fault lines alongside porous rock trap oil.

Isolated areas of porous rock among impermeable rock can form oil traps.

Beds of salt may rise beneath rock to form a dome, trapping oil.

Oil becomes trapped in porous rock between layers of impermeable rock.

HOW DO OIL AND GAS FORM?

OIL AND NATURAL gas are the remains of living organisms that inhabited the sea millions of years ago. They sank to the seabed and became buried by layers of mud and sand, in a similar way to the plants that formed coal. As the remains became more deeply buried, they were broken down by bacteria, heat, and pressure and gradually turned into oil and gas. These fuels are trapped in layers of porous rock, either beneath the seabed or deep below land that was once covered by sea. Geologists call oil and natural gas "petroleum."

The plastic used to make these toys was made from oil.

WHAT IS OIL USED FOR?

OIL IS SUCH a valuable resource because it has many uses. Crude oil (its natural state) is refined into different types of oil. Fuel oil comes in many forms: gasoline for motor vehicles; gas oil for diesel and heating fuel; kerosene for aircraft jet engines. These and other oil products can be processed to make chemicals used in plastics, lubricants, drugs, and solvents.

HOW ARE OIL AND GAS TRANSPORTED?

OIL AND GAS are carried around the world in two ways–by ship and through miles and miles of pipelines. Oil tankers are usually very large, capable of carrying over 22 million gallons (100 million liters) of oil. Pipelines carry oil and gas from fields and platforms directly to refineries to be processed or transferred to oil tankers.

Pipelines carry oil and gas across great distances. One of the largest is the Trans-Alaska Pipeline, which stretches for over 800 miles (1,290 km) between the north and south coasts of Alaska.

fast facts

WHAT IS GAS USED FOR?

Gas is used as a domestic heating fuel, but it is also refined in a similar way to oil to produce useful chemicals.

WILL WE EVER RUN OUT OF OIL?

Oil will not last forever. It is thought that current oil supplies will begin to run out by around 2040.

WHY DOES GAS SMELL?

Gas in its natural form–methane–has its own smell, but when it is refined for use in the home, the smell disappears. A scent is then added to make gas leaks easy to detect.

WHEN WAS PLASTIC INVENTED?

The first usable plastic was "Bakelite," developed in 1909 by Henrik Baekeland.

HOW IS OIL FOUND?

Oil and gas are found by surveying and analyzing the shock waves of test explosions. Exploratory drilling is then carried out. On land, oil sometimes rises to the surface, giving a clue to its location under the ground.

WHAT IS RENEWABLE ENERGY?

Hydroelectric power is produced by turbines and generators when water is held behind huge dams.

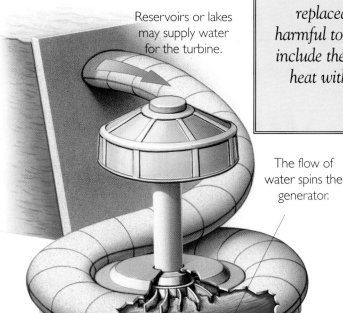

Reservoirs or lakes may supply water for the turbine.

The flow of water spins the generator.

Renewable energy systems use resources that are constantly being replaced. Unlike fossil fuels, they are usually cleaner and less harmful to the environment. Examples of renewable energy sources include the sun, wind, and geothermal energy (energy derived from heat within the Earth). We can also get renewable energy from trees, plants, water, and even waste products.

HOW IS WATER USED FOR POWER?

WATER IS used to generate electricity in three ways. Hydroelectric power is one of the most commonly used forms of renewable energy, accounting for around 7% of the world's electricity production. Specially built dams feed falling water into turbines that drive electricity generators. A similar system controls the flow of water in tidal areas, with a barrier built across an estuary or river. Wave power can also be harnessed by using floating generators that transform wave movement into electricity.

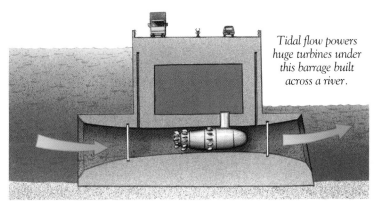

Tidal flow powers huge turbines under this barrage built across a river.

WHAT IS GEOTHERMAL ENERGY?

IN VOLCANICALLY ACTIVE areas of the world, heat energy inside the Earth is used for power. Geothermal power plants use the heat produced by molten rocks to create hot water and steam. The steam powers turbines, while the hot water is piped to homes. Iceland and New Zealand are two countries where geothermal energy is used.

Geothermal power plants use very deep wells to reach volcanically heated water.

HOW IS THE WIND USED TO GENERATE ELECTRICITY?

THE POWER of the wind can be used to generate electricity with huge wind turbines. The blades of a wind turbine drive a generator that produces electricity. Large groups of wind turbines, called wind farms, are built in areas where the wind blows fairly constantly. Flat, open areas of land and coastal areas are popular locations for wind farms. The electricity produced by these farms is fed into the electricity supply along with that coming from other sources.

Modern technology is making wind farms a viable source of electrical power.

WHAT IS SOLAR POWER?

SOLAR POWER SYSTEMS convert light energy from the sun into electricity using photo-voltaic cells. These cells are similar to those used to power pocket calculators, but used on a larger scale they can provide electricity for homes and businesses in areas away from a regular power supply. Most solar power systems work by charging batteries that store the electricity for later use, or act as a backup system for a conventional power supply. Solar power is also used to heat water.

This experimental car uses solar power. The entire surface of the vehicle is covered in photovoltaic cells that create enough electricity to power the wheels. It is highly energy-efficient but not very practical.

CAN WASTE PRODUCTS BE USED FOR ENERGY?

SOME POWER STATIONS can burn waste products that would otherwise be buried in the ground. Even waste that is already buried can be put to use by harnessing the methane gas that decaying matter gives off. Once purified, the gas can be piped to homes, or used in power stations. However, while it solves the problem of what to do with garbage, burning waste releases gases into the atmosphere, creating a pollution problem of its own.

WHERE DOES NUCLEAR ENERGY COME FROM?

NUCLEAR POWER PLANTS use radioactive materials such as uranium or plutonium to power their steam turbines. The atoms of these materials decay, producing heat energy inside a nuclear reactor. Nuclear energy is a "clean" fuel, in that it does not produce the polluting gases that fossil fuels do. However, disposing of used nuclear fuel is hazardous, expensive, and poses serious environmental risks.

The two dome structures in this nuclear power station hold the reactors in which the energy to drive its generators is produced.

fast facts

WHAT IS BIOMASS ENERGY?

Biomass energy is derived from burning natural materials such as wood. Wood chips can also be processed to produce a gas to be burned.

WHAT IS LPG?

LPG stands for Low Pressure Gas– an alternative to gasoline.

WHAT IS ETHANOL?

Ethanol is a type of alcohol derived from grain, which may prove to be a useful fuel.

WHY IS NUCLEAR ENERGY DANGEROUS?

Nuclear fuels emit radiation, which can cause cancer in people and animals. If it enters the atmosphere, it can damage plants and trees and make large areas of land uninhabitable.

WHAT IS A SALTER DUCK?

In the 1970s, engineer Stephen Salter developed a method of harnessing power with his "ducks"–paddles that float on the water surface and transform wave energy into electricity.

HOW DO INDUSTRIES USE RAW MATERIALS?

Most of the world's industries work with raw materials extracted from the Earth. Besides fossil fuels, minerals such as salt, clay, and sulfur, and metals including copper and iron ore are all extracted for industrial purposes. The extraction of such materials is described as primary industry; activities that convert them into other products are known as secondary industries.

Trees are cut into logs, which are then broken into wood chips.

Chemicals and dyes are added, depending on the type of paper being produced.

HOW ARE TREES USED TO MAKE PAPER?

TREES ARE MADE up of thousands of tiny fibers. The paper-making process extracts these fibers and arranges them in a crisscross pattern. Wood is broken up into small pieces and then chemically treated to break it down into fibers. Most paper is produced from softwood trees such as spruce and pine.

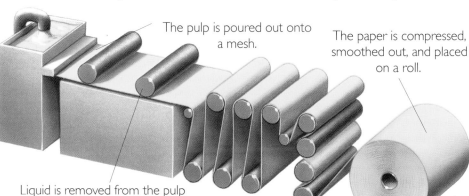

The pulp is poured out onto a mesh.

The paper is compressed, smoothed out, and placed on a roll.

The wood chips are pulped in water and treated with alkalis or acids to release the fibers. Used paper may be added at this point.

Liquid is removed from the pulp by squeezing it through rollers.

WHAT ARE CERAMICS?

CERAMICS ARE materials made from stony or earthy material taken from the ground. Some ceramics, such as pottery and bricks, are molded into shape and then baked (fired) to make them set. Glass is a type of ceramic that is heated first and then molded into shape. Some ceramic materials are able to withstand very high temperatures and are used for specialized applications in industry and engineering.

HOW DOES MINING FOR MINERALS AFFECT THE ENVIRONMENT?

MINING CAN CREATE a number of environmental problems. In the search for useful minerals, other substances are often discarded in the landscape. If these substances are toxic and they enter the water supply, wildlife and people may be affected. Mining can also cause serious physical damage to a landscape.

Clay pots are made from a mixture of kaolin (china clay), which has a smooth texture, and ball clay, which gives strength. Once shaped, the pottery is baked in a kiln.

This iron-ore mine in Brazil has made a huge impact on the landscape.

How is iron turned into steel?

IRON HAS BEEN extracted from iron ore since around 1500 B.C. Most iron is now turned into steel, because this is a much more flexible metal. Steel is made by removing more carbon from the iron and adding other metals, depending on the type of steel being produced. Steel is made in an oxygen furnace. Molten iron mixed with scrap steel is poured into a furnace, and oxygen is blown over it. The oxygen mixes with the carbon and removes it in the form of carbon monoxide.

Molten iron

Scrap

1 Molten iron and scrap steel is poured into the furnace.

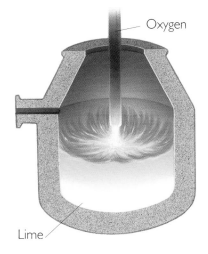

Oxygen

Lime

2 Oxygen is added to produce carbon dioxide. Lime added to the mix helps remove impurities.

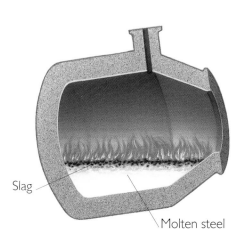

Slag

Molten steel

3 Impurities float on the surface of the molten steel as "slag."

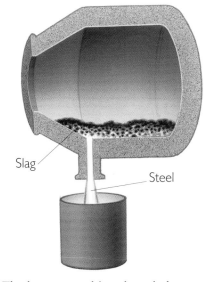

Slag

Steel

4 The slag is separated from the steel when it is poured out of the furnace.

Why is glass so useful?

GLASS IS ONE of the world's oldest manmade materials. It is made from sand that is heated, mixed with other materials, and then shaped as it cools. Glass is easily shaped, cheap to make, and easy to recycle over and over again. It has a huge range of uses, from buildings and optical instruments to bottles and glasses. Modern communication systems rely heavily on fiber-optic cables, which are made from very fine glass fibers.

fast facts

Where does most of the world's gold come from?

Much of the world's supply of precious metals comes from the countries of southern Africa. Gold exports account for around 30% of South Africa's earnings.

Do any countries not have any raw materials?

Japan is one of the world's leading producers of electronics, cars, and ships, yet it has to import almost all of its raw materials.

Where does silicon come from?

Silicon is the most common solid element on Earth, although it is fairly difficult to extract from the rocks and clays in which it is found. It is a semimetal, or semiconductor, which means that it conducts electricity in certain conditions. Silicon is used to make electronic components such as microchips.

Where does most of the world's timber come from?

The United States is the world's largest producer of timber, providing around 14% of the global supply of wood.

Where does aluminum come from?

Aluminum is the most common metal on Earth, but it is difficult to extract in a pure form. Most aluminum comes from bauxite–an ore found in rocks that contain aluminum, oxygen, and silicon. Aluminum is useful because it is both lightweight and strong.

Glass is used to make fiber-optic cables, which allow information to be sent around the world at the speed of light.

WHY IS WATER SO IMPORTANT?

All living things depend on water for their survival; life on Earth would not exist without it. A supply of clean water is essential for people, not only to drink but for sanitation and health reasons. There is plenty of water on Earth, but not everyone has access to the same amount. Demand for water is always increasing, and supplies in many parts of the world are overstretched. In such areas, supplying fresh water can be time-consuming and expensive. For many people, a safe, regular supply of water is taken for granted, but without it life, and indeed industry, would come to a halt.

HOW DOES WATER GET INTO OUR HOMES?

WATER IS SUPPLIED into most homes by underground pipes. It starts its journey in a lake or man-made reservoir and passes through a process of purification before coming out of the tap in your home.

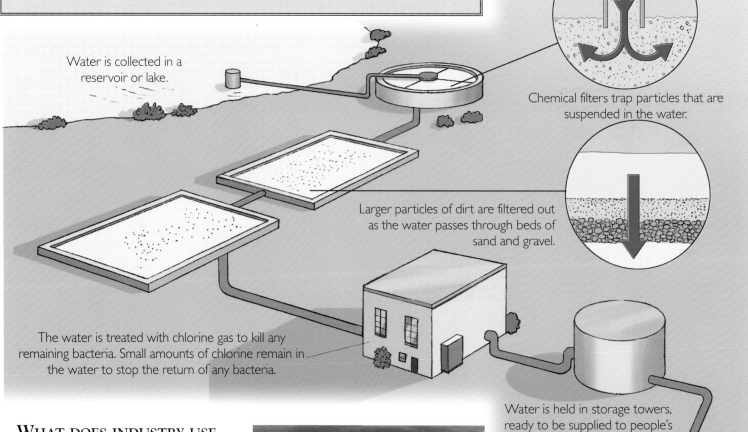

Water is collected in a reservoir or lake.

Chemical filters trap particles that are suspended in the water.

Larger particles of dirt are filtered out as the water passes through beds of sand and gravel.

The water is treated with chlorine gas to kill any remaining bacteria. Small amounts of chlorine remain in the water to stop the return of any bacteria.

Water is held in storage towers, ready to be supplied to people's homes through the water lines.

WHAT DOES INDUSTRY USE WATER FOR?

WATER HAS an enormous range of industrial uses, which means that industry needs a huge amount of water. Companies that produce chemicals use water as a solvent to dissolve other substances and also as a coolant. Power stations use water to generate steam for their turbines, and, of course, water is used in all industries for cleaning.

The electricity-generating industry is one of the biggest users of water. Most power stations use water to produce steam to drive their turbines; nuclear power stations also use it to cool their reactors. This hydroelectric power station uses water directly to power huge turbines.

WHY IS WATER PURIFIED?

HARMFUL BACTERIA that may cause serious diseases and death need to be removed from water before it can be used for domestic purposes. Dirt particles are removed because they can wear away pipes or damage industrial equipment.

HOW DO COUNTRIES WITH LITTLE RAINFALL GET WATER?

IN PARTS of the world that receive little rainfall, access to water can be difficult. In such areas, wells may be dug deep underground, or water can be piped from natural springs. Some countries even process seawater at a desalination plant. The seawater is heated, and only pure water evaporates. When it condenses, it is collected, leaving the salt behind in a concentrated form.

WHERE DOES MINERAL WATER COME FROM?

MINERAL WATER comes from natural water sources under the ground. The types of minerals in the water depend on the type of rock over which the water has been running–different areas produce mineral water containing different types of minerals. Calcium, sodium, and sulfur are examples of minerals commonly found in mineral water. Sources of mineral water are most often in mountainous and hilly regions.

WHAT DISEASES CAN UNCLEAN WATER CAUSE?

MANY MILLIONS of people in developing countries do not have access to clean drinking water and sanitation. In the countryside, people may be forced to use the same ponds, streams, rivers, and lakes for drinking and for sewage. In cities, water supply and sewage systems are often inadequate and, in both cases, people may be exposed to serious illnesses such as malaria, cholera, and yellow fever.

Many people in the Western world drink bottled mineral water in the belief that it is healthy.

fast facts

HOW IS WATER QUALITY MEASURED?

Water quality is measured by what is in the water. Bacteria, phosphates, and metals may all be present, and the amount of such substances in the water will determine its quality. Water used for drinking needs to be of better quality than that used to water land.

WHAT ARE MINERAL DEPOSITS?

The greenish-white crusts sometimes found in teakettles and steam irons are mineral deposits left by the water. Water with a high mineral content is "hard water."

WHICH COUNTRIES USE THE MOST WATER?

Not surprisingly, countries with large populations use most of the world's water. Between them, the U.S., the Commonwealth of Independent States (formerly USSR), India, and China use 45% of the world's water supply.

WHAT IS ALUMINUM HYDROXIDE?

This is a chemical used in water treatment to remove impurities.

WHAT IS THE WATER CYCLE?

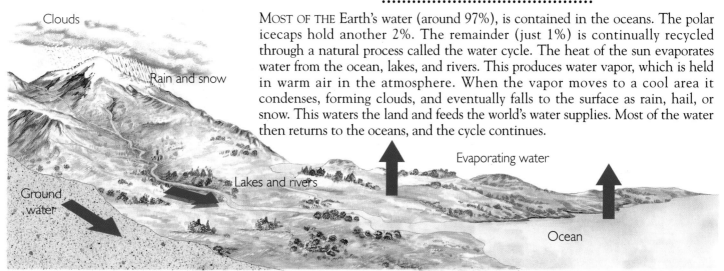

MOST OF THE Earth's water (around 97%), is contained in the oceans. The polar icecaps hold another 2%. The remainder (just 1%) is continually recycled through a natural process called the water cycle. The heat of the sun evaporates water from the ocean, lakes, and rivers. This produces water vapor, which is held in warm air in the atmosphere. When the vapor moves to a cool area it condenses, forming clouds, and eventually falls to the surface as rain, hail, or snow. This waters the land and feeds the world's water supplies. Most of the water then returns to the oceans, and the cycle continues.

Clouds

Rain and snow

Ground water

Lakes and rivers

Evaporating water

Ocean

HOW LONG HAVE PEOPLE BEEN FARMING?

The first farmers grew and cultivated crops in the Middle East around 12,000 years ago. Different varieties of wheat and barley were the main crops. They were grown, as they are today, to produce grain to make bread. Knowledge of farming spread from the region into Europe and Asia, while the native peoples of North and South America began farming around 7000 B.C.

WHAT IS INTENSIVE FARMING?

DEMAND FOR FOOD in the modern world means that the production of crops and livestock needs to be maximized. Many farms use a range of machinery and chemicals to practise what is known as intensive farming. Tractors plow fields and plant seeds, and combine harvesters cut the crops at harvest time. Animal pests are controlled with pesticides, and weeds are destroyed with herbicides. Intensive farming methods often raise concerns about animal welfare, because livestock may be kept indoors in cramped conditions for long periods of time.

Springtime is when the fields are plowed, to get ready for crops to be planted.

Combine harvesters are used to harvest grain.

Seeds are sown by machinery that automatically covers them with soil.

Pesticides and herbicides are applied with a sprayer.

WHAT IS SUBSISTENCE FARMING?

IN MANY DEVELOPING countries, subsistence farming is a common way of life. Farmers usually grow just enough to food to feed themselves and their families, occasionally selling or trading surplus produce at local markets. They keep just a few animals, sometimes for their meat, but more often to work the land.

In some countries, farming methods are used that have remained unchanged for thousands of years. In such circumstances, the way of life is hard and is very dependent on the weather and the quality of the harvest.

WHAT IS THE MOST WIDELY GROWN CROP?

GRAIN, IN the form of wheat, corn (maize), or rice, is the most important food crop in the world. As the basic ingredient of bread, wheat is grown throughout the world, often in very large quantities. Rice is grown in paddy fields throughout Asia, forming the basic food-stuff in that part of the world. Intensive farming methods mean that the amount of grain grown per acre (the yield) in the United States is four times that produced from the same area in Africa.

WHAT IS SELECTIVE BREEDING?

ONLY VARIETIES of crops that grow and taste the best have been cultivated over time, resulting in improved size, flavor and appearance of crops. Certain breeds of animals have been bred to produce livestock that yields more meat. This is known as selective breeding.

Modern breeds of cattle have been developed through years of selective breeding.

HOW DOES A COMBINE HARVESTER WORK?

A COMBINE HARVESTER is an important machine on a modern grain farm. It allows a very large amount of grain to be harvested very quickly. A combine harvester is called that because it does both of the processes involved in harvesting the grain—cutting the crop and separating the grain from the plant. Before the combine harvester, one or both of these jobs were done by hand or by two separate machines.

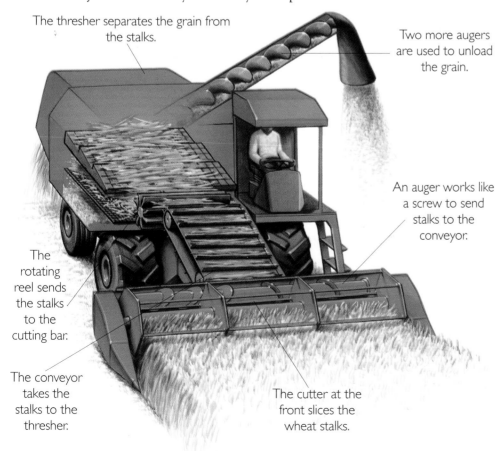

The thresher separates the grain from the stalks.

Two more augers are used to unload the grain.

An auger works like a screw to send stalks to the conveyor.

The rotating reel sends the stalks to the cutting bar.

The conveyor takes the stalks to the thresher.

The cutter at the front slices the wheat stalks.

WHAT IS GENETIC MODIFICATION OF FOOD?

The genetic modification of food sets out to improve crops and live-stock by changing their genetic make-up. Crops can be bred to be resistant to pesticides or extreme weather conditions, allowing them to be grown more efficiently, or in places where they could not grow before. Many people are concerned about the effects this may have on the environment and public health.

WHAT IS ORGANIC FARMING?

Organic farming is very different from intensive farming. It uses natural fertilizers and pesticides rather than artifical ones. Animals are often allowed to enjoy a more natural life than in "factory" farming.

WHAT IS A FOOD MOUNTAIN?

Sometimes the amount of a crop grown for a market exceeds the demand. Large quantities of the foodstuff may be stockpiled, giving us the term "food mountain."

WHAT ARE CASH CROPS?

Cash crops are those grown specifi-cally for trade and economic reasons. Coffee and rubber grown in devel-oping countries may be described as "cash crops."

HOW DOES A FAMINE HAPPEN?

Famines usually occur in areas that rely heavily for food on crops grown locally. If weather conditions result in a poor harvest, there may be a severe shortage of food in the whole area.

WHAT IS AGROFORESTRY?

Agroforestry is a system of growing trees and crops together.

WILL THE WORLD EVER RUN OUT OF FISH?

Fishing is a very important global industry, but it can only exist as long as there are fish to catch. In some parts of the world, stocks of fish have decreased dramatically, due in part to modern fishing methods. As demand for fish has increased, greater numbers of boats have fished the same areas. Technology has also made locating fish easier. Using nets too fine to allow small fish to escape has reduced the numbers of younger fish, which affects breeding and future stocks. While it is unlikely that stocks of fish will run out completely, many countries place strict controls on fishing in an attempt to limit the damage.

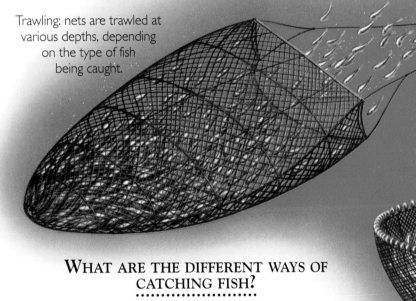

Trawling: nets are trawled at various depths, depending on the type of fish being caught.

Purse-seining: the nets are towed in a large circle to catch the fish.

WHAT ARE THE DIFFERENT WAYS OF CATCHING FISH?

THE FISHING INDUSTRY uses several different methods to catch large numbers of fish. Most involve the use of nets. Trawling uses a cone-shaped net towed behind the fishing boat (known as a trawler). Purse-seining involves surrounding a school (group) of fish with a net and drawing the net lines together. Drift nets may be as long as 60 miles (95 km). Left to drift in the water, they can catch many millions of fish at once.

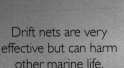

Drift nets are very effective but can harm other marine life.

WHERE ARE THE BEST PLACES TO CATCH FISH?

THE AREAS OF SEAS and oceans where most fish are caught are called fishing grounds. Most of the world's fishing grounds are found above the continental shelf–relatively shallow areas around the coastlines of the world. Fish are attracted to these areas because ocean currents create feeding grounds there.

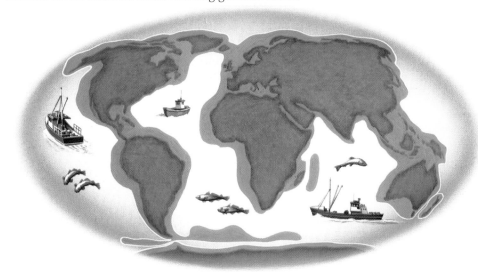

The blue areas of this map show where most of the world's fish are caught.

HOW ARE SHELLFISH CAUGHT?

SHELLFISH SUCH as crabs and lobsters are caught with baskets or netting pots. These baskets or pots sit on the seabed, with their position marked on the surface by a floating buoy. The opening of the basket or pot is designed so that the fish can get inside easily but cannot get out.

Shellfish are caught in fairly shallow waters close to the coastline. The fishermen set down the pots or baskets and return later to retrieve the catch.

WHAT ARE FISH FARMS?

SOME FISH are bred in controlled conditions called fish farms. Fish farmers build special pens in lakes, ponds, or estuaries. Here, they hatch fish from eggs and keep them until they are big enough to sell. Also known as "aquaculture," fish-farming is becoming more common. Freshwater fish farms breed salmon, carp, and trout. Oysters and other shellfish are popular in coastal fish farms.

Fish farms are an efficient way of supplying stocks of fish. This farm in Iceland is used to produce salmon, one of the most commonly farmed fish.

fast facts

WHICH COUNTRIES CATCH THE MOST FISH?

Japan's fishing fleet travels all over the world and catches millions of tons of fish. Russia and China are also big fishing countries.

ARE WHALES STILL CAUGHT?

Some countries, including Japan, Canada, and Norway, continue to catch whales, though controls are strictly enforced.

ARE THERE ANY BY-PRODUCTS OF FISH?

Fish are caught for their oil, and fish bones are used to make some kinds of fertilizer.

WHICH ARE THE MOST POPULAR FISH?

Commercial fishing involves all types of fish. The small pelagic types such as pilchards and herring are the main sources of fish meal and oil products. Atlantic cod is an important food fish for Europe and North America, and pollock is the major catch for Russia and Japan.

WHAT WAS THE COD WAR?

In the 1970s, Britain and Iceland argued about which areas of the North Atlantic their fishing fleets could work. British navy and Icelandic coast guard ships were involved. The dispute became known as the "Cod War."

HOW MUCH OF THE WORLD'S FOOD COMES FROM FISH?

Fishing supplies the world with around 20% of its food.

WHAT IS "DOLPHIN-FRIENDLY" TUNA?

"Dolphin-friendly" tuna is tuna fish caught using methods that do not harm dolphins.

IS EARTH THE ONLY PLANET THAT SUPPORTS LIFE?

As far as we know, the Earth is the only planet in our Solar System that can support life. It has all the things necessary for life as we know it—water, carbon, oxygen, nitrogen, and an abundant supply of food. Life on Earth is incredibly diverse, and the systems that support it are very complex.

Despite the efforts of astronomers and other space scientists, we have not yet found evidence of life on a planet other than our own.

HOW DO SCIENTISTS STUDY THE BIOSPHERE?

SCIENTISTS WHO study the relationships between different forms of life on Earth are called ecologists. They divide up the biosphere into different, related sections, which makes the relationships easier to understand. These sections are the *niche*, the *habitat*, and the *ecosystem*.

WHAT IS THE BIOSPHERE?

THE BIOSPHERE is the part of the Earth in which life exists. It covers an area that stretches from the very bottom of the oceans to some distance above the surface of the Earth.

An ecosystem is a particular part of the biosphere that contains living things.

A habitat is an area in which communities of different species live together.

A niche is where a plant or animal exists within its habitat, and includes its relationship to other plants and animals.

HOW BIG IS AN ECOSYSTEM?

AN ECOSYSTEM is any area that can support different living things, so it can be almost any size. A droplet of rain may contain bacteria and other microscopic living things that live off one another, and could therefore be described as an ecosystem.

An ecosystem may be as small as a droplet of water or as large as a forest.

DOES THE EARTH RECYCLE ITS RESOURCES?

THE EARTH is continually recycling the essential ingredients for life–carbon, oxygen, nitrogen, and water. All plants and animals play their part in this recycling process.

All living things need the oxygen in the atmosphere.

Plants and trees take in carbon dioxide and give out oxygen during the day.

Carbon is the basis for all living things and is found in carbon dioxide gas.

At night, plants and trees take in oxygen and give out carbon dioxide.

Living things use the nitrogen in the atmosphere to create proteins.

Animals breathe in oxygen and give out carbon dioxide.

Bacteria in the soil help release nitrogen and carbon dioxide back into the environment.

Decaying plant matter and animal wastes release nitrogen into the soil.

WHAT DOES THE OZONE LAYER DO?

OZONE IS a very important gas in the Earth's atmosphere. It screens out some of the harmful ultraviolet rays that come from the sun. The ozone layer is a very fine layer of the gas that surrounds the Earth at a height varying between 9 and 30 miles (15 and 50 km).

Ozone makes up a very small part of the Earth's atmosphere.

fast facts

WHAT IS BIODIVERSITY?

If a habitat or ecosystem has a large number of different species living within it, it is said to have a high degree of biodiversity. Ecologists use biodiversity as a measure of the relative ecological "health" of an area.

WHAT WOULD EARTH BE LIKE WITHOUT LIFE?

If there were no longer any life on Earth, the atmosphere would probably be very similar to that of the planet Mars–dry and low in oxygen. All the nitrogen in the atmosphere would move to the oceans.

WHAT IS THE GAIA THEORY?

The idea that the Earth is a single living organism that looks after itself is known as the Gaia theory. Named for the Greek goddess called "Mother Earth," it was developed by the scientist James Lovelock in the 1970s.

HOW LONG HAVE HUMANS BEEN ON EARTH?

Humans have lived on Earth for around 35,000–40,000 years. In the context of the history of the Earth, which is around 4.6 billion years old, it is a very short period of time.

WILL LIFE ON EARTH EVER END?

This is a question that is often asked. Dinosaurs lived for around 10 million years, until they were wiped out by a major catastrophe, generally thought to have been an asteroid colliding with our planet. Such an event, or the long-term ecological destruction of the Earth, could see the elimination of certain species, but some kind of life would probably replace them.

WHO WAS ERNST HAECKEL?

The German biologist Ernst Haeckel coined the word "ecology" in 1869.

HOW HAS HUMANKIND ENDANGERED THE EARTH?

Human beings have affected the Earth's environment like no other species on the planet. The destruction of rainforests, pollution from industry and transportation, and wasteful use of resources are just some of the ways in which people have put the Earth in danger.

Oil spillages at sea can cause serious damage to coastlines and marine wildlife. Cleaning up afterwards is costly and time-consuming.

WHAT IS THE GREENHOUSE EFFECT?

THE "GREENHOUSE EFFECT"–or global warming–is a natural process in which gases in the atmosphere trap the sun's heat and warm the Earth. Industrial activities, such as burning fossil fuels, have added to the levels of carbon dioxide and other "greenhouse gases" in the atmosphere, increasing the greenhouse effect and causing the Earth to get hotter than it would have done naturally.

Some heat is reflected back by Earth, clouds, and the atmosphere.

Heat from the sun

Some heat radiates back into space.

Heat is trapped in the atmosphere.

The Earth is warmed by heat trapped in the atmosphere.

The atmosphere warms up.

The Earth is warmed by the sun.

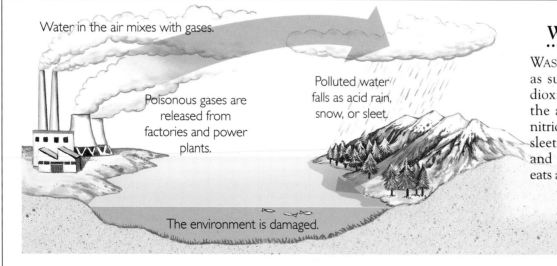

Water in the air mixes with gases.

Poisonous gases are released from factories and power plants.

Polluted water falls as acid rain, snow, or sleet.

The environment is damaged.

WHAT IS ACID RAIN?

WASTE GASES from factories, such as sulfur dioxide and nitrogen dioxide, combine with water in the air to produce sulfuric and nitric acid. This falls as acid rain, sleet, or snow. It pollutes rivers and lakes, kills trees, and even eats away at buildings.

WHAT ARE CFCs?

CFCs (CHLOROFLUOROCARBONS) are another example of greenhouse gases. They are found in aerosol sprays, refrigeration and air-conditioning systems, and certain types of foam packaging. Awareness of the damage caused by CFCs means that some products are now labeled as "CFC Free."

Some aerosol sprays contain CFCs, but awareness of the damage they cause has led to the use of safer alternatives.

IS THERE A HOLE IN THE OZONE LAYER?

GIVEN THE RIGHT CONDITIONS, CFCs can also damage the ozone layer. The CFCs combine with very cool air, producing chlorine–a substance that eats away at ozone. Ozone loss is worst in the area above the South Pole, where a complete "hole" was confirmed in 1985. Reduced ozone levels mean that more of the sun's harmful ultraviolet rays will reach the Earth's surface, affecting human and animal health, and damaging food crops.

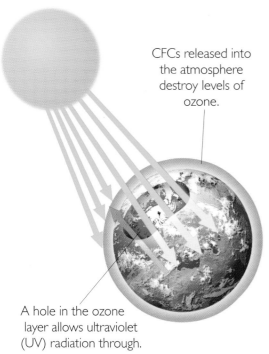

CFCs released into the atmosphere destroy levels of ozone.

A hole in the ozone layer allows ultraviolet (UV) radiation through.

You need to protect yourself from exposure to UV radiation when you're in the sun. UV rays cause sunburn and can eventually cause skin cancer.

WHAT CAN I DO TO HELP PROTECT THE ENVIRONMENT?

EVERYONE CAN do things to help save the environment–here are a few things you could do. Using recycled paper and cardboard is a good way to start; so is making sure all the glass, cans, and paper your family uses is sent for recycling. Try to use public transportation instead of traveling by car, and encourage others to do the same. Switch off lights and other electrical appliances when they are not in use. Make sure that any aerosol products you use do not contain CFCs.

High levels of traffic in cities are the main cause of smog. Some countries have attempted to deal with the problem by restricting traffic and encouraging the use of cleaner fuels. Smog, and air pollution in general, continues to be a major problem and is the cause of some respiratory diseases, such as asthma.

fast facts

WHERE DOES MOST ACID RAIN FALL?

Acid rain tends not to fall in the regions where it is created, because it is carried away by weather systems. Scandinavian counties are affected by pollution created by the heavily industrialized areas of Britain, eastern Europe, and Germany. It is thought that half of the acid rain that falls in Canada comes from its neighbor, the United States.

ARE GOVERNMENTS DOING ANYTHING TO HELP SAVE THE EARTH?

In the last 50 years, people have become aware of environmental problems and some countries have entered agreements to reduce the use of CFCs, cut levels of vehicle emissions, and control industrial pollution. The problem is that many governments and companies avoid employing environmentally friendly systems if they are expensive.

WHAT IS A CATALYTIC CONVERTER?

Emissions from gasoline engines contain harmful chemicals, such as carbon monoxide and nitrogen oxide, which produce smog and affect people's health. A catalytic converter attached to a vehicle's exhaust converts these chemicals into less harmful carbon dioxide, nitrogen, and water.

WHAT IS A LANDFILL SITE?

Most household garbage is buried in a hole in the ground called a landfill site.

WHAT IS SMOG?

Many of the world's large cities suffer from smog (literally smoke + fog). Exhaust emissions from motor vehicles are the main source of smog. The situation is made worse in strong sunlight, when warm air above the level of smog traps it at ground level.

WILL THE WORLD'S POPULATION CONTINUE TO GROW?

Around a thousand years ago, the world's population began to increase dramatically, with the sharpest increase occurring during the 20th century. In the year 2000, the world's population reached six billion, and its growth shows no sign of stopping. Many people fear that an ever-increasing population will lead to serious problems with food supply and overcrowding.

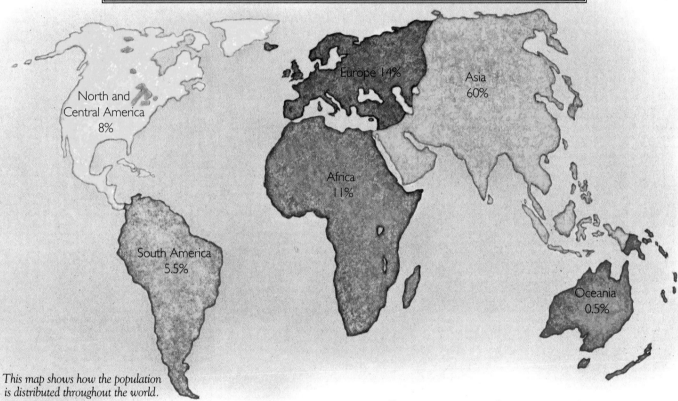

North and Central America 8%

Europe 14%

Asia 60%

Africa 11%

South America 5.5%

Oceania 0.5%

This map shows how the population is distributed throughout the world.

WHICH COUNTRY HAS THE GREATEST POPULATION?

CHINA HAS been the world's most populated country for some time. This vast country is home to over one billion people–around one-sixth of the world's total. In an effort to control the growth in numbers of people there, the government has encouraged families to have only one child.

IS THE WORLD'S POPULATION GETTING OLDER OR YOUNGER?

THE AVERAGE age of a population varies from country to country. In the more developed parts of the world, the population is generally older. High standards of health care allow people to live longer, and families tend to have fewer children. In poorer countries, life expectancy is shorter and many babies die at birth. As a result, families have more children, which means that the population is generally younger.

WHAT IS URBANIZATION?

IN THE MODERN WORLD, more and more people live in towns and cities. This is mainly because of employment opportunities–there are generally more jobs available in urban areas–but also because modern building methods allow more people to live in a smaller area. Roughly half of the world's population lives in cities, and this proportion is expected to increase.

More and more people are moving to the world's cities in search of jobs. This is especially true in developing countries, where cities are becoming very overcrowded.

WHY DO SOME PEOPLE MIGRATE TO OTHER COUNTRIES?

THE MOST common reason that people move to other countries is to seek work. Modern North America was founded through mass immigration–its population grew from 31 to 92 million between 1860 and 1910. Some people may leave their home country because of war, or for political or religious reasons. These people are known as refugees.

The first European immigrants arrived in America in 1620. They sailed in a small ship called the Mayflower. *The Pilgrims, as they are known, named their settlement Plymouth, after the town in England from which they set sail.*

During the 19th and 20th centuries, millions of immigrants arrived in the United States from Europe. The first thing many saw on their way into New York was the Statue of Liberty. Nearby Ellis Island was the site of the U.S.'s main immigration station for many years.

fast facts

CAN POPULATION GROWTH BE CONTROLLED?

In developing countries, where population growth can create serious social problems, education about birth control and contraception is an important step in controlling the situation.

HOW MANY PEOPLE ARE BORN EACH DAY?

It is estimated that around 255,000 people are born each day–that is three new babies every second.

WHAT IS A CENSUS?

Information about a population is gathered through a census. This provides the government of a country with various details about the people who live there, such as the number of people living in a household, the type of work they do, and their ethnic background. This helps build a picture of the population, so that the information can be used to plan services such as health and education.

WHAT IS THE WORLD'S MOST POPULATED CITY?

Tokyo, Japan's capital city, is the world's largest metropolitan area, with a population of around 28 million people.

WHERE WILL POPULATION INCREASE MOST IN THE NEXT DECADE?

It is estimated that most population growth will occur in the developing countries of Africa, Asia, and Latin America–places that are least likely to be able to cope with it.

WHAT IS FAMILY PLANNING?

Family planning combines education and medicine to help families plan the number of children they have.

WHAT ARE INDIGENOUS PEOPLES?

The human race is made up of many different nationalities and groups of people. Indigenous people are those who are native to a certain area. The term is often used to describe the original inhabitants of areas that are now populated by people from other parts of the world.

WHO ARE THE NATIVE AMERICANS?

AROUND 20,000 YEARS AGO, the first settlers of North America arrived from Asia. They were able to travel over land, because at the time, the two continents were joined together. These early settlers gradually formed different tribes and spread themselves throughout the whole country. When the first Europeans arrived in the 15th century, they thought they had landed in Asia, and called the Native Americans "Indians." The relationship between the Indians and the new settlers was difficult, and many battles were fought.

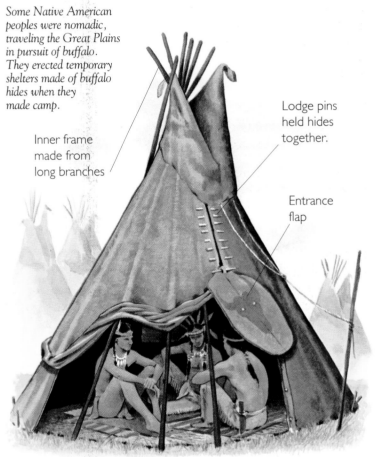

Some Native American peoples were nomadic, traveling the Great Plains in pursuit of buffalo. They erected temporary shelters made of buffalo hides when they made camp.

Inner frame made from long branches

Lodge pins held hides together.

Entrance flap

Many Native Americans live on reservations–areas of land set aside especially for them by the U.S. government during the 19th century.

The Inuit traditionally build temporary hunting lodges, called igloos, from blocks of ice.

WHO ARE THE INUIT?

THE INCREDIBLY HARSH environment of the Arctic is home to a group of people who settled there around 4,000 years ago. They inhabit parts of Siberia, Alaska, Canada, and Greenland. Those who live in North America are known as Inuit, which literally means "real men." Many Inuit continue their traditional lifestyle–hunting for food and furs to sell–but being part of both modern and traditional worlds can be hard, especially for young people.

WHO ORIGINALLY LIVED IN AUSTRALIA?

THE FIRST PEOPLE to live in Australia arrived there about 40,000 years ago from Southeast Asia. These people were named "Aborigines" (people who have lived there since early times) by the European settlers who arrived in Australia during the 18th century. Life has been difficult for many Aboriginal Australians, forced to adapt to the settlers' ways of life. Today, youngsters are being taught about their own rich heritage.

WHAT IS THE DREAMTIME?

THE NATURAL environment is very important to Australian Aborigines. This is because they traditionally believe that the world was created by human, animal, and plant ancestors in something called the Dreamtime. The Dreamtime is celebrated and communicated through art, songs, dancing, and storytelling.

WHO LIVED ON EASTER ISLAND?

ONE OF THE great mysteries of the world is the identity of the people who inhabited Easter Island in the South Pacific. The island is famous for the mysterious stone statues found there. It is believed that they were carved by tribes of people who lived there during neolithic times (more than 1,000 years ago). Very little is known about these people, but they are thought to be the ancestors of the people of the islands of Polynesia.

There are more than 600 ancient statues on Easter Island. Some of them are over 65 feet (20 m) tall.

The fortress city of Machu Picchu was an Inca stronghold. Built over a series of terraces in the spectacular setting of a remote Peruvian mountain, it remained undiscovered by the Spanish conquistadors.

HOW ARE CIVILIZATIONS WIPED OUT?

GROUPS OF PEOPLE can be wiped out when their way of life is threatened by a sudden change of circumstances. One of the best known examples of this happened in the early 16th century, when Spanish conquistadors conquered the Incas and Aztecs of South America. More than 70 million indigenous people were wiped out by diseases such as smallpox and measles, which were brought from Europe by the Spanish. With no history of these diseases, the Incas and Aztecs had few natural defenses against these illnesses.

fast facts

WHAT IS COLONIALISM?

During the 19th century, many European countries set out to gain influence in countries around the world. This "colonialism" was usually done for economic or military reasons, and often resulted in the exploitation of the native peoples.

WHO WERE THE LAST PEOPLE TO BE "DISCOVERED"?

Tribes of people living in the forests of Papua New Guinea were unknown to the West until the 1930s.

WHERE DID THE MAORIS COME FROM?

The Maoris arrived in New Zealand around 1,000 years ago from the islands of Polynesia, thousands of miles away in the Pacific Ocean. According to Maori legend, they arrived in just seven small canoes.

WHERE DO PYGMIES LIVE?

There are many groups of Pygmies–"small people"–many of whom live in the rainforests of Central Africa.

WHO ARE THE MASAI?

The Masai are a nomadic tribe of cattle herders who roam around the borders of Kenya and Tanzania in Africa.

WHAT IS RELIGION?

A religion is a set of beliefs that attempts to make sense of the things in life that are difficult to understand, such as why we are here. Human beings have always sought explanations about the world, and various religions have developed in order to provide some answers. Most religions are based around the teachings of one God or several gods—supreme beings who created the world and determine what happens in it. Religions have been an extremely powerful force in human history, inspiring art and culture and shaping countries and empires.

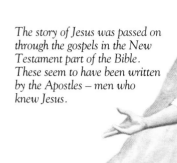

The story of Jesus was passed on through the gospels in the New Testament part of the Bible. These seem to have been written by the Apostles – men who knew Jesus.

WHAT DO CHRISTIANS BELIEVE?

CHRISTIANITY is a religion that has one God. Its followers–Christians–believe that Jesus Christ was the son of God and that he lived to show people the way to eternal life with God through the forgiveness of sins (wrongdoing). A key Christian belief is that Jesus was killed by his enemies and then rose from the dead to join God in heaven. Christianity is the world's largest religion, with more followers than any other.

WHO WAS MOHAMMED?

MOHAMMED WAS a 7th-century prophet who founded the religion of Islam. Islam's followers–Moslems (or Muslims)–believe that many prophets, including Jesus Christ and Moses, have carried the word of one God, named Allah. For Moslems, Mohammed was the greatest prophet of all. His word is revealed in the Koran –the sacred book of Islam.

WHICH WAS THE FIRST RELIGION TO HAVE ONE GOD?

JUDAISM, the religion of the Jewish people, was the first to have only one God. Jews believe that Judaism began in the Middle East about 4,000 years ago, when God's word was revealed to Abraham, the father of the Jewish people. God told Abraham that the Jews would be his chosen people in return for obeying his laws and spreading his message. Throughout their history, Jewish people have suffered persecution in many parts of the world.

The city of Jerusalem is a holy city for Christians, Moslems, and Jews. Partly for this reason, it has become a place of tension and conflict instead of peace and understanding.

WHAT IS BUDDHISM?

BUDDHISM BEGAN in northern India about 2,500 years ago. It was founded by an Indian prince called Siddhartha Gautama, who had become upset by the suffering of the world. After traveling and meditating for three years, he adopted the name Buddha, which means "Enlightened One." Buddhists, like Hindus, believe in reincarnation and karma. The ultimate aim of all Buddhists is to achieve Nirvana–a state of absolute peace.

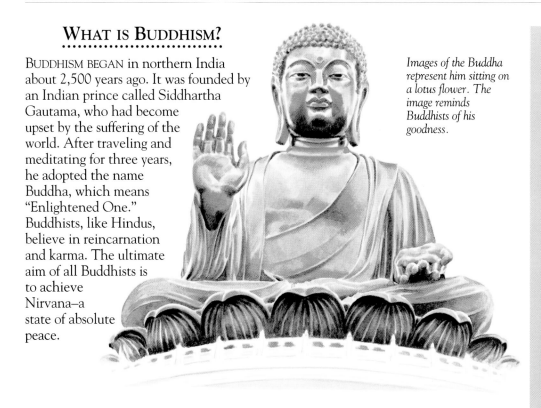

Images of the Buddha represent him sitting on a lotus flower. The image reminds Buddhists of his goodness.

WHERE DID HINDUISM ORIGINATE?

HINDUISM IS one of the world's oldest religions. It began in India some 5,000 years ago and developed gradually from various early beliefs in the region. Those who follow the Hindu religion worship many different gods, and there are lots of different Hindu sects. Most Hindus believe in reincarnation–that a person's soul moves to another body after death. Those who lead good lives are reborn in a higher state; those who do not may return as an animal or insect.

Shiva rules over life and death.

Vishnu brings peace and order.

Brahma is the creator.

Vishnu, Brahma, and Shiva are the three most important Hindu gods.

fast facts

WHAT IS ANIMISM?

Early religions were based around the belief that a spirit or god existed in everything. This is called animism.

WHAT IS A MISSIONARY?

Missionaries are people who travel to spread the word of their own religion to those who have not adopted its beliefs.

WHAT IS SECULARISM?

Secularism is the belief that people should be taught things without a religious emphasis.

WHAT IS A SECT?

A sect is a group of people with particular views within a religion. They sometimes demand strict conformity and may be shunned by the mainstream leaders of their religion.

WHAT IS SHINTOISM?

This is a Japanese religion based on the worship of the gods of nature.

WHEN DID SIKHISM BEGIN?

THE SIKH FAITH is a relatively new religion, which began in about A.D. 1500. Its founder, Guru Nanak, came from the Punjab region of northern India. He and nine other "gurus" set out the basic beliefs of Sikhism in the Guru Granth Sahib–the religion's sacred book. Sikhs believe that God is found in all things.

WHAT IS MEDICINE?

All human beings are likely to suffer from disease or illness at some point in their lives. Medicine is a science that attempts to identify, prevent, and treat diseases that affect humans. Diseases are usually treated with drugs or surgery, although preventive treatments, such as vaccinating against diseases before they occur, are an important part of medical science today.

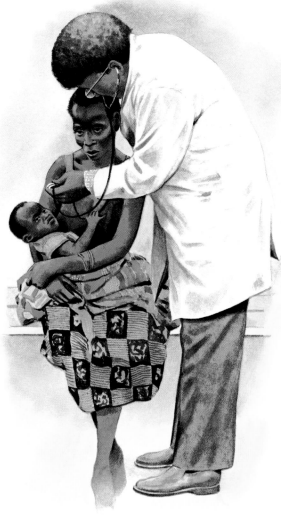

HOW HAS TECHNOLOGY CHANGED MEDICINE?

MODERN TECHNOLOGY allows doctors and other medical specialists to make a more accurate diagnosis of a problem and to treat patients more effectively. Scanners can produce an x-ray or ultrasound image of the whole body, making it possible to identify problems and begin treatment at an early stage. This helps increase the patient's chances of making a good recovery.

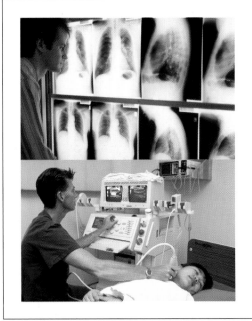

Ultrasound and x-ray machines are just two examples of the way technology has revolutionized modern medicine.

Visiting a doctor is taken for granted by most people in the Western world. In some countries, however, there may only be one doctor for many thousands of people.

HOW ARE DRUGS PRODUCED?

MODERN MEDICINE uses thousands of different types of drugs, which come from a variety of sources. They can be broadly divided into those that are derived from natural sources such as plants and herbs, and those that are produced artificially from chemicals. A recent development involves genetically engineering certain bacteria to produce a drug for a specific purpose.

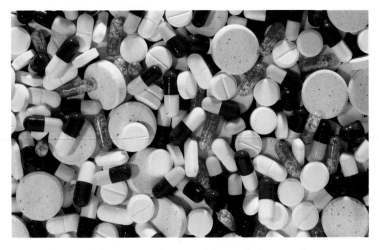

The production of pharmaceuticals is one of the world's biggest industries.

WHAT CAUSES DISEASE?

DISEASES ARE CAUSED in many different ways. Infectious diseases are those that can be passed from person to person. They are usually caused by tiny organisms called viruses and bacteria. Influenza (flu) is a disease caused by a virus; typhoid and cholera are caused by bacterial infections. Certain diseases are passed on to children by their parents at conception. These are called hereditary diseases.

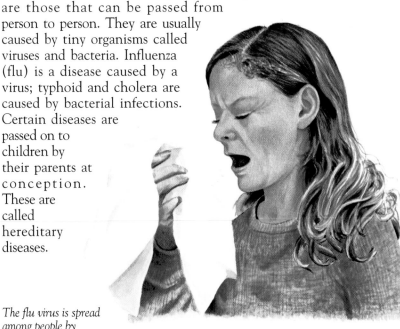

The flu virus is spread among people by coughing and sneezing.

WHICH PEOPLE ARE MOST AT RISK FROM DISEASE?

SOME PEOPLE MAY be more at risk from disease than others. In many developing countries, people may be short of food or may not have access to clean water. In such circumstances, they are at risk from nutritional diseases such as scurvy and rickets, as well as those that thrive in areas with poor sanitation, such as cholera and hepatitis. In industrialized nations, the population may have an increased risk of cancer and heart disease, brought about by high-fat diets and unhealthy lifestyles.

Despite having good medical services, people in the West risk their health through an unbalanced diet.

WHAT IS IMMUNIZATION?

PEOPLE CAN be protected from certain diseases by being given a weakened version of the germ that causes a disease. This is called immunization. A successful immunization program has completely eliminated the disease of smallpox. Immunization programs are especially important for developing countries.

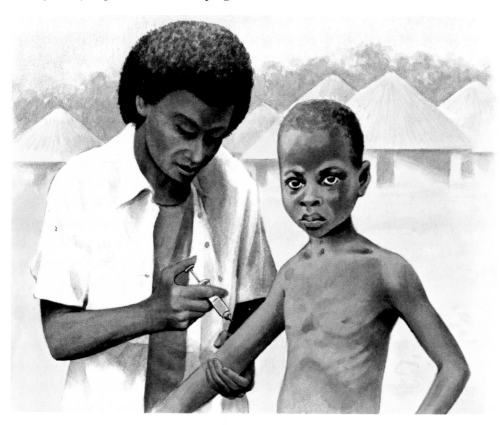

WHAT ARE ANTIBIOTICS?

SPECIAL DRUGS called antibiotics are used to treat diseases caused by bacteria. Early antibiotics were made from molds and fungi, but today they are produced artificially from chemicals. Antibiotics work by breaking down the cells of the bacteria. There is some concern that the continued use of antibiotics could create problems for the future because the bacteria are becoming resistant to the drugs.

Antibiotics, created in laboratories, have been very effective in controlling bacteria-based diseases.

WHEN DID PEOPLE FIRST BUILD HOUSES?

In very early times, people probably lived in caves, moving from one cave to another as they roamed around, hunting for food. It is thought that some of the first people to settle down in one place did so in what is now Israel, around 13,000 years ago. The Natufians, as they are known, built circular huts made of mud, reeds, and wood. They lived in these and used them to store grain.

Wooden chalets in Alpine regions have steep-sloped roofs to prevent snow from piling up on them.

Wood is a plentiful material in cold, forested areas and makes an ideal building material.

WHY DO BUILDINGS VARY BETWEEN COUNTRIES?

THE CONSTRUCTION and style of houses vary greatly from country to country. This is due mainly to a combination of the materials available locally and the type of weather that the region experiences.

Mud houses often have small windows and thick walls, which help keep out the fierce heat of the day.

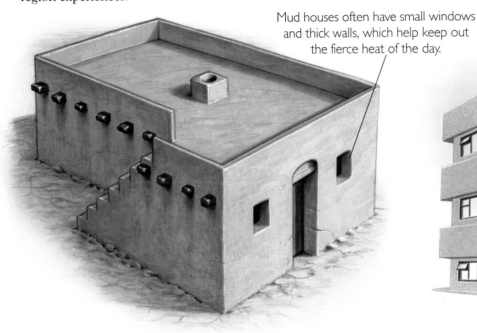

In very hot countries, houses are often made of mud. Low levels of rainfall mean that the mud stays hard.

Space is limited in large towns and cities, so the best option is to build upward. Apartments can house large numbers of people in a small area.

DOES ANYONE STILL LIVE IN CAVES?

THERE ARE some parts of the world where people still live in caves. However, most are far removed from the prehistoric dwellings of our ancestors. Indeed, many of them are in spectacular locations and have all the facilities of any other modern home.

This is a modern cave dwelling in Matmata, Tunisia, Africa.

Reinforced concrete is made by combining liquid concrete with steel rods.

A crane is used to lift building materials into position.

These skyscrapers dominate the skyline in an area of Paris, France. Very tall buildings offer architects the chance to use interesting shapes and surfaces.

HOW DOES A SKYSCRAPER STAY UP?

SKYSCRAPERS–very tall buildings–are a familiar sight in many of the world's large cities. Ordinary buildings are constructed in such a way that the walls provide support for the whole structure. A skyscraper is so tall, and the weight of the building is so great, that a frame of steel or concrete is needed to support it. The foundations of the skyscraper are also important. Beams (piles), also made of steel or concrete, are driven into the ground with a powerful machine called a pile driver.

The strength of the frame allows lightweight materials such as glass and aluminum to be used on the outside of a skyscraper.

HOW ARE TUNNELS BUILT?

TUNNELS ARE built for many different reasons, such as carrying water and sewage beneath cities or providing access for people, trains, and motor vehicles. "Cut-and-cover" is a common method of building tunnels in urban areas–a deep trench is dug and then covered over. Long transportation tunnels, which may go through mountainsides or underwater, are usually made with enormous boring machines. As a rotating cutting head cuts out rock at the front of the machine, sections of tunnel lining are fitted in behind. Often two machines are used, one starting at each end.

Subways keep pedestrians safe.

Transportation tunnels carry cars and trains.

Service tunnels carry water or sewage.

fast facts

WHAT WAS THE WORLD'S FIRST SKYSCRAPER?

The first building to be called a skyscraper was the 10-story Home Insurance Building in Chicago, Illinois. It was completed in 1885.

HOW DO WE FIND OUT ABOUT RUINED BUILDINGS?

Archeologists can tell us a lot about buildings from the past. The foundations, walls, and other parts of a building's structure can be uncovered by digging through layers of earth. Using knowledge of other buildings, archeologists can build up a picture of what the building looked like.

WHAT WILL HOUSES BE LIKE IN THE FUTURE?

A big feature of houses in the future will be energy conservation. They will probably be better insulated and use alternative fuel sources.

WHAT IS ARCHITECTURE?

Architecture refers to the style and design of a building. Architects aim to design buildings that are visually attractive and comfortable to inhabit.

WHAT IS A SHANTYTOWN?

Cities in developing countries are often surrounded by "shantytowns" –groups of makeshift houses built by those who have nowhere else to live.

WHAT IS ADOBE?

Bricks of sun-baked mud used to build houses are called adobe.

WHAT IS A YURT?

A yurt is a type of tent used by nomads in Mongolia, Asia.

HOW IS INFORMATION SENT AROUND THE WORLD?

Satellites receive signals from transmitters on Earth and send them back to various receivers.

Today, we can access information in ways that could only be dreamed about just 50 years ago. Information can travel around the world via television, radio, telephone, and computer networks, all of them connected by satellite or cable links. Modern communication systems, or media, allow almost anyone to transmit and receive verbal, visual, and written information wherever they are in the world.

Signals are used for communication and provide navigation assistance for ships and planes.

WHAT WERE THE EARLIEST FORMS OF COMMUNICATION?

Early people probably communicated through a combination of primitive sounds and basic sign language. Languages may have evolved through a need for survival–warning others of danger, for instance. They developed gradually as people used the spoken word for instruction and entertainment. Oral communication, particularly through storytelling, was and still is an important part of a society's culture.

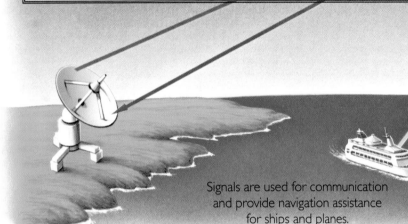

WHAT ARE MASS MEDIA?

CERTAIN FORMS of media, particularly television and newspapers, are able to communicate to thousands, or even millions of people at the same time. These mass media can have a very powerful influence on their audience, and often reflect the particular viewpoint of the media owner.

In early times, news could only travel as fast as a messenger could travel. Smoke signals were one of the first attempts at long-distance communication.

WHY DO COMPANIES ADVERTISE?

COMPANIES USE all forms of media to advertise their products and services. Advertising began simply as a way of telling people about a product, but it is now much more sophisticated. It is used to present the image of a company in a certain way and also to target a particular audience that the company feels it can attract. In this way, the company associates itself with a certain lifestyle. Advertising is a huge business, with large companies investing huge sums of money in anything from sports sponsorship to putting their logo on the side of a milk carton.

We are exposed to advertising almost everywhere. These electronic billboards are advertising products in Tokyo, Japan.

HOW DOES THE INTERNET WORK?

THE INTERNET is a global network of millions of computers which can communicate with one another. Information can be sent and received across the network in the form of text, pictures, video, and sound. Home computers often connect to the Internet using a normal phone line and a modem—a device that connects the computer to an Internet Service Provider (ISP). Businesses and other large organizations may have their own network, known as a Local Area Network (LAN), which connects to an ISP with a high-speed link.

Local ISPs   Regional ISPs   Global ISPs

LAN

Internet Service Providers (ISPs) connect computers used in homes, businesses, schools, and other organizations to the Internet. The Internet is all of these networks of computers connected together.

HOW HAS TELEVISION CHANGED OUR LIVES?

TELEVISION WAS undoubtedly the most important communications invention of the 20th century. Its ability to bring visual information directly into millions of homes made people aware of world events in a way that they never were before. It quickly overtook movies as the main form of entertainment, and modern satellite, cable, and digital television now provides people with an incredible choice of programs, 24 hours a day.

fast facts

WHEN DID TELEVISION BROADCASTING BEGIN?

Scottish engineer John Logie Baird demonstrated a mechanical "visual wireless" in 1926, but the first television service began in Britain in 1936.

WHAT IS PROPAGANDA?

Propaganda is the spreading of information, usually to promote a certain kind of religious or political thinking. The use of mass media to spread propaganda has had a very powerful and influential effect.

CAN YOU WATCH TELEVISION IN SPACE?

When television signals are transmitted, they pass through the atmosphere and into space. This means that even astronauts can tune in to their favorite TV shows!

WHAT WAS TELSTAR?

Telstar was the name of the first satellite to send television pictures. It was used to transmit live images from the U.S. to Europe in 1962.

WHAT WAS CUNEIFORM?

Cuneiform was an early form of writing that used symbols to represent the sounds of words.

The Apollo moon landing of July 1969 was a global television event—over 700 million people tuned in to watch live pictures of the landing.

WHAT IS A SOCIETY?

A society is a community of people. All societies around the world are based on families, but the way societies are organized and governed varies from country to country. Religion, politics, economics, and climate all influence the way a society develops and organizes itself.

HOW DO FAMILIES DIFFER?

THE WAY families live together can vary hugely from country to country and even within the same country. The term "nuclear family" describes an arrangement where two parents bring up their children in the same home. Extended families are those where several generations live together. In some societies, men and women may live separately most of the time, each with defined social roles.

The nuclear family is a common living arrangement in some parts of the world.

In extended families, many relatives live, and very often work, together.

HOW ARE COUNTRIES GOVERNED?

IN THE MODERN WORLD, most countries are led by governments. A government makes decisions on behalf of the population to organize public services, maintain law and order, and manage the economy. It is also responsible for the defense of the country. A government collects taxes from its people to finance its activities. In a democracy, the people choose the government by voting for candidates in an election. An autocratic government is not elected by its people and is usually ruled by one person.

WHAT IS A PARLIAMENT?

IN MANY DEMOCRATIC countries, such as the United Kingdom, political issues are debated in an elected assembly. The political party with the most elected members forms the government, headed by the prime minister. Laws and decisions are passed (or rejected) on the basis of votes cast by the members of parliament (MPs). Many parliamentary systems have two assemblies. The United Kingdom has the House of Commons and House of Lords. The House of Commons has more power and makes most of the decisions.

The speaker chairs debates.

Members of the government, including the prime minister, sit together.

Representatives of the opposition parties sit opposite the government.

In the United Kingdom, debate between MPs takes place in a formal room called the "Chamber."

WHAT IS A REPUBLIC?

A REPUBLIC is a country where the head of state (the leader) is a president elected by the people. The president appoints heads of administrative departments to help make decisions. Their decisions are discussed by an assembly of elected representatives, who can pass or block the laws. In the U.S., the assembly is called Congress. Congress may suggest its own laws, which the president has the power to overrule. Most republics have a third level of government, a judiciary, which reviews the laws. The highest judiciary in the U.S. is the Supreme Court.

The Capitol Building in Washington, D.C. houses Congress, the elected representatives of the United States government.

Karl Marx was a German philosopher.

WHAT IS COMMUNISM?

COMMUNISM is a type of political and economic system devised by the German thinker Karl Marx in the 19th century. The idea of the communist system was that property and wealth should be shared by the people and that everyone should be treated equally. Unfortunately, many countries that adopted Communism found it difficult to put these high ideals into practice. Many people lost their freedom, and the governments struggled to control the economy.

Defense lawyer | Judge | Prosecution lawyer | Witness | Defendant on trial | Jury

In some countries, ceremonial dress, such as gowns and wigs, is still worn by officers of courts of law.

HOW ARE PEOPLE TRIED FOR CRIMES?

IN MANY COUNTRIES, someone accused of a serious crime will be tried in a court of law in front of a judge and jury. The jury is chosen at random from the general public and is usually made up of 12 people. The accused person–the defendant–is represented by a lawyer, who tries to convince the jury that his or her client is not guilty. The prosecution lawyer tries to establish guilt. Judges are usually appointed by the state. They advise the jury and decide on punishment if the defendant is found guilty.

fast facts

WHAT DOES "GOVERNMENT" MEAN?

The word government is taken from a Latin word–*gubernare*–meaning "to steer."

WHY DOES A COUNTRY NEED LAWS?

The laws of a country are usually decided on by the government and enforced by the police and a legal system. Laws are designed to protect society from crime, and to settle disagreements over such things as money and property.

WHO INVENTED POLITICS?

Politics has its origins in ancient Greece. The philosopher Plato was the first to discuss government and politics in *The Republic*, over 2,000 years ago. Democratic traditions and the discussion of ideas became central to the way Greece was governed.

WHO MADE THE FIRST LAWS?

The first laws were probably made by the Babylonians, whose civilization flourished in the Middle East around 4,000 years ago. The laws covered things like property, slaves, and wages. Penalties were enforced for those who broke the laws.

WHAT IS CAPITAL PUNISHMENT?

In some countries, people may be sentenced to death if they have committed a very serious crime. This is called capital punishment. Many countries have abolished the death penalty, and in places where it still exists, it is often never applied. In the United States, convicts facing the death penalty can spend many years in prison on "death row" while their sentence is subject to appeal.

WHAT IS INDUSTRY?

Industry organizes the production of things that people need to live their lives, from essential items such as food and water, to luxury goods like toys and chocolate. Without industry, we would have to make everything we need ourselves. Not all industries produce goods. Service industries offer a service–washing clothes, for example–in return for money.

WHAT IS MANUFACTURING?

MANUFACTURING FORMS the basis of what most people think of as "industry." It means using materials to make a product. There are often many stages of manufacturing between the raw material and the finished product. Many industries involve the assembly of component parts that have been made by any number of separate companies.

WHAT IS AN ASSEMBLY LINE?

IT IS RARE in modern manufacturing for something to be made from start to finish by one person. Most factories use an assembly line to manufacture their products. Each worker has a specific task in the production process–adding a particular component or operating a certain machine, for example. As each task is completed, the product passes along the line for the next stage of production. Some assembly lines, especially in the automotive industry, are entirely or partly automated. Robots play a large part in putting together many products.

The car body is assembled from component parts.

The body is sprayed in the paint plant.

The assembled body is treated and prepared for painting.

The body is attached to the chassis, and the engine is put in.

The interior and other components are added, and the car is ready to be driven away.

WHAT IS MASS PRODUCTION?

MASS PRODUCTION is manufacturing goods on a large scale. It aims to produce the maximum number of goods for the lowest possible cost. The use of assembly lines and automation makes it possible to manufacture near-identical, interchangeable parts. Modern techniques of mass production were pioneered by the American automobile manufacturer Henry Ford. Production of the Model T Ford revolutionized the way all manufacturing industries operated.

Over 15 million Model T Fords were made between 1908 and 1927. It was the first car to be made by mass production. The car was inexpensive, reliable, and cheap to run. It brought motoring to those who could not previously afford it.

WHAT WAS THE INDUSTRIAL REVOLUTION?

AROUND THE middle of the 18th century, changes took place that greatly affected the way people lived and worked. The Industrial Revolution, as it is known, began in Britain and spread to Europe and then to the United States. New machines and inventions allowed goods to be produced more quickly, and huge factories were built, leading to the rapid growth of industrial towns. People began to move from the country to towns and cities in search of work, but often ended up living in miserable conditions.

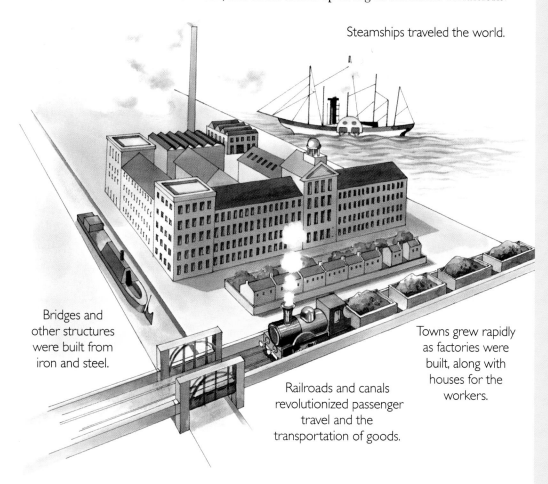

Steamships traveled the world.

Bridges and other structures were built from iron and steel.

Railroads and canals revolutionized passenger travel and the transportation of goods.

Towns grew rapidly as factories were built, along with houses for the workers.

WHEN WERE TOOLS FIRST USED?

THE EARLIEST human beings began to use tools around 35,000–40,000 years ago. Sharpened flints were used to skin animals and to make implements from wood and bone.

HOW ARE GOODS MOVED AROUND THE WORLD?

ALL FORMS of transportation are used to move goods around the world. Cargo planes are by far the quickest method, but are very expensive. Where large amounts of goods need to be transported over great distances, ships are the cheapest method. Container ships carry metal containers of a standard size, which can hold almost anything. Once the ship docks, the containers are easily transferred to trains or trucks. For shorter sea journeys, trucks and their cargoes are driven onto Ro-Ro (roll on, roll off) ferries in one port and driven off at another.

Container ships are the main way of transporting goods across the world. The largest ships can carry several thousand containers.

fast facts

WHAT IS A UNION?

A union is a body that represents groups of workers who work in the same or similar industries. Its role is to make sure the workers have fair pay and working conditions. Sometimes, a union may call a strike–stopping work–to try to enforce its demands.

WHAT DID THE FIRST FACTORIES MAKE?

The first factories were used in the textile industry. The cotton mills, as they were known, produced cloth with machines powered by water and steam.

WHO WAS ROBERT OWEN?

Robert Owen was a British factory owner at the height of the Industrial Revolution. Unlike many of his contemporaries, he was concerned about the rights of his workers and fought to improve their working conditions.

WHAT IS NATIONALIZATION?

When an industry is brought under the control of the state, it is said to have been nationalized.

WHAT IS THE WORLD ECONOMY?

Most of the world's countries trade goods and services with one another. The transactions that take place make up the world economy. The global marketplace exists partly because countries need things that they cannot produce themselves. Also, richer countries buy goods from places where the costs of production are low and the goods are cheap. Modern transportation and communications have allowed the world economy to develop.

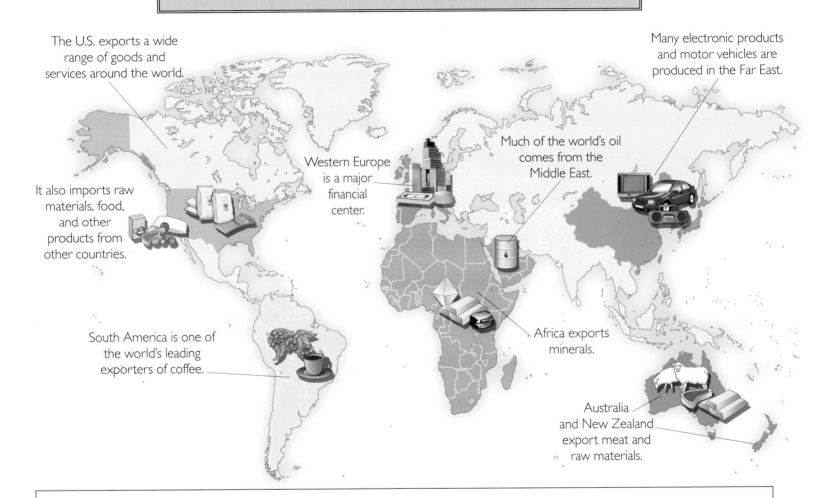

The U.S. exports a wide range of goods and services around the world.

It also imports raw materials, food, and other products from other countries.

Western Europe is a major financial center.

Much of the world's oil comes from the Middle East.

Many electronic products and motor vehicles are produced in the Far East.

South America is one of the world's leading exporters of coffee.

Africa exports minerals.

Australia and New Zealand export meat and raw materials.

WHAT IS A BALANCE OF PAYMENTS?

THE GOODS OR SERVICES that one country sells to another are called exports; the things that it buys from other countries are called imports. Imports need to be paid for with the money made from exports–the balance between the two is called the balance of payments. Not all countries can afford to pay for everything they need, so they borrow money from wealthier countries and large banks. This has led in part to the large gap between the world's richest and poorest countries. Many so-called "developing countries" need to use all the money they make from trade just to repay the interest on loans.

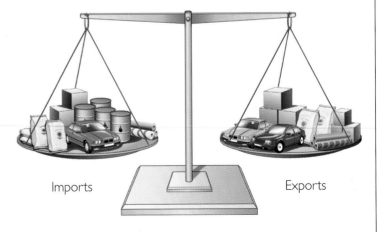

Imports   Exports

HOW IS PAPER MONEY PRINTED?

PAPER MONEY needs to be designed and made in such a way that it is very difficult to forge. Bills have extremely complicated designs, with pictures and backgrounds made up of very fine lines and patterns. These are printed from hand-engraved steel plates. The bills are also printed on a special type of paper, which is very durable and has a strip of plastic or metal embedded in it.

HOW HAS SHOPPING CHANGED IN THE PAST CENTURY?

SHOPPING HABITS have changed enormously in the past 100 years. At one time, most goods were purchased from various specialized shops–meat from a butcher and vegetables from a greengrocer, for example. In many countries, it is now more common for households to buy everything from one store and to visit shopping malls, where individual stores are housed under one roof. Also, since the late 1990s, the Internet has allowed more and more people to shop without leaving home.

HOW DID OUTDOOR MARKETS BEGIN?

OUTDOOR MARKETS have been around for thousands of years–since long before the first shops. They were set up in towns where trading routes crossed. Salesmen, known as peddlers, traveled between markets, buying and selling goods. People also sold surplus goods or things they had made. Goods were often exchanged for other goods, a practice known as bartering, and people always argued, or haggled, over a price.

Outdoor markets are still common all over the world. They are often good places to find bargains, if you know what to look for. In some countries, it is still common to negotiate a price with the vendor.

fast facts

WHAT IS A STOCK MARKET?

Companies may allow people to invest in them by offering "shares." These are known as stocks and are bought and sold on a stock market.

WHAT IS A TRADE AGREEMENT?

Countries often sign trade agreements with each other to try to ensure economic stability. They may set a price for a certain product and restrict or exclude other countries. Breaking trade agreements can lead to fierce disputes and, sometimes, war.

WHAT IS A MINT?

A mint is a factory where both coins and paper money are produced. Coins are usually made of copper, nickel, brass, or a combination of all three metals. They are stamped with a design, the coin's value, and its year of manufacture–a process known as minting.

WHAT IS THE "BLACK MARKET"?

The "black market" involves the trade of illegal goods, such as drugs, and transactions that avoid taxation and other official controls.

WHEN WAS MONEY INVENTED?

It is thought that "money" in the form of various weights of silver was used in Mesopotamia over 4,000 years ago. The first coins were probably used in what is now Turkey around 2,700 years ago.

WHAT IS A "CRASH"?

A very large and rapid drop in the price of shares is called a crash.

WHAT IS A "TAKEOVER"?

When one company buys another, it is called a takeover.

GLOSSARY

Architecture The style and design of buildings.

Biosphere The parts of the Earth's atmosphere, land, and water where living things can exist.

CFCs (Chlorofluorocarbons) Chemicals used in aerosols, refrigerators, and air conditioning systems that are partially responsible for damaging the ozone layer.

Civilization A group of people or a nation that, through its organization, customs, and culture, has become historically important.

Coke Fuel produced by refining certain types of coal to remove impurities. Used as an industrial and domestic fuel.

Community A group of people identified by belonging to a certain group, organization, or place.

Coral A marine organism, which has a skeleton made from calcium carbonate (lime) extracted from the sea in which it lives. Large numbers of coral skeletons build up to form coral reefs.

Crust The rocky outer layer of the Earth.

Deforestation The destruction and clearing of forests without replanting for agricultural and other uses.

Democracy A system in which a country's government is chosen by the people.

Desertification A process in which areas of land turn to desert. It is caused by climate change, some intensive farming methods, and deforestation

Ecology The science of the relationship between living things and the environment in which they live.

Ecosystem A community of living organisms and the particular area in which they exist.

Erosion The process by which rocks and soils are broken up, worn down, and taken away. It can be caused by the action of wind, water, glaciers, or a change in the rock itself.

Geology The science of the Earth, its history, and its structure.

Glacier A huge mass of ice, which forms in areas where layers of snow and ice build up over long periods.

Igneous A type of rock formed from solidified lava.

Immigration The movement of people into a country for the purpose of settling there permanently.

Irrigation Diverting water supplies to land or crops by digging channels or building pipelines.

Magma Molten rock that lies beneath the Earth's surface. Lava is magma that emerges through a volcano.

Media Means by which information is communicated, often to large numbers of people at the same time.

Metamorphic A type of rock formed by the effects of heat and pressure over time.

Mineral A naturally occurring, non-living substance with a certain chemical makeup. Rocks are made from one or more minerals.

Oceanography The study of the oceans and the living things that inhabit them.

Ozone A highly reactive gas that forms a layer in the atmosphere. It protects life on Earth from the sun's damaging ultraviolet rays.

Pangaea A name for the Earth's original "supercontinent" that existed around 220 million years ago.

Petroleum The term scientists give to naturally occurring oil and gas.

Plateau An area of very level ground. Plateaus may be found at the bottom of rift valleys.

Sedimentary rock A type of rock formed when layers of material are compressed over long periods.

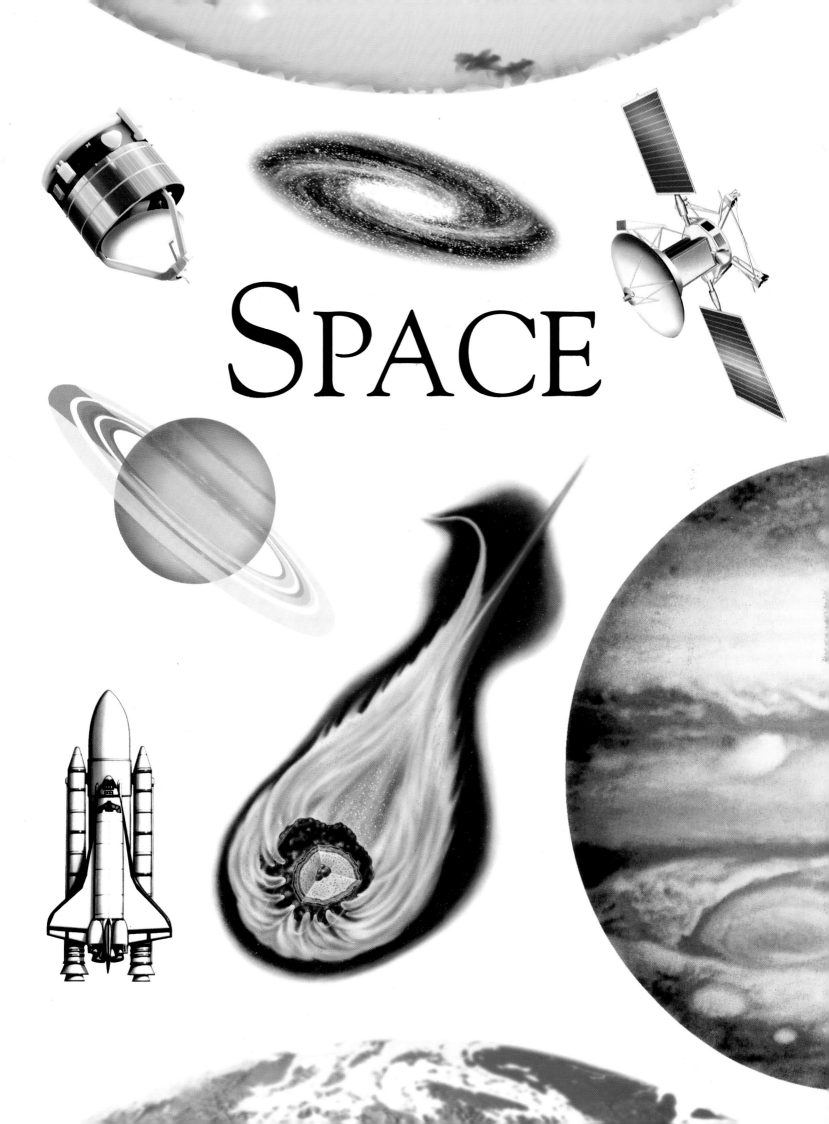

SPACE

WHAT DOES THE UNIVERSE CONTAIN?

The universe contains literally everything–from you and me to the most distant stars. It is everything and anything that exists, occupying an unimaginably vast area. Distances in space are so immense that light from the farthest galaxies takes over 10 billion light years to reach Earth, even though light travels fast enough to go around the Earth several times every second. Everything you can see in the night sky lies in our universe, from the sun to far-off gas clouds like the Eagle Nebula (right).

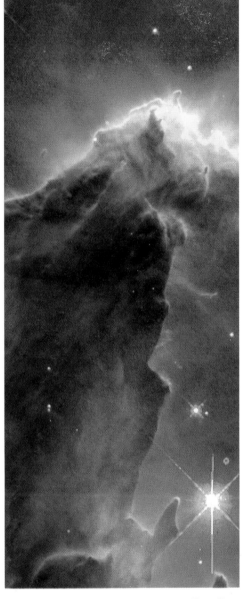

HOW DID THE UNIVERSE BEGIN?

ALTHOUGH NOBODY can be sure how the universe began, most scientists believe that it was born from an enormous explosion 13 billion years ago. This explosion, called the "Big Bang," was the point where space and time came into existence and all of the matter in the cosmos started to expand. Before the Big Bang, everything in the universe was compressed into a minuscule area no bigger than the nucleus of an atom. The Big Bang was an unimaginably violent explosion that sent particles flying in every direction. A process called cosmic inflation caused the universe to expand into an area bigger than the entire Milky Way in less than a second. Moments later, the temperature began to decrease, and the universe began to settle down. Stars and galaxies began to form roughly one billion years after the Big Bang.

The temperature of the universe during the first second of its existence was over 100 million trillion trillion degrees. During this second, the building blocks of the universe formed.

After three minutes the universe cooled to one billion degrees. Protons and neutrons began to combine, forming heavier elements such as helium.

300,000 years after the Big Bang, the temperature dropped to 3,000 degrees. Electrons began to join with atomic nuclei to form neutral atoms.

These incredible cloud patterns are actually stellar nurseries, where stars are being born all the time. Everything that can be seen in the night sky is part of the known universe.

CAN WE PROVE THERE WAS A BIG BANG?

THE IDEA OF THE "Big Bang" was first suggested in the 1920s by an astronomer named Edwin Hubble. He discovered that the universe was expanding and suggested that it must have been much smaller in the past. The most convincing argument for the Big Bang lies in the presence of cosmic background radiation. This is an echo of the energy released by the Big Bang, and was detected in 1965 by two astronomers. Scientists believe that the only possible source of this radiation is the dying heat of the Big Bang.

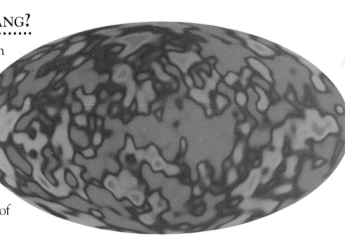

In 1992 the COBE satellite took this microwave image of the universe. The ripples are the afterglow of the Big Bang.

DOES THE UNIVERSE HAVE AN EDGE?

ALTHOUGH WE KNOW THE UNIVERSE is expanding, nobody knows for sure what it is expanding into. Some scientists claim that it is not expanding into anything, because nothing exists outside the universe. Instead, space itself is stretching to accommodate the expanding matter. The universe has no outside edge, and no center because the force of gravity distorts everything within it.

Gravity affects everything in the universe, even space itself. If the universe contained enough matter, then space could bend so much that it doubled back on itself. A spaceship leaving Earth and traveling in a straight line would never find the edge of the universe…

…but would arrive back at Earth trillions of years later. This concept is called a closed universe. Although it extends forever, it has no edges.

HOW DO WE KNOW IF THE SIZE OF THE UNIVERSE IS CHANGING?

ASTRONOMERS CAN GAUGE the movement of a star using a technique called the Doppler effect. All stars and galaxies emit electromagnetic radiation. The wavelengths of any form of electromagnetic energy are affected by movement–the radiation emitted by an object moving toward an observer is squeezed, moving toward the blue end of the spectrum where wavelengths are shorter (blueshift). The wavelengths of an object moving away are stretched, and move toward the red end of the spectrum (redshift). Most of the stars and galaxies in the universe have redshifted, meaning that everything is drifting apart.

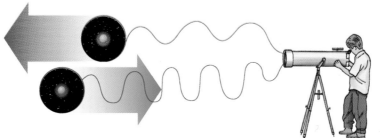

The electromagnetic energy from a star moving away from Earth is stretched, making it appear red.

fast facts

IS THE BIG BANG THE ONLY THEORY ABOUT HOW THE UNIVERSE BEGAN?

There have been only a handful of alternative theories to the Big Bang. The Steady State theory suggested that the universe had no beginning and that, although it is expanding, it stays in perfect balance all the time.

WHAT IS A CELESTIAL OBJECT?

Any object seen in the sky, such as a planet, moon, star, or galaxy, is called a celestial object.

HOW BIG IS THE UNIVERSE?

In 1995 the Hubble Space Telescope took a photograph of a speck of the sky no bigger than a grain of sand. In this small space alone were thousands of galaxies. If the entire sky is as densely populated as this, then the universe must be large enough to contain over fifty billion galaxies.

WHAT IS THE MOST DISTANT THING IN THE UNIVERSE?

Quasars–the powerful cores of remote galaxies–are the most distant things in the universe. Some were formed over twelve billion years ago.

WHERE IS EARTH IN THE UNIVERSE?

It is impossible to pinpoint exactly where the Earth lies in the universe because of the distortion of space. However, astronomers are able to tell where Earth lies in relation to its surroundings.

Our planet orbits one of 200 billion stars in the galaxy called the Milky Way. The Milky Way stretches over 100,000 light years.

The Milky Way itself is part of a collection of galaxies called the Local Group, the diameter of which is over 5 million light years.

The Local Group is part of one of millions of Local Superclusters that stretch across hundreds of millions of light years.

WHAT IS THE SOLAR SYSTEM?

The Solar System is everything that orbits our star, the sun. Caught in the sun's immense gravitational pull are nine planets, over 60 moons, and millions of asteroids, meteoroids, and comets. Pluto is the farthest planet from the sun, but the Solar System does not end there. Surrounding the planets is a vast sphere of comets—the Oort cloud. Objects beyond this are pulled away from the Solar System because the sun's gravity is not strong enough to hold them.

Mercury, 36 million miles (57.9 million km) from the sun

Venus, 67 million miles (108.2 million km) from the sun

Earth, 93 million miles (150 million km) from the sun

Mars, 142 million miles (228 million km) from the sun

WHAT IS AN ORBIT?

AN OBJECT'S ORBIT is the path it takes around another, more massive object in space. Each of the nine planets in the Solar System is held in orbit by the sun's gravitational pull. However, the planets do not orbit the sun in circular paths but in elliptical (oval) ones. Orbit lengths, and the orbital period (the time it takes a planet to complete one orbit) increase with successively distant planets.

Inner planets: Mercury, Venus, Earth, and Mars

Outer planets: Jupiter, Saturn, Uranus, Neptune, and Pluto

Jupiter, 484 million miles (779 million km) from the sun

Saturn, 886 million miles (1.4 billion km) from the sun

Uranus, 1.8 billion miles (2.9 billion km) from the sun

Neptune, 2.8 billion miles (4.5 billion km) from the sun

Pluto, 3.7 billion miles (5.9 billion km) from the sun

WHAT IS THE DIFFERENCE BETWEEN THE INNER AND THE OUTER PLANETS?

THE PLANETS in the Solar System form two very different groups—inner and outer. The inner planets, often called terrestrial planets, are composed mainly of rock and metal, with solid surfaces, no rings, and few satellites. The outer planets, called Jovian planets or gas giants, are much larger than their inner neighbors. They are composed primarily of hydrogen and helium, have very deep atmospheres, rings, and lots of satellites.

ARE PLANETS AND MOONS THE ONLY THINGS IN THE SOLAR SYSTEM?

PLANETS AND MOONS are just a few of the objects orbiting the sun. Astronomers already know of thousands of large rocky bodies called asteroids (shown right), and icy objects called comets. Millions of smaller rocks, called meteoroids, also orbit the sun.

HOW DID THE SOLAR SYSTEM FORM?

OUR SOLAR SYSTEM formed from the force of an exploding star. When some stars reach the end of their lives, they explode into a supernova, sending shock waves of energy deep into space. Roughly 4.6 billion years ago, a shock wave from a supernova, traveling at 19 million miles per hour (30 million kmph), hit a cloud of ice, dust, and gas. The force of the impact caused the cloud to flatten and rotate. From this spinning disk, our Solar System began to form.

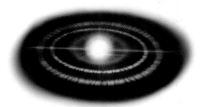

1 A dying star exploded, shedding energy and material into space. When the shock wave hit a nearby cloud of debris and gas, it enriched it with elements such as carbon.

2 The cloud began to rotate and shrink, causing many of the particles within it to group at its center. As they impacted against each other, they heated up, becoming a protosun.

3 Throughout the cloud, pieces of debris collided against each other and joined together. These rocky lumps grew larger and larger, and gradually formed into planets.

4 When the center of the cloud reached 50 million°F (10 million°C), nuclear reactions began, and the sun was born. The force of the explosion blew away the loose dust and gas.

WHAT ARE PLANETS MADE OF?

ALL OF THE planets in the Solar System formed from the same cloud of debris. The inner planets have solid cores of iron, surrounded by rocky mantles, topped with a very thin silicate crust. The gas giants have solid cores of rock and ice, but these are much smaller in proportion to those of the inner planets. Jupiter and Saturn are made of hydrogen and helium, which becomes denser toward their centers. Uranus and Neptune both have mantles of icy water, methane, and ammonia.

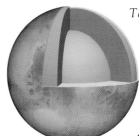

Terrestrial planets like Mars are made up of rock and metal. The only gases are those found in their small atmospheres.

Jupiter and Saturn are roughly 90% hydrogen and 10% helium. This is very close to the makeup of the original gas cloud from which the Solar System formed.

WHY ARE PLANETS SPHERICAL?

WHEN THE PLANETS were forming, they were in a molten state. In any object, gravity pulls from the center, and parts of the object at the same distance from the center are pulled inward with equal force, creating a sphere. This will only happen to objects with sufficient mass, such as planets and stars. Smaller objects, such as asteroids, have a weaker gravitational force, so they cannot pull themselves into a spherical shape. Gravity is also responsible for denser materials being pulled to the center of a star or planet.

HOW BIG IS THE SOLAR SYSTEM?

Measured from opposite ends of the Oort Cloud, the Solar System is roughly 1.6 light years in diameter. It fills a volume of 15 trillion kilometers.

WHICH PLANET HAS THE LONGEST ORBIT?

The orbits of the planets increase the farther they are from the sun. This makes Pluto the planet with the longest orbit. It takes 247.68 Earth years to complete one circuit of the sun. This is so long that it has not even traveled half its orbit since its discovery in 1930.

WHY IS PLUTO THE ODD PLANET OUT?

Pluto is a mystery to astronomers because it is so different from both the inner and the outer planets. It is much smaller than any other planet in the Solar System and made of rock, metal, and snow.

WHICH PLANET HAS THE HIGHEST VOLCANOES?

Venus, Earth, and Mars all have enormous volcanoes, but those on Mars are the most impressive. Because of its smaller size, Mars has weaker gravity than Earth or Venus, allowing the lava from volcanic eruptions to build up higher. Also, Mars's crust is in a fixed position, meaning that volcanoes are formed in the same place many times, each lava flow adding to the height of the last.

WHERE DO ASTEROIDS AND COMETS COME FROM?

After the planets formed, a great deal of loose material remained, but it was no longer being thrown together with the force needed to create planets. This debris became asteroids and comets.

WHY IS THERE LIFE ON EARTH?

Earth is the only place in the Solar System where scientists have encountered life. Conditions on our planet are perfect for sustaining life—the surface temperature averages around 59°F (15°C), allowing water to exist in liquid form. Water is a vital ingredient for life, and its presence on Earth has enabled an incredible variety of creatures to live on every part of the planet. Also, Earth is large enough to contain a protective atmosphere, but not big enough to become a suffocating gas planet like Jupiter or Saturn.

The Earth began to form around 4.6 billion years ago. It started life as a huge ball of liquid rock. Gradually, the surface began to cool and harden.

HOW DID LIFE DEVELOP ON EARTH?

FOR MUCH OF ITS EARLY HISTORY, Earth was a bubbling, volcanic ball—much too hot to sustain life. Over millions of years, the surface of the planet began to cool and harden, releasing enormous clouds of steam and gas. The moisture in these clouds eventually became rain, forming the seas. Scientists believe that the first life forms originated in shallow pools of water, where different chemicals were concentrated to form single-celled organisms. These gradually evolved into more complex life forms. All living creatures on Earth are still evolving.

Simple organisms began to form in shallow pools around four billion years ago.

These organisms gradually evolved into fish. Some of these fish made their way onto land, where they became amphibians.

As the Earth became drier, some amphibians evolved into reptiles that could survive better on dry land. Around 220 million years ago the first dinosaurs appeared. They are believed to have been wiped out by a huge meteorite around 65 million years ago.

The first mammals evolved around 200 million years ago. Early ancestors of humans only appeared less than two million years ago. Today, millions of different species cohabit our planet.

WILL THERE ALWAYS BE LIFE ON EARTH?

LIKE ALL STARS, our sun will eventually die. In around five billion years its supply of hydrogen will run out, and it will become a red giant, expanding to well over thirty times its current size. As it grows, the sun will engulf all the inner planets, making them much too hot for life to survive.

WHAT IS THE ECOSPHERE?

THE ECOSPHERE is a narrow band around the sun where the temperature is neither too hot nor too cold for life to exist. Earth is the only planet in this zone, and is therefore the only planet in the Solar System able to support life. Mercury and Venus are too close to the sun for water to exist in liquid form. The remaining planets lie well beyond the ecosphere, where it is too cold for life. The temperature on Pluto can go as low as –370°F (–223°C)!

HOW DID LIFE BEGIN ON EARTH?

NOBODY KNOWS WHAT conditions are needed for life to begin. Some scientists have suggested that living cells may have been brought to Earth by a comet. When the Giotto probe investigated Halley's comet in 1986, it found molecules that were similar to living cells. If a comet like this collided with Earth at the right time, then life may have taken hold. Another theory is that powerful lightning bolts flashing through Earth's early atmosphere may have caused chemical reactions, which created living cells.

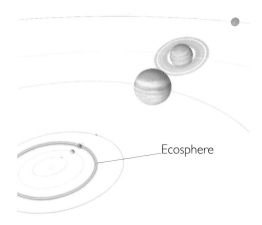

Ecosphere

HOW LONG HAVE HUMANS LIVED ON EARTH?

HUMAN BEINGS are late arrivals on planet Earth. Humankind's earliest ancestor–*Australopithecus afarensis*–appeared over two million years ago. Neanderthals had evolved by 400,000 years ago, and *Homo sapiens*, modern humans, only existed around 100,000 years ago. Just how short a time this is can be seen when we look at the history of the Earth as a clock, with 12 o'clock midnight being the time that Earth was formed 4.6 billion years ago. Each hour on the clock represents 383 million years.

For the first two hours the planet was forming. Primitive life evolved over billions of years (blue). Dinosaurs appeared at 11.30, lasting less than 30 minutes (purple). Mammals (green) have been around for a very short time, and humans (yellow) for less than a minute.

fast facts

WHAT IS EVOLUTION?

All living creatures exist as they do now because of evolution. This is a process of natural change in a species over many generations. This change enables it to adapt to its surroundings, and therefore to increase its chances of survival. Over many years, the changes that are most successful survive.

CAN WE SEE EVOLUTION AT WORK?

Evolution occurs very gradually and over many generations, so it is very difficult to see. However, scientists experimenting with mice have found that, in cold conditions, some evolve with thicker coats and are therefore more likely to survive.

WHAT IS THE OXYGEN CYCLE?

All plants and animals on Earth depend on each other because of something called the oxygen cycle. Animals breathe oxygen because it is needed to release energy from food. When the oxygen is used up, it is breathed out as carbon dioxide. All plants on Earth need carbon dioxide in order to survive, and they, in turn, change it back into oxygen.

HAS THE EARTH ALWAYS LOOKED THE WAY IT DOES TODAY?

EARTH IS THE ONLY planet in the Solar System whose surface is split into geological plates. These plates are constantly moving, carried on oceans of rocky mantle no faster than two centimeters each year. 250 million years ago all the plates on Earth were compressed together in a giant super-continent called Pangaea. Over millions of years this land mass was pulled apart as forces caused the plates to move away from each other.

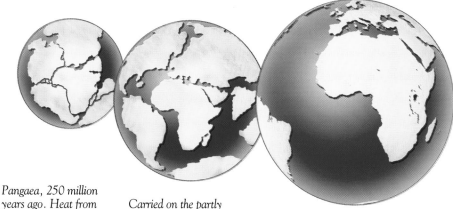

Pangaea, 250 million years ago. Heat from inside the planet caused the individual plates to move slowly apart.

Carried on the partly molten rock of the mantle, the plates move no faster than human hair grows.

The continents will continue to move. If we were able to look at earth in another 250 million years, it would look totally different.

IS THERE ICE ON MERCURY?

Mercury is the closest planet to the sun, and as a result is a dry, barren planet scorched by solar heat. Parts of Mercury's surface often exceed 840°F (450°C) when the planet is closest to the sun. However, at night, temperatures can drop by over 1,100°F (600°C), and some scientists believe that there is actually ice in deep craters that never see the sun. Radar imaging of the planet has revealed areas of high reflectivity near the planet's poles. This may be frozen water carried to Mercury by meteorites.

IS MERCURY A DEAD PLANET?

PLANETS ARE BORN from the countless collisions of rocks and space debris that were part of the early Solar System. The heat from these impacts remains deep within the core of the planet, released through volcanic eruption. Mercury's cratered appearance shows that there has been no volcanic activity on the planet for billions of years. This makes Mercury a dead planet.

WHY DOES MERCURY GET SO COLD?

DESPITE BEING the closest planet to the sun, often orbiting less than 60 million kilometers away from the star, temperatures on Mercury can drop below –290°F (–180°C). This is because Mercury is too hot and too small to be able to hold on to much gas. With no clouds to stop heat from escaping into space at night, temperatures on Mercury plummet.

WHY IS MERCURY HEAVY?

ALTHOUGH MERCURY is the second smallest planet in the Solar System, it is heavier than Mars, and almost as heavy as Earth. The reason is that Mercury has an enormous core of iron – almost 2,237 miles (3,600 km) in diameter.

Craters on Mercury are not as deep as those on the moon. This is because material ejected by meteorite impacts does not travel so far, due to Mercury's stronger gravity.

There is no wind or water on Mercury, as on Earth's moon, meaning that its scarred landscape has remained unchanged since the early days of the Solar System.

WHY IS MERCURY DIFFICULT TO SEE?

BECAUSE IT IS so close to the sun, Mercury is a very difficult planet to explore. It is normally obscured by the sun's glare, which prevents even observatories such as the Hubble Space Telescope from peering at it because of the risk to light-sensitive equipment. Mariner 10 is the only probe to have visited Mercury, but even it could only photograph half the planet.

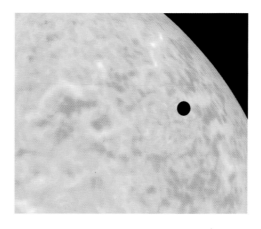

WHAT IS UNUSUAL ABOUT MERCURY'S ORBIT?

MERCURY ORBITS THE SUN more quickly than any other planet, but turns slowly on its axis, completing one rotation in 59 Earth days. The planet spins three times for every two complete orbits of the sun, meaning that anybody born on Mercury would technically be two years older each day!

WHY IS MERCURY SCARRED?

MERCURY IS ONE of the most heavily scarred objects in the Solar System. Thousands of meteor craters cover the planet, including the largest—the Caloris Basin. This was formed when a piece of rock 60 miles (100 km) wide collided with Mercury 3.6 billion years ago. Mercury is also shaped by wrinkles and cracks that formed when the surface of the planet cooled and shrank (right).

HOW ARE MERCURY'S SURFACE FEATURES NAMED?

Mercury's surface features are all named after men and women famous for their contributions to the arts. The Beethoven crater is the second largest on the planet, and there are smaller landmarks named after writers, such as Milton; philosophers, such as Sophocles; and musicians, including Mozart and Vivaldi.

DOES MERCURY HAVE ANY ATMOSPHERE AT ALL?

Mercury has a very slight atmosphere consisting of atoms blown from its surface by the power of the solar wind—charged particles released from the sun.

WHO DISCOVERED MERCURY?

Mercury was known about in ancient times, but the eighteenth-century astronomer Johan Hieronymous Schroeter was the first to make detailed illustrations of Mercury's surface.

HOW DO CRATERS FORM?

Craters form when smaller objects from space collide with a planet or moon. These objects, called meteorites, travel at very fast speeds and are often pulled toward larger objects by their gravitational pull.

When a meteorite collides with a planet or moon, it does so with tremendous force. The impact creates an enormous dent in the ground. Vast quantities of dirt and debris are blasted upward, making the hole much bigger than the meteorite.

The dirt and debris form rings of mountains around the crater. Chunks of rock make smaller crater holes. Some impacts can be so powerful that they send shock waves through the planet, creating mountain ranges on the other side.

WHY IS VENUS A KILLER PLANET?

Early astronomers claimed that Venus was Earth's sister planet. They believed that the light and dark areas they saw on the planet through their telescopes were oceans and continents. Modern astronomy has proved that nothing could be further from the truth! The light and dark areas are Venus's suffocating atmosphere—a layer of clouds containing sulfuric acid released by volcanic eruptions. The temperature on Venus can rise to 867°F (464°C), and the heavy layers of cloud make the air pressure on the surface over 100 times that of Earth.

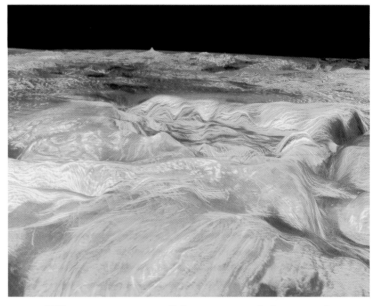

HOW CAN WE SEE PAST VENUS'S CLOUDS?

VENUS'S ATMOSPHERE is formed from clouds of carbon dioxide, nitrogen and sulfuric acid. This heavy layer of clouds is over 18 miles (30 km) deep in some places, meaning that no part of the planet's surface can be seen with the naked eye. Only since the 1970s have scientists been able to "look" past these clouds to see the solid ground beneath. This has mainly been done with equipment mounted on space probes. Radar technology allows probes to record the geography of the planet, and to produce a map of surface features.

WHAT WAS THE MAGELLAN MISSION?

THE MOST DETAILED information about Venus was acquired by a space probe called Magellan. Launched in 1989, Magellan traveled to Earth's neighbor and spent three years building a complete map of the planet. Flying as low as 183 miles (294 km) above the surface, Magellan bounced radar pulses off the solid ground beneath and sent the data back to Earth to be analyzed. It measured strips of land 14 miles (24 km) wide and 6,000 miles (10,000 km) long each time it circled the planet, while its altimeter measured its height above the surface.

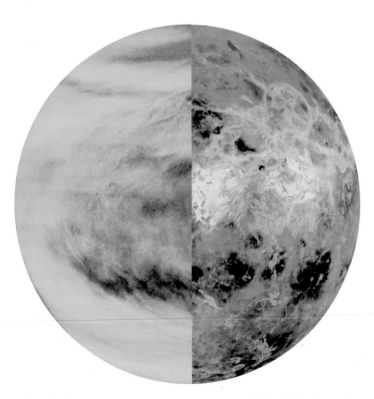

To the naked eye, Venus appears as a mass of cloud, like the left-hand side of the image above. With the data from Magellan, scientists can see what Venus looks like beneath the clouds (right-hand side above).

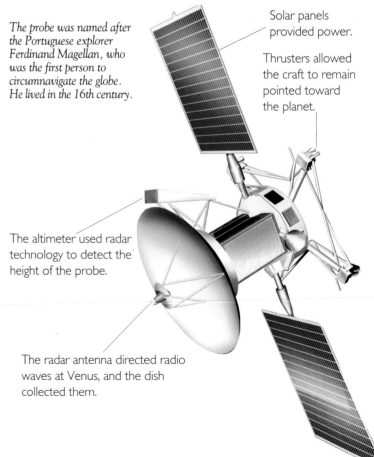

The probe was named after the Portuguese explorer Ferdinand Magellan, who was the first person to circumnavigate the globe. He lived in the 16th century.

Solar panels provided power.

Thrusters allowed the craft to remain pointed toward the planet.

The altimeter used radar technology to detect the height of the probe.

The radar antenna directed radio waves at Venus, and the dish collected them.

HOW DOES RADAR TECHNOLOGY WORK?

RADAR WORKS IN THE same way as an echo. When you shout loudly at a distant wall, you will hear the echo of your voice a few seconds later. This is because the sound waves hit the solid wall and bounce back toward you. Radar uses high-frequency waves that travel much faster and much farther. The radar sends out a short burst of radio waves and then listens for an echo, which tells it how far away the target is, and what it is made of.

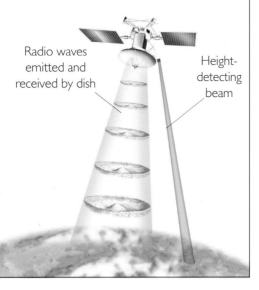

Radio waves emitted and received by dish

Height-detecting beam

WHERE DOES THE TERM "RADAR" COME FROM?

The word "radar" is made up of the initial letters of the phrase "RAdio Detecting And Ranging."

HOW BIG ARE VENUSIAN VOLCANOES?

One of the largest volcanoes on Venus is Maat Mons, which rises over 5.5 miles (9 km) above the surrounding terrain. Its diameter measures over 120 miles (200 km). It lies in a region called Aphrodite Terra, which contains several enormous volcanoes.

WHICH PLANET HAS THE LONGEST DAY?

It takes Venus 243 Earth days to spin once, giving the planet a longer day than any other in the Solar System.

CAN VENUS BE SEEN FROM EARTH?

Venus's clouds reflect a great deal of the sun's light, which means that the planet can usually be seen clearly from Earth. In fact, Venus is often called a star because it is the brightest object in the sky in the early morning or late evening (depending on the season).

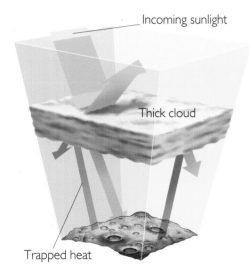

Incoming sunlight

Thick cloud

Trapped heat

WHY IS VENUS LIKE A GREENHOUSE?

LESS THAN 20% of sunlight falling on Venus breaks through the clouds. Despite this, Venus has the hottest surface temperature of any planet in the Solar System. This is because infrared radiation (heat) released from the planet cannot escape back into space. The atmosphere traps heat inside, like the glass in a greenhouse, meaning that the temperature is over 750°F (400°C), greater than it would be if Venus had no atmosphere.

WHY ARE THERE SO MANY VOLCANOES ON VENUS?

VENUS IS covered by hundreds of thousands of volcanoes. This is because the planet's surface is a thin skin floating on hot, molten rock. This lava is vented wherever possible, meaning that, unlike Earth, Venus has volcanoes everywhere. Most of them are around 2 miles (3 km) wide and 395 feet (90 m) high, but there are over 160 much larger than this. Some volcanoes on Venus are over 60 miles (100 km) in diameter! The volcanic activity on Venus means that the surface of the planet is always changing.

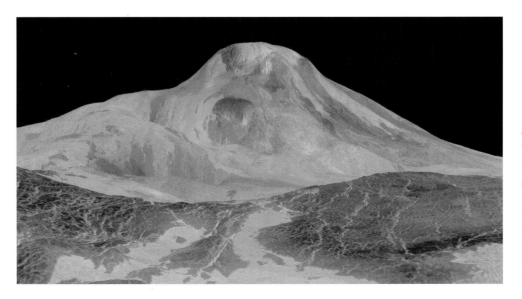

HOW LONG CAN PROBES SURVIVE ON VENUS?

Over twenty spacecraft have landed on Venus since 1970, sending back information about the planet's composition, pressure, and weather. Once they have landed, however, the probes do not have long to complete their tasks. The Russian lander Venera 13, which sent back the picture on the left, lasted just over two hours on the surface before it was destroyed by the planet's immense pressure.

HOW FAR AWAY IS THE MOON?

The moon is Earth's closest neighbor in space. Its orbit around Earth is elliptical, rather than circular, which means that its distance from us varies. At its closest point to Earth (its perigee), the moon is 225,600 miles (363,300 km) away. However, at its farthest distance from the planet (its apogee) it is 252,000 miles (405,500 km) away. Incredibly, the moon's orbit is slowly carrying it away from Earth at a rate of around 2 inches (5 cm) a year.

WHAT IS THE MOON MADE OF?

ALTHOUGH THE MOON'S interior structure is difficult to study, scientists believe that it has a small iron core. Surrounding this is a partially molten zone called the lower mantle. Above this lies the mantle, which is made up of dense rock, and the crust, which is also made of rock. Together, the mantle and the crust form the lithosphere which can be up to 500 miles (800 km) thick. There are only two basic regions on the moon's surface–dark plains called *maria* and lighter highlands. These heavily cratered highlands are the oldest parts of the moon's crust, dating back over four billion years. The darker plains are craters that were filled with lava.

IS THE MOON HOT OR COLD?

THE MOON EXPERIENCES temperatures both hotter and colder than those on Earth. When the sun is directly overhead, the temperature on the moon's surface is higher than the boiling point of water, 212°F (100°C). However, at night, the moon becomes very cold, with temperatures dropping to –280°F (–173°C). Earth and the moon are approximately the same distance from the sun, and therefore receive the same amount of heat. But the lack of an atmosphere on the moon means its temperature range is much more extreme. The sun's radiation is not filtered out by gases in the atmosphere, and there are no clouds to stop heat from escaping at night.

HOW DID THE MOON FORM?

NOBODY KNOWS EXACTLY HOW the moon formed. The most common theory is that shortly after Earth formed, it was hit by an object the size of Mars. The impact was so powerful that it sent billions of tons of molten material into space. This debris was held in orbit around Earth, and eventually solidified to form the moon.

A large object strikes the young Earth, ejecting material into space.

Caught by Earth's gravity, this material clumps together to form a solid sphere. Over millions of years, it cools and hardens.

| *Waxing crescent* | *First quarter* | *Waxing gibbous* | *Full moon* | *Waning gibbous* | *Last quarter* | *Waning crescent* |

WHY DOES THE MOON HAVE PHASES?

LIKE THE EARTH, half of the moon is always lit by the sun, while half remains in darkness. Its orbit around the Earth, and Earth's orbit around the sun, mean that we see the moon with different amounts of sunlight on its surface. Although its shape appears to be changing, only the position of the sun's light on the moon's surface is changing. These phases follow a cycle from a new moon, where the dark side is facing us and the moon appears invisible, to a full moon, where the entire sunlit part is visible.

WHY IS THE SKY ALWAYS BLACK ON THE MOON?

IF YOU ARE STANDING ON THE MOON, the sky would always appear black, whether it was night or day. This is because there is no atmosphere to scatter sunlight. On Earth, atoms of oxygen and nitrogen in the atmosphere have an effect on sunlight passing through them. Light scatters when it passes through particles that are one-tenth as large as the light's wavelength. The atoms of oxygen and nitrogen are one-tenth the size of the blue wavelength, so blue light is scattered more effectively than other colors.

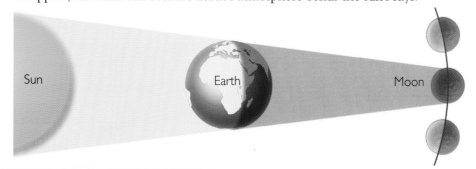

WHY DO WE ALWAYS SEE THE SAME SIDE OF THE MOON?

The moon takes the same time to rotate on its axis as it does to orbit the Earth. Because of this, we always see the same side of the moon. The far side remained a mystery to astronomers until 1959, when the Russian Luna 3 space probe traveled behind the moon and sent back photographs.

DOES THE MOON PRODUCE LIGHT?

The moon has no light of its own. It shines because it is reflecting light from the sun.

HOW POWERFUL IS THE MOON'S GRAVITY?

The gravitational pull of the moon is so strong that it is actually slowing the Earth's rotation. This is only happening at a rate of less than two seconds a year, but over thousands of years it can have a serious effect. Scientists studying the growth lines of coral fossils have discovered that a day on Earth was around three hours shorter 350 million years ago.

WHAT HAPPENS DURING A LUNAR ECLIPSE?

A LUNAR ECLIPSE OCCURS when the Earth comes directly between the sun and the moon. As the moon moves through Earth's shadow, the planet prevents direct sunlight from reaching the surface of the moon. The moon does not disappear, but turns red because Earth's atmosphere bends the sun's rays.

Sun · Earth · Moon

HOW DOES THE MOON AFFECT EARTH?

DESPITE BEING much smaller than the Earth, the moon still has a great deal of influence on its parent planet. Its gravity is constantly pulling on Earth's surface. This is not noticeable in relation to solid ground, but can clearly be seen in the movement of Earth's tides. Twice a day, the oceans on Earth rise and fall. This is because the moon's gravitational pull is strongest on the side of Earth that is facing the moon. Oceans on this side will be pulled into a bulge–high tide. Water on the opposite side is least affected by the moon's gravity, so it flows away from Earth in another bulge, resulting in another high tide. Areas of Earth at right angles to the moon, will have low tide.

The moon's gravity pulls the oceans into a tidal bulge. When the sun and the moon are in line, their combined gravitational pull creates larger bulges and a greater tidal rise and fall–called spring tides.

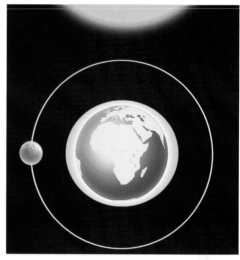

When the sun and moon are at right angles to one another, their gravitational pulls tend to cancel out one another. This produces smaller tidal pulls that are known as neap tides.

HAS THERE EVER BEEN LIFE ON MARS?

Of all the planets in the Solar System, Mars most resembles Earth. Its day is only slightly over 24 hours, and it is tilted at the same angle as our planet, meaning that seasons are very similar to ours. Early on in its history, Mars had water on its surface. Oceans formed, kept warm by volcanic activity, and primitive life may have started here. Today, freezing conditions on Mars, and the planet's thin atmosphere, mean that life can no longer exist on the planet's surface.

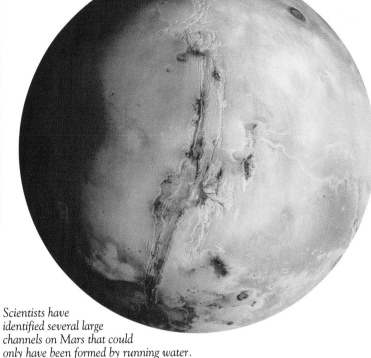

Scientists have identified several large channels on Mars that could only have been formed by running water.

ARE THERE CANALS ON MARS?

IN THE 19TH CENTURY, the astronomer Giovanni Schiaparelli claimed that Mars was covered by a network of channels. Many people believed that these were canals created by an intelligent civilization to help carry water from the polar regions to drier areas around the equator. Recent photographs of Mars have shown that there are many channels on the planet, but scientists believe these were created naturally by running water billions of years ago.

DOES MARS HAVE AN ATMOSPHERE?

WHEN MARS FIRST FORMED it had a very thick atmosphere. However, the gases have long since disappeared into space due to the planet's weak gravity. Mars's atmosphere is now very thin, and made mainly of carbon dioxide.

WHY IS MARS KNOWN AS THE RED PLANET?

MARS HAS been known as the red planet for thousands of years. The ancient Romans named the planet Mars because it reminded them of their god of anger and war. Mars gets its striking color from large amounts of iron oxide (rust) in its soil.

WHAT IS SPECIAL ABOUT THE METEORITE ALH84001?

THE MOST CONVINCING evidence for life on the red planet comes from a Martian meteorite that landed on Earth around 13,000 years ago. This meteorite contained microscopic structures that could have been formed by living organisms.

WHAT IS TERRAFORMING?

TERRAFORMING IS THE process of changing the environment of a planet to make it more like Earth. Many scientists have proposed terraforming Mars as a way of dealing with over-crowding on Earth. Nobody knows exactly how terraforming would work, and whether it would have a damaging effect on Mars's natural environment, but in theory, Mars could be transformed into a second Earth, where many forms of life could live naturally. The diagrams to the right show how it could be done.

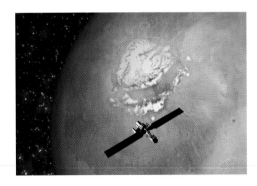

Before they started, scientists would need to know more about Mars. Probes would visit the planet to find out how much water it contains, and whether there is enough carbon dioxide in its atmosphere to support plant life.

Once these factors are ascertained, the first major step would be to warm the planet by creating a greenhouse effect. This could be done by unfreezing the carbon dioxide locked in the planet's polar caps, either by giant mirrors, or with nuclear waste.

IS THERE STILL WATER ON MARS?

WHEN MARS FIRST formed it had a much thicker atmosphere than it does today. Because the planet's gravity is not very strong, this atmosphere gradually escaped into space. The climate became increasingly cold, and all the water on Mars froze. Today, the water on Mars exists only as an icy, permafrost layer deep in the soil. Temperatures in Mars's polar regions are so low that carbon dioxide in the atmosphere freezes, covering sheets of water ice with a layer of frosty crystals of dry ice.

WHAT IS THE SURFACE OF MARS LIKE?

MARS HAS ONE of the most dramatic surfaces of any planet in the Solar System. Enormous volcanoes dominate the landscape, the largest of which–Olympus Mons–is over 15.5 miles (25 km) tall. This is three times larger than Mount Everest on Earth! The giant canyon called Valles Marineris is long enough to stretch across the entire United States.

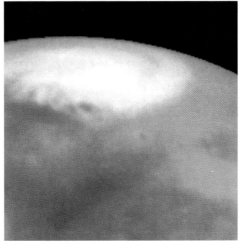

CAN ANYBODY LIVE ON MARS?

AS IT EXISTS TODAY, Mars is a planet hostile to life. Unlike Earth, Mars has no ozone layer to protect life from the Sun's lethal ultraviolet radiation. There is no breathable oxygen in the air, and giant dust storms are common around the planet. The first astronauts to live on Mars will probably do so in large domes that can contain an artificial, Earth-like atmosphere.

This photograph was taken by the spacecraft Pathfinder, which landed on Mars in 1997.

fast facts

DOES MARS HAVE MOONS?

Mars is orbited by two tiny moons called Phobos and Deimos (which mean "fear" and "panic"). They are so different from Mars that scientists believe they were asteroids captured by the planet's gravitational pull.

WHAT WERE THE VIKING LANDERS?

In 1976, two Viking spacecraft landed on Mars. They were designed to carry out numerous experiments on the planet to determine if there were any signs of life. The landers tested the soil, looking for gases that could have been produced by living organisms. The Viking landers found no conclusive evidence of life on Mars, but some scientists still believe that microscopic organisms may exist there.

After many centuries, Mars would have a suitable atmosphere. Tiny, car-sized factories on the surface would pump certain chemicals and gases such as nitrogen into the air, allowing plants to grow. Eventually, an ozone layer would develop.

Although the temperature and air pressure would be bearable to humans, they would initially have to carry oxygen tanks because of the lack of breathable air. Eventually, oxygen produced by plants would allow humans to exist naturally.

Gravity on Mars is only one-third that of Earth, which means that people born on Mars might not be able to visit Earth because their bodies would not be able to cope with the pressure. The first Martians to visit Earth could be humans!

WHAT ARE ASTEROIDS?

Planets and their moons are not the only objects in our Solar System. Billions of small rocky bodies, called asteroids, also orbit the sun. An asteroid, often called a minor planet, is a small body made up of rock and metal left over from the formation of the Solar System. Asteroids can range in size from almost 610 miles (1,000 km) in diameter to the size of a small car.

WHAT IS THE ASTEROID BELT?

MOST OF THE ASTEROIDS in the Solar System orbit the sun in a band between Mars and Jupiter. This band is nearly 340 million miles (550 million km) wide and is called the asteroid belt. There are billions of asteroids in this zone, each moving independently around the sun and spaced many thousands of miles from each other.

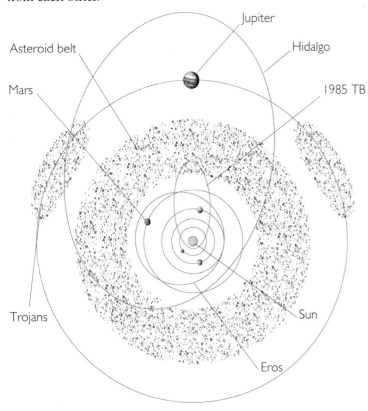

WHAT IS BODE'S LAW?

BODE'S LAW states that there is a pattern in the way the planets are spaced from the sun. Bode started with the number 0, then took 3, and began doubling: 0, 3, 6, 12, 24, 48, 96, 192, 384, 768. He then divided each number by 10 and added 4. The numbers that he discovered were similar to planetary distances from the sun in astronomical units. According to Bode's theory, there should be a planet between Mars and Jupiter.

HOW DID THE ASTEROID BELT FORM?

THERE ARE MANY THEORIES about how the asteroid belt developed. Some astronomers believe that it is the remains of a planet that was torn apart billions of years ago. Conversely, others argue that the asteroids in the belt are pieces of a planet that never formed. According to this theory, the immense gravitational pull of the young planet Jupiter prevented the rocks from forming one large body.

HOW CLOSE DO ASTEROIDS FLY TO EARTH?

ALTHOUGH MOST ASTEROIDS DRIFT harmlessly around the sun for billions of years, some are occasionally knocked out of their orbits. Some of these asteroids pass very close to Earth. In 1994, an asteroid measuring 32 feet (10 m) in diameter passed within 65,000 miles (105,000 km) of our planet–around one third of the distance to the Moon. If a large asteroid were to collide with Earth, the impact could be powerful enough to annihilate all life on the planet. Vast waves of water, dust, and fire would flatten cities in seconds, and billions of tons of dust entering the atmosphere would block out the sun's light for hundreds of years.

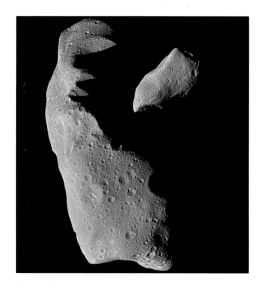

HOW CAN WE FIND OUT MORE ABOUT ASTEROIDS?

SCIENTISTS ARE INTERESTED in finding out more about asteroids. Many are thought to contain minerals and metals that could benefit industries on Earth. The Near Earth Asteroid Rendezvous (NEAR) space probe (below) visited two asteroids, Mathilde and Eros, in 1997 and 1998. It took photographs that showed that Mathilde is entirely covered by craters. Soon, expeditions may be launched from Earth to mine asteroids in space.

CAN ASTEROIDS HAVE MOONS?

ALTHOUGH ASTEROIDS ARE very small compared to planets, some have a powerful enough gravitational pull to attract natural satellites. As the spacecraft Galileo traveled toward Jupiter in 1993, it flew by an unusual pair of asteroids called Ida and Dactyl. Ida is 35 miles (56 km) long, and was found to have a moon, Dactyl, that is smaller than 1 mile (1.6 km) across (above).

COULD JUPITER BECOME A STAR?

Jupiter formed from the same cloud of gases as the sun. If this giant planet had continued to grow, its core would have ignited into a nuclear furnace, and Jupiter would have become a star. Theoretically, Jupiter could still become a star. If it expands to forty times its present mass, then self-sustaining nuclear reactions will begin within its core–the defining factor of a star.

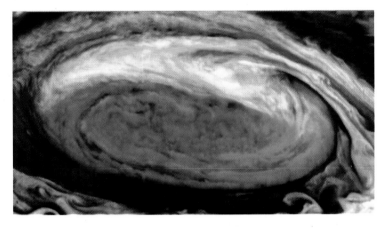

WHY DOES JUPITER HAVE BANDS OF CLOUDS?

THERE ARE THREE LAYERS of clouds on Jupiter, each made of different molecules. The outer cloud deck is made from ammonia, the middle deck from a combination of ammonia and sulfur, and the inner deck from ordinary water clouds. Heat from Jupiter's interior, and the planet's rapid rotation, cause ferocious winds that create the cloud patterns. The white bands are areas of rising gas, called zones. The dark bands are called belts, and are areas of falling gas. In these belts we are seeing much further into Jupiter, so they appear darker.

WHAT IS JUPITER'S RED SPOT?

THE GREAT RED SPOT is Jupiter's fiercest storm. It is a hurricane over three times as large as Earth that has been raging continuously for over 300 years. Made from gases such as ammonia and clouds of ice, it towers 5 miles (8 km) over surrounding clouds. Damp air rising inside the Great Red Spot causes the clouds to rotate, coming full circle every six Earth days.

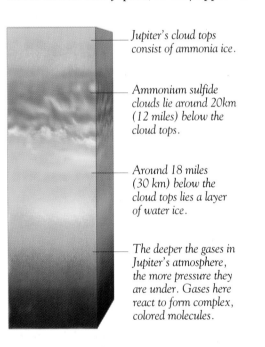

Jupiter's cloud tops consist of ammonia ice.

Ammonium sulfide clouds lie around 20km (12 miles) below the cloud tops.

Around 18 miles (30 km) below the cloud tops lies a layer of water ice.

The deeper the gases in Jupiter's atmosphere, the more pressure they are under. Gases here react to form complex, colored molecules.

Voyager 1

WHAT WERE THE VOYAGER MISSIONS?

SEVERAL PROBES have flown as far as Jupiter. In 1973, the Pioneer 10 probe flew by the giant planet taking close-up photographs. The Voyager 1 and 2 probes, launched in 1977, flew by the four gas planets–Jupiter, Saturn, Uranus and Neptune–taking pictures and measurements. The primary Voyager missions were completed in 1989, but both craft are now continuing into the depths of the outer Solar System at a speed of over 35,000 mph (56,300 kmph). Even at this speed it could take the probes over 30,000 years to reach the outer edges of the Solar System!

WHY ARE JUPITER'S MOONS SO VARIED?

Jupiter has at least 16 moons. Twelve of these are smaller than 125 miles (200 km) in diameter, but the four enormous Galilean moons are of great interest to astronomers.

Callisto has more scars than almost any other body in the Solar System. These craters were caused by meteorite impacts billions of years ago. Callisto may have a salty ocean beneath its crust of ice.

Ganymede is Jupiter's largest satellite–bigger even than the planets Mercury and Pluto. Its surface is dark and covered with craters.

Io is the most volcanic world in the Solar System. It is caught in a gravitational tug-of-war between Jupiter, Ganymede, and Europa. The conflicting pressures mean that heat is generated as molecules on the planet collide with each other, creating numerous violent volcanoes, molten sulfur lakes, and enormous lava flows.

Europa is completely covered with a sheet of ice.

HOW DID JUPITER GET ITS RINGS?

JUPITER HAS A VERY FAINT system of rings that was discovered by the Voyager space probes in the 1970s. There are three distinct rings, all formed by material knocked off the planet's four inner moons. Adrastea, Metis, Amalthea, and Thebe all orbit very close to the planet, and are constantly bombarded by meteorites. The dust blasted from these tiny moons is added to the planet's rings.

DOES JUPITER HAVE A SURFACE?

NONE OF THE GAS GIANTS has a surface like the terrestrial planets. Instead, the gases that make up Jupiter are put under more and more pressure the deeper they are, so that they gradually change from a gas into a liquid. Further in, the pressure is so great that the gases are squeezed into solid form.

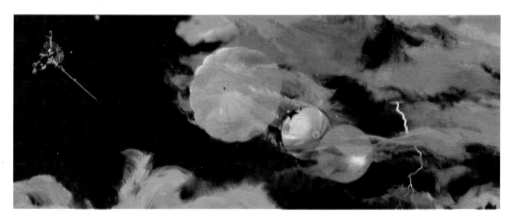

Jupiter has no surface on which to land a space probe, so any craft investigating the giant planet's atmosphere must take a suicidal journey deep into its interior. In 1995, NASA's Galileo Orbiter dropped a small probe into Jupiter's atmosphere. It took readings and measurements for almost an hour before being crushed by the intense pressure.

fast facts

HOW FAST DOES JUPITER SPIN?

Considering its size, Jupiter spins incredibly quickly, rotating fully in 9 hours and 55 minutes. The speed of its rotation makes Jupiter bulge at its equator.

WHAT IS A PLANET'S MAGNETOSPHERE?

A magnetosphere is the bubble around a planet where the magnetic field is strong enough to block the solar wind. Jupiter's magnetosphere is over 20,000 times stronger than Earth's, and stretches past Saturn.

IS THERE LIFE ON EUROPA?

Scientists believe that beneath Europa's icy crust there may be a liquid ocean. Volcanic activity may have allowed this ocean to form under the crust, with heat from the moon's core rising up through thermal vents in the ocean bed. It is possible that primitive aquatic life may have developed here.

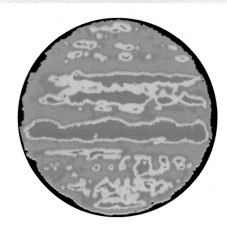

WHY DOES JUPITER GIVE OUT SO MUCH HEAT?

Jupiter has been contracting and cooling down since its birth 4.6 billion years ago. It was once an incredible 435,000 miles (700,000 km) in diameter–over five times its present size. Jupiter shrinks by around 1 inch (2.5 cm) each year, and as it does so, it generates an enormous amount of heat. Scientists now know that Jupiter gives out more heat than it receives from the sun.

WHAT ARE SATURN'S EARS?

In 1610, when Galileo Galilei first began to look at Saturn through his homemade telescope, he thought that Saturn's rings were actually two moons. He called these moons "Saturn's ears." Forty-five years later, the astronomer Christiaan Huygens realized that these moons were actually a series of beautiful rings surrounding the planet. With the photographs provided by the Pioneer and Voyager probes, scientists now know more about these rings than ever before.

WHAT ARE SATURN'S RINGS MADE OF?

SATURN'S RINGS are made of millions of tiny individual satellites, or moonlets. Each of these particles is like a dirty snowball of ice, dust, and rock. These range in size from less than a centimeter to over a kilometer in diameter.

Each tiny particle in Saturn's rings is a natural satellite of the planet. Some scientists believe that Saturn's gravity may eventually cause the rings to group together and form a moon.

HOW MANY RINGS DOES SATURN HAVE?

THE VOYAGER SPACE PROBES took many pictures of Saturn's rings, showing that they are made up of countless hundreds of ringlets. These have been separated into different divisions. Three of these divisions can be seen from Earth: the outer A ring, the bright B ring and the inner C ring. The E ring is farthest from Saturn, stretching nearly 310,000 miles (500,000 km) from the planet. None of the rings is ever more than 0.9 miles (1.5 km) thick.

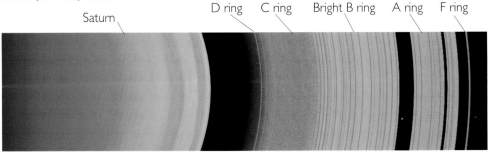

Saturn   D ring   C ring   Bright B ring   A ring   F ring

DO OTHER PLANETS HAVE RINGS?

FOR A LONG TIME astronomers believed that Saturn was the only planet with rings. However, in 1977, astronomers studying Uranus noticed that as it moved through the sky, the light from stars behind it twinkled, suggesting the presence of rings. In 1986, the Voyager 2 space probe flew past the planet and photographed 11 very faint, black rings. Both Jupiter and Neptune have ring systems that are very difficult to spot from Earth.

This false-color image of Uranus's rings was taken by Voyager 2 as it flew by the planet. The ring systems of the planets appear beautifully colored because the ice refracts sunlight in the same way as a lawn sprinkler.

ARE THERE STORMS ON SATURN?

ALTHOUGH SATURN IS considered a more beautiful planet than its neighbor Jupiter, its weather is no less violent. It spins so quickly that it bulges at its center, creating 1,000 mph (1,600 kmph) winds. Every 30 Earth years, a giant raging storm breaks out on Saturn, spreading across the entire planet. Storms such as these start when bubbles of hot gas rise up in the atmosphere.

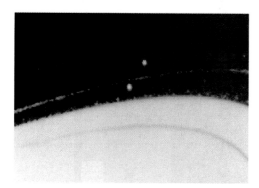

WHAT ARE SHEPHERD MOONS?

TWO OF SATURN'S MOONS–Pandora and Prometheus–are known as shepherd moons. They orbit either side of the narrow F rings, and have earned their name because their gravitational pull prevents the particles in this ring from straying out into space.

Pandora and Prometheus, shown left, were discovered in 1980 by Voyager 1.

fast facts

HOW MANY MOONS DOES SATURN HAVE?

Saturn has the largest family of moons in the Solar System. Astronomers know of over 20 already, but there may be more. These range from Titan, which is the second largest moon in the Solar System after Jupiter's Ganymede, to tiny Pan, which is less than 12 miles (20 km) in diameter.

WHAT IS THE CASSINI MISSION?

The Cassini probe was launched in 1997 on a seven-year journey to Saturn. It will spend four years in orbit there, taking photographs and measurements of the planet, its rings, and its moons.

WHY WOULD SATURN "FLOAT"?

Although Saturn is the second largest planet in the Solar System, it is the least dense–its average density is less than three-quarters that of water. The particles that make up Saturn are spread so thinly that if the planet were placed in a large enough ocean, it would float!

HOW DO RINGS FORM?

NOBODY KNOWS FOR sure how planets get their rings. In the 19th century, the French mathematician Edouard Roche suggested that if any large object, such as a moon or comet, got too close to a planet, it could be torn apart by the planet's tidal force. The object would be pulled one way by its orbit and another by the planet's gravity. Once it reached the "Roche limit," it would break apart into tiny fragments.

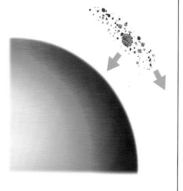

WHY ARE SCIENTISTS INTERESTED IN TITAN?

ONE OF SATURN'S satellites, Titan, is the only moon in the Solar System to have a substantial atmosphere. It is covered by thick clouds, and scientists believe conditions beneath these clouds may be similar to those on Earth billions of years ago. Although temperatures on the planet are believed to be well below freezing level, some scientists believe that internal heating may allow areas of liquid water to exist on the moon's surface. Some believe that primitive life may even exist on the moon. The European Space Agency's Huygens probe has been designed to parachute down through Titan's atmosphere in order to investigate the moon firsthand (right).

WHY IS URANUS LIKE A BARREL?

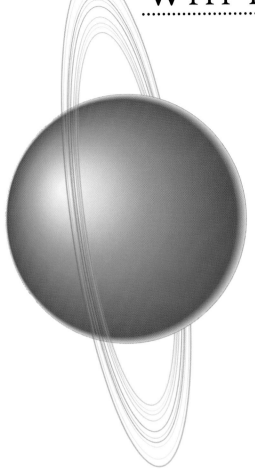

Uranus is the third largest planet in our Solar System. It is unusual because it appears to lie on its side. Because the planet's axis is tilted, Uranus "rolls" around the sun like a barrel, rather than spinning like a top. Its 11 faint rings and 17 moons spin around it like cars on a Ferris wheel. Nobody knows exactly why Uranus behaves this way. Many believe the planet was struck by an enormous object billions of years ago, and the impact knocked the planet on its side.

IS THERE ANY ACTIVITY ON URANUS?

THE SURFACE OF URANUS may look as motionless as that of a billiard ball, but in reality the planet is just as turbulent as Jupiter and Saturn. Like its larger neighbors, Uranus has bands of clouds that blow around the planet at incredible speeds, but because of an overlying layer of methane in the upper atmosphere, they are very faint. Only enhanced infrared pictures, like those taken by the Voyager space probe (right), show the weather on Uranus.

HOW ARE URANUS'S MOONS UNUSUAL?

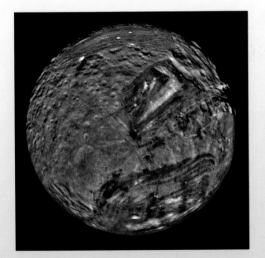

ALTHOUGH URANUS IS DEVOID OF SURFACE FEATURES, its many moons display a fascinating portrait of a violent history. The cracked and distorted surfaces of Uranus's moons are believed to have been caused by water. As liquid water rose from the interior of the moons, it froze and expanded, causing the crust to buckle outward. Miranda, one of Uranus's larger outer moons, has one of the most chaotic surface patterns of any body in the Solar System. The moon, shown left, resembles a patchwork, with parts of its core now on the surface, and parts of the crust buried deep underground. Scientists believe that this is because the moon was at one time pulled apart, and has gradually re-formed.

WHY ARE URANUS AND NEPTUNE BLUE?

URANUS'S COLOR COMES FROM the presence of methane clouds in the planet's atmosphere. Methane absorbs red light, reflecting only blue and green. Neptune's upper atmosphere contains more methane than Uranus's, which gives the planet's clouds their striking blue color.

HOW WAS NEPTUNE DISCOVERED?

NEPTUNE'S DISCOVERY WAS UNUSUAL in that it was found by calculations rather than with a telescope. Astronomers observing Uranus noticed that it was drifting off the expected path of its orbit. Two mathematicians, working independently of each other, thought that this was because the gravitational pull of an unknown planet was disturbing Uranus's orbit. The calculations of both men led to the planet being discovered in 1845.

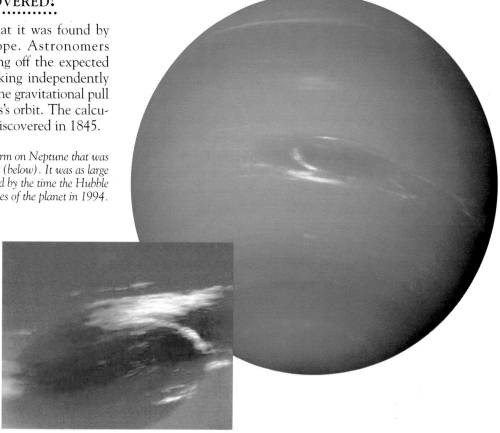

Voyager 2 found a raging storm on Neptune that was named the Great Dark Spot (below). It was as large as Earth, but had disappeared by the time the Hubble telescope took pictures of the planet in 1994.

WHAT IS THE WEATHER LIKE ON NEPTUNE?

NEPTUNE BOASTS one of the most violent weather systems known. When the Voyager 2 spacecraft flew by in 1989, it discovered that winds around the planet's equator reached speeds of 1,240 mph (2,000 kmph)–faster than anywhere else in the Solar System. Heat from inside the planet means that Neptune's atmosphere is turbulent and constantly changing.

WHAT IS THE COLDEST BODY IN THE SOLAR SYSTEM?

TRITON, ONE OF NEPTUNE'S MOONS, has been found to be the coldest world in the Solar System. Parts of its surface reach temperatures as low as –391°F (–235°C), which is only 100°F (38°C) above the coldest temperature possible–absolute zero. Voyager 2 discovered that the moon is also geologically active. In several places, pockets of nitrogen gas explode from vents, sending plumes of gas, dust, and ice up to 5 miles (8 km) into the air. Wind blows the plumes into long streaks that can stretch for 90 miles (150 km).

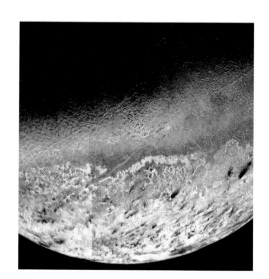

WHY ARE URANUS AND NEPTUNE ICE GIANTS?

SCIENTISTS STUDYING URANUS and Neptune discovered that these planets were very different from Jupiter and Saturn. They are much younger than their bigger neighbors, and therefore unable to feed on the enormous clouds of hydrogen and helium that made Jupiter and Saturn so large. Uranus and Neptune have been called ice giants as opposed to gas giants because beneath their cloud tops they may have oceans of water, heated by the energy from their cores.

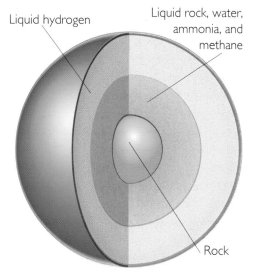

Liquid hydrogen

Liquid rock, water, ammonia, and methane

Rock

IS PLUTO REALLY A PLANET?

Pluto is the most mysterious planet in the Solar System because it is the one that astronomers know least about. Many have questioned Pluto's status as a planet, arguing that it is too small, and its orbit too elliptical, to be classified as such. Pluto may be the largest of the asteroids in the Kuiper Belt. Or it may once have been one of Neptune's moons that broke free of its parent's gravity. However, there are no plans to demote Pluto yet.

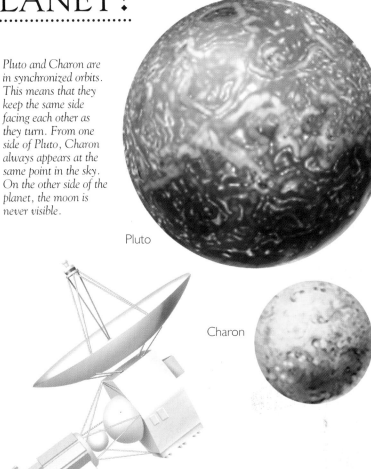

Pluto and Charon are in synchronized orbits. This means that they keep the same side facing each other as they turn. From one side of Pluto, Charon always appears at the same point in the sky. On the other side of the planet, the moon is never visible.

Pluto

Charon

Pluto-Kuiper Express

HOW MUCH DO WE KNOW ABOUT PLUTO?

BECAUSE PLUTO is so far away from Earth, it is very difficult to explore the planet using telescopes. Even the Hubble Space Telescope cannot make out the planet in very much detail. So far, no probes have visited the ninth planet. However, NASA's Pluto-Kuiper Express is due to fly by the planet between 2006 and 2008.

WHAT ARE CONDITIONS LIKE ON PLUTO?

AT NEARLY 3.67 billion miles (5.9 billion km) from the sun, Pluto is a cold, dark world, even in the middle of the day. The sun appears over 1,000 times fainter from the surface of Pluto than it does from Earth–little more than a bright star. Because of this, surface temperatures average around –382°F (–230°C). In the summer, Pluto has a slight atmosphere because the surface warms up enough to turn some of the ice to gas. As Pluto moves away from the sun, the gas freezes and becomes ice again.

WHAT IS A DUAL PLANET SYSTEM?

PLUTO'S ONLY MOON, Charon, is more than half the diameter of Pluto, making it the biggest moon in relation to its parent planet in the Solar System. They are only 12,430 miles (20,000 km) apart, and are caught in a gravitational headlock that scientists call a dual-planet system. They are so similar in size that they can be thought of as a double planet, as shown below.

WHAT LIES BEYOND PLUTO?

THE SOLAR SYSTEM does not end at Pluto but stretches outward in all directions for billions of miles. Many scientists believe that the boundary of the Solar System could be an immense cloud of comets, called the Oort cloud, which surrounds the planets like a spherical cage. Scientists believe that there are over ten trillion comets in this spherical halo, stretching nearly 5 million million miles (8 million million km) from end to end.

IS THERE A TENTH PLANET?

SOME SCIENTISTS ARE CONVINCED that the orbits of Uranus and Neptune are being distorted by the gravitational pull of a planet beyond Pluto. The recent discovery of minor members beyond Pluto that could be responsible for this distortion makes the existence of a tenth planet unlikely. New planets are always being discovered, however, not in our Solar System, but orbiting other stars.

fast facts

IS PLUTO ALWAYS THE MOST DISTANT PLANET?

Pluto's highly elliptical orbit means that it is not always the most distant planet from the sun. For a 20-year span in each 248-year orbit, Pluto comes closer to the sun than Neptune. It was like this between 1979 and 1999.

WHAT IS PLUTO MADE OF?

Pluto is a tiny ball of ice and rock, a great deal smaller than Earth. It has a large rocky core and a small mantle of water ice below the surface. Pluto's thin crust is made up of rock and frozen methane. Pluto is only 1,413 miles (2,274 km) in diameter–only one-fifth the size of Earth.

HOW DID PLUTO GET ITS MOON?

Nobody really knows how Pluto came to have so large a moon. Some believe that both Pluto and Charon are former moons of Neptune that escaped and found their own orbit around the sun. The most common theory, however, is that Charon is made up of ice that was knocked off Pluto during a collision.

WHO DISCOVERED PLUTO?

Pluto was discovered in 1930 by the astronomer Clyde Tombaugh.

The Oort cloud, named after the Dutch astronomer Jan Oort, is made up of trillions of comets. Objects outside the Oort cloud are pulled away from the Solar System because the sun's gravity is not strong enough to hold them.

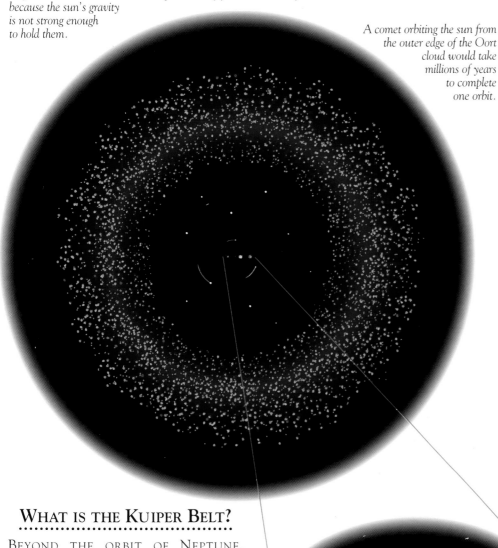

A comet orbiting the sun from the outer edge of the Oort cloud would take millions of years to complete one orbit.

WHAT IS THE KUIPER BELT?

BEYOND THE ORBIT OF NEPTUNE, stretching deep into the outer Solar System, lies a belt of celestial bodies made of rock and ice. The astronomer Gerard Kuiper first suggested the existence of this zone of cometlike objects, and so it was named the Kuiper Belt. There are at least 70,000 minor members in the Kuiper Belt with a diameter of over 62 miles (100 km). The largest of these is 1992QB1, otherwise known as Smiley, which is 137 miles (220 km) across.

If all the planets in the Kuiper Belt joined together, they would form an object roughly the size of Earth. The mass of all the objects in the Oort cloud is roughly the same as three Earths.

HOW DO COMETS GET THEIR TAILS?

Although all comets seen from Earth have tails, they do not always look like this. When a comet is a long distance from the sun, it exists purely as a lump of ice, frozen gas, and rocky dust. However, as the comet's orbit takes it closer to the sun, the temperature rises, and the ice begins to melt. Gas and dust are released, forming a huge cloud around the comet. This cloud is blown by the solar wind to form a tail.

A comet usually has two tails, a blue gas tail and a yellow or white dust tail. A comet's tails can stretch for hundreds of millions of miles into space.

The nucleus is the only solid part of a comet. It is made up of ice, dust, and rock.

The coma is formed of gas released by melting ice in the nucleus. It can measure 62,000 miles (100,000 km) across.

WHAT ARE COMETS MADE OF?

ALL COMETS BEGIN their lives as dirty snowballs. They are relics from the birth of the Solar System around 4.6 billion years ago, and are made up mainly of ice, gas, and rock. As the comet approaches the inner Solar System, the sun's heat causes the ice to evaporate. It turns into gas and forms a glowing head around the nucleus.

HOW MANY TAILS DOES A COMET HAVE?

COMETS USUALLY HAVE two tails—one of gas and one of dust. The gas tail is generally blue, and is pushed away from the sun by particles in the solar wind. The dust tail is yellow or white, and although it too is pushed away from the sun, the star's gravity causes the tail to curve.

DOES A COMET'S TAIL ALWAYS FOLLOW THE NUCLEUS?

BECAUSE OF THE SOLAR WIND, a comet's tail always points away from the sun. If a comet is traveling away from the sun, its tail will be in front of the nucleus, as shown below.

HOW CLOSE HAS A PROBE FLOWN TO A COMET?

THE SPACE PROBE GIOTTO was the first to visit a comet up close. In 1986, it flew into Halley's comet and photographed the nucleus in incredible detail. It was able to gather data for almost 10 hours before dust and gas hitting the probe put the cameras out of action. From just 373 miles (600 km) away, Giotto determined that Halley's nucleus measures 9 miles by 5 miles (15 km by 8 km), and is made up of ice and dust.

Giotto was named after a 14th-century Italian artist who painted a comet on the wall of a chapel in Padua, Italy, in 1303. The probe was equipped with 10 instruments that photographed and analyzed Halley's comet.

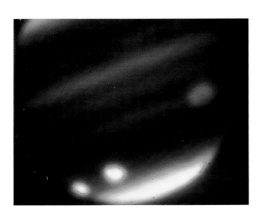

HOW WILL SCIENTISTS FIND OUT MORE ABOUT COMETS?

SEVERAL MORE PROBES have been designed and built to visit comets in the near future. Stardust, above, will investigate and photograph comet Wild 2 in early 2004. It will bring a sample of dust and gas back to Earth for scientists to study.

WHEN WAS THE FIRST RECORDED SIGHTING OF A COMET?

UNLIKE MANY OTHER minor bodies in the Solar System, comets have been known about for thousands of years. The Chinese recorded Halley's comet as far back as 240 B.C. The famous Bayeux Tapestry, which was made to commemorate the Norman conquest of England in 1066, shows Halley's comet (right).

Comet

WHAT HAPPENS WHEN A COMET HITS A PLANET?

IF A COMET collided with Earth, the results could be disastrous—possibly meaning the end of all life on our planet. Comets can often be caught by the strong gravitational pulls of planets. In 1994, the Shoemaker-Levy 9 comet crashed into Jupiter's atmosphere. It impacted at more than 124,000 mph (200,000 kmph), creating balls of fire larger than Earth.

fast facts

HOW LONG DO COMETS HAVE THEIR TAILS?

Comets develop new tails each time their orbit takes them close to the sun. Their tails only last for a short time, often less than two months.

WHICH COMET IS THE MOST FREQUENT?

The most frequent cometary visitor is comet Encke, which passes by the sun every 3.5 years. Halley's comet orbits every 76 years. In contrast, the Great Comet of 1864 will pass by Earth only once every 2,800,000 years.

WHAT KIND OF ORBITS DO COMETS HAVE?

MOST COMETS HAVE very long orbits that cover millions of miles. They travel into the Solar System from about one light year away, before swinging around the sun and heading back out into space for thousands of years. These are called long-period comets. Some comets, particularly those that are trapped by the gravity of large planets, orbit the sun in fewer than 200 years. These are called short-period comets.

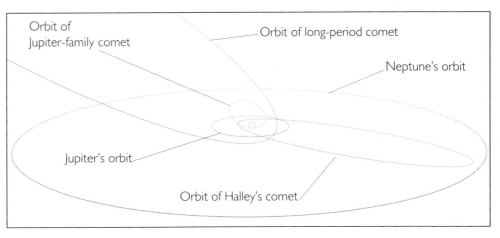

Orbit of Jupiter-family comet

Orbit of long-period comet

Neptune's orbit

Jupiter's orbit

Orbit of Halley's comet

HOW MANY METEORITES LAND ON EARTH?

Amazingly, thousands of rocks from space hit the surface of Earth each day. Every year our planet gains nearly 10,000 tons in weight due to meteoroids entering the atmosphere. Many of these are minuscule grains of dust, but some can be many yards long. The world's largest known meteorite was discovered in Namibia, Africa, in 1920 (right). It weighs an incredible 120,000 pounds (55,000 kg).

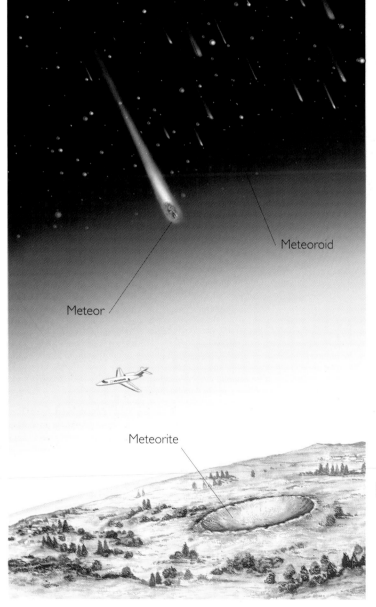

Meteoroid

Meteor

Meteorite

WHAT IS THE DIFFERENCE BETWEEN A METEOROID, A METEOR, AND A METEORITE?

SPACE IS TEEMING with millions of tiny pieces of rock and dust left over from the formation of the Solar System 4.6 billion years ago. These fragments are called meteoroids. They range in size from minuscule dust particles no larger than one-millionth of a gram to large rocks weighing many tons. Meteoroids travel through space and are often caught by Earth's gravitational pull. When a meteoroid enters Earth's atmosphere, it begins to heat up because of friction. As it heats up, it starts to glow, becoming a meteor–better known as a shooting star. Most meteors burn up in the atmosphere before they reach the ground. Those that hit the Earth's surface are called meteorites.

WHAT ARE METEORITES MADE OF?

THERE ARE THREE MAIN types of meteorite. More than 90% of meteorites found on Earth are made of stone. Stony meteorites are divided into chrondites, which contain particles of solidified rock, and achrondites, which do not. Iron meteorites are composed of iron and nickel. Fewer than 1% of meteorites are a mixture of rock and iron, and are called stony-iron meteorites.

Iron meteorite

Stony-iron meteorite

Stony meteorite

WHY DO METEOR SHOWERS OCCUR?

A GREAT DEAL OF the material that makes up meteorites comes from short-period comets. As comets travel close to the sun, they lose material, creating a trail of debris behind them. These trails, called meteoroid streams, can take many hundreds of years to form, but gradually build up to contain a large amount of loose dust and rock fragments. If Earth's orbit carries it through one of these streams, hundreds of meteoroids will enter the atmosphere in a very short time, creating a meteor shower.

WHY ARE THERE SO FEW CRATERS ON EARTH?

UNLIKE MANY of the planets, moons, and smaller bodies in the Solar System, Earth appears to be covered by very few craters. In the early days of the Solar System, Earth was as much a target for meteorites as any other planet, and suffered intensive cratering in the first one billion years of its existence. However, unlike bodies such as Mercury and the moon, Earth has many geological processes that "hide" craters. Constant weathering and erosion from winds and water wear away or cover up craters. Some may also be hidden by vegetation or lie under the sea, although in the last hundred years, aerial photography and other forms of imaging have given us a clearer view of many remaining craters.

CAN SCIENTISTS PREDICT METEOR SHOWERS?

BECAUSE EARTH PASSES THROUGH meteor streams at roughly the same time each year, meteor showers can be predicted highly accurately. Astronomers have now even worked out which comets are responsible for each annual shower. Two meteor showers come from the trail left by Halley's comet: the Orionids in October, and the Eta Aquarids in May. Although meteors in a shower fall to Earth over a large distance, perspective makes them seem to be falling from the same point in the sky, called the radiant.

HOW FAST DO METEORITES IMPACT WITH THE EARTH?

THE AVERAGE METEORITE enters the Earth's atmosphere at around 31 miles per second (50 km per second), but particles in the atmosphere slow the speeding rocks down. All but the largest meteorites decelerate to around 93 mph (150 kmph) by the time they impact. Larger meteorites are not slowed down by atmospheric friction and hit the ground traveling at deadly speed.

HOW ARE METEOR SHOWERS NAMED?

Meteor showers are named after the constellation in which their radiant is located. For example, the Orionids appear to fall from the Orion constellation (the hunter).

HAS ANYBODY EVER BEEN HIT BY A METEORITE?

Although ancient Chinese records describe deaths by meteorite impacts, no human in the last 1,000 years has been killed by one. However, some have been known to crash into houses and yards, and in 1992 an empty car was flattened by a falling meteorite.

WHERE IS THE WORLD'S LARGEST CRATER?

The largest crater on Earth lies near the city of Progreso, in Mexico. It is almost 180 miles (300 km) in diameter, and was created when a 6-mile-wide (10 km) meteorite impacted with the Earth around 65 million years ago. Many think that this impact was responsible for the death of the dinosaurs, and of 70% of all life on Earth.

HOW MUCH DAMAGE COULD A METEORITE IMPACT DO?

WE KNOW THAT EARTH is bombarded by thousands of meteorites every day, none of which does our planet much damage. Any meteorite up to 33 feet (10 m) in diameter usually burns up in the atmosphere before it reaches Earth, separating into tiny fragments. If a meteorite larger than this falls to Earth, it can cause considerable damage–impacting with the energy of five nuclear warheads. Approximately once every 1,000 years, a larger meteorite does fall to Earth, and several large craters caused by such impacts can still be seen. One such was the nickel-iron meteorite that created the Barringer Crater in Arizona (shown on the left from the air). The meteorite was an incredible 148 feet (45 m) wide, creating a crater nearly 1 mile (1.5 km) in width. However, it would take an impact by an object roughly 3 miles (5 km) wide to cause mass extinctions and threaten life on Earth.

HOW HOT IS THE SUN?

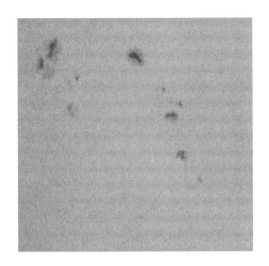

Temperatures in and around the sun vary considerably. On the sun's surface, called its photosphere, the temperature is around 10,000°F (5,500°C). Above this lies a hotter section of the atmosphere called the chromosphere, where temperatures can reach 27,000°F (15,000°C). Temperatures in the core of the sun can exceed an incredible 27 million°F (15 million°C).

HOW DOES THE SUN GENERATE ENERGY?

LIKE ALL STARS, the sun generates nuclear energy. In the sun's core, the temperature is so high that particles of gas cannot form completely. Instead, atomic nuclei and electrons travel around at very high speeds, moving so fast that if they collide, they join to form new particles. This process is called nuclear fusion, and it converts hydrogen into helium while also releasing vast amounts of energy. The sun converts over four million tons of matter into energy every second.

WHY DOES THE SUN HAVE SPOTS?

THE SURFACE OF THE SUN often appears to be dotted with small dark patches. These are called sunspots. They form when the sun's magnetic field blocks the heat rising from inside the sun. Sunspots are actually very bright but appear dark because of their surroundings.

Once the energy has been released in the core, it travels outward in the form of radiation such as gamma rays.

Energy travels through the radiative zone and the convective zone. As it moves, each photon of radiation collides with gas particles, losing energy with each impact. Because of this, radiation from the core can often take thousands, even millions of years to reach the surface of the sun. The radiation has lost so much energy by this time that it leaves as visible light and infrared radiation.

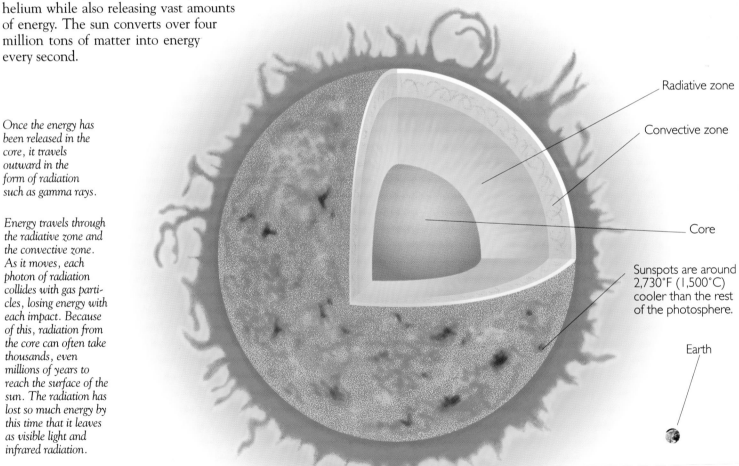

Radiative zone

Convective zone

Core

Sunspots are around 2,730°F (1,500°C) cooler than the rest of the photosphere.

Earth

WHAT ARE SUNQUAKES?

SUNQUAKES ARE violent eruptions on the sun around areas of hot gas. These explosions send out shock waves more powerful than the detonation of a billion tons of high explosives.

At least 109 Earth-sized planets would fit side by side across the diameter of the sun.

HOW BIG IS THE SUN?

THE SUN is a large ball of gas 900,000 miles (1.4 million km) in diameter. It is so large that, if it were hollow, one million Earth-sized planets could fit inside it!

WHAT IS AN ECLIPSE?

A SOLAR ECLIPSE occurs when the moon comes directly between the Earth and the sun. When this happens, the sun's light is blocked, and the moon's shadow falls on Earth. During an eclipse, the moon and the sun appear to be exactly the same size in the sky, because although the moon is much smaller, it is also much closer. Total eclipses occur once every 18 months around our planet. However, it is estimated that any one place on Earth only sees a total eclipse every 360 years.

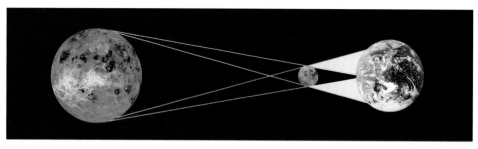

As a solar eclipse occurs, people in different locations on Earth will see different things. Anybody inside the complete shadow of the moon, called the umbra, will see a total eclipse. Anybody in the outer shadow, called the penumbra, will witness a partial eclipse. A solar eclipse will reach a point of totality, where the sun is completely covered by the moon. This lasts for up to seven minutes.

During a total eclipse, the moon covers up the sun completely. All that can be seen of the star is its faint outer atmosphere, the corona, like a cloud of gas around a dark center. As the moon appears to devour the sun, a brilliant bright spot can be seen on the edge of the moon. This is caused by the last fingers of sunlight filtering through mountain ranges on the moon.

HOW DOES SOLAR WIND AFFECT EARTH?

THE SUN is constantly sending out a stream of charged particles into space, called the solar wind. The strength of the solar wind varies. It is usually at its strongest when the number of sunspots is highest. As these particles pass by Earth, some are trapped by the planet's magnetic field, interacting with gases in the atmosphere. The reaction between particles and gases creates a multicolored light show that can be seen from Earth.

HOW HIGH CAN SOLAR PROMINENCES SHOOT?

GIANT JETS OF flaming hydrogen can often be seen erupting from the chromosphere. These are called solar prominences. They shoot from the sun at incredible speeds. The average length of a prominence is 60,000 miles (100,000 km), but many can reach distances of over 310,000 miles (500,000 km). Some prominences, like the one on the left, make giant loops, following the magnetic field of the sun.

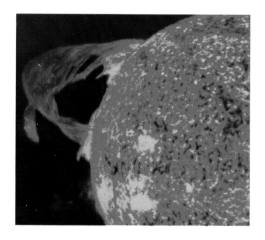

WHAT IS AN ANNULAR ECLIPSE?

THE MOON'S ORBIT around Earth is elliptical rather than circular, which means that sometimes the moon appears slightly smaller in the sky than the sun. If this happens during an eclipse, a ring of brilliant sunlight remains visible, like a circle of fire around the moon. This is called an annular eclipse (the word *annular* means "ring-shaped").

HOW CAN WE OBSERVE THE SUN?

BECAUSE OF ITS extreme brightness, it is very dangerous to look at the sun directly or through a telescope. Professional astronomers use tower telescopes to record the sun's activity. These are large telescopes with moving mirrors (heliostats) that reflect light down a long shaft to data-recording instruments on the ground.

fast facts

IS THE SUN ON FIRE?

Scientists in the early 19th century believed that the sun was an enormous lump of burning coal. However, scientists today know that the sun is not actually on fire, but is powered by nuclear reactions.

HOW FAST DOES THE SUN ROTATE?

Because the sun is a giant ball of gas, all parts do not rotate at the same speed or in the same way as a planet or a moon. The inner part of the sun rotates every 27 days, whereas the sun's equator rotates roughly every 25 days. Areas near the sun's poles take around 35 days to make one complete rotation.

WHAT IS A SOLAR FLARE?

Solar flares are powerful explosions from the sun, caused by sudden releases of energy heating up matter in the sun's atmosphere. Flares eject charged particles into space. These particles carry so much radiation that when they reach Earth they can cause magnetic storms and interfere with radio communications. If a particularly powerful flare hit Earth, it could strip the planet of its protective ozone layer.

WHERE ARE STARS BORN?

Stars are born in giant stellar nurseries of gas and dust called molecular clouds. The gas that forms these vast clouds is much thinner than the atmosphere on Earth, yet there is just enough gravity to force clumps of gas and dust to contract into a ball. This is the beginning of a star. It will continue to grow until it is large enough for nuclear reactions to begin in its core. A molecular cloud remains dark until the light from new stars illuminates the surrounding gas, turning it into a nebula.

DO STARS COME IN DIFFERENT SIZES?

ALTHOUGH THE STARS in the night sky may appear to be similar in size, they can vary greatly. Red supergiants are the largest stars, growing up to 500 times the size of the sun. Stars like the sun are the most common in the night sky. When these stars die, they become white dwarfs, shrinking to the size of Earth. Neutron stars are even smaller than this, their gravitational pull so strong that they have shrunk to a few miles in diameter.

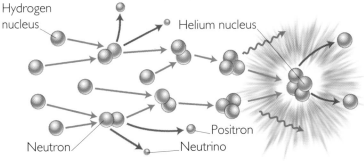

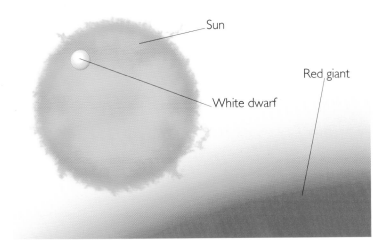

WHAT IS CORE FUSION?

A STAR PRODUCES ENERGY by nuclear fusion. Inside the core of the star, the temperature is so hot that particles cannot form properly, leaving a soup of atomic nuclei and electrons. These nuclei travel at incredibly fast speeds and often collide. If two hydrogen nuclei (protons) collide, they join together in a process called nuclear fusion, creating heavy hydrogen (deuterium). If another hydrogen nucleus collides with the deuterium, a light variety of helium is formed, called helium-3. If two helium-3 nuclei collide, an ordinary helium nucleus (helium-4) is formed. At each stage of the process, vast amounts of energy are released in the form of particles called positrons and neutrinos, and in packets of radiation called gamma-ray photons.

HOW LONG IS A STAR'S LIFE SPAN?

A STAR'S LIFE CYCLE can last millions, if not billions, of years. All stars begin in the same way—from material in a giant cloud of gas and dust called a molecular cloud. Stars remain alive as long as there is enough hydrogen to make helium, so a star's life span depends on its mass. Stars like the sun will burn steadily for around 10 billion years before running out of hydrogen. Larger stars convert hydrogen much more quickly and therefore have much shorter lives.

A giant cloud of gas and dust begins to contract under its own gravitational pull.

The cloud separates into clumps. As each clump shrinks, its core begins to heat up.

When the core reaches critical density, nuclear reactions begin with a violent release of energy.

The new star shines steadily, converting hydrogen into helium by nuclear fusion.

HOW DO LARGE STARS DIE?

LARGE STARS, with a mass much greater than our sun's, die a very violent death. As the hydrogen in a large star is used up, nuclear reactions produce heavier and heavier elements until a large iron core develops. This core eventually collapses under its own immense gravity, and the force of this collapse creates a tremendous explosion called a supernova. Most of the star's matter is blown into space by this explosion, leaving a tiny, dense remainder–either a neutron star or a black hole.

The matter inside a neutron star is so densely packed that a single thimbleful would weigh more than the Eiffel Tower in Paris, France.

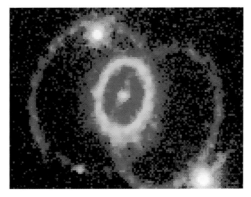

Supernova explosions can be brighter than a billion suns, and are so violent that they send shock waves of energy into space at millions of miles per hour.

WHAT ARE NEUTRON STARS?

WHEN A STAR explodes into a supernova, all that remains is a very small, extremely dense ball. This star is not made of gas, but rather of a liquid center of subatomic particles called neutrons, surrounded by a solid iron crust. The matter in a neutron star is packed so tightly that the star is often only a few miles in diameter.

fast facts

WHAT IS A PULSAR?

After the power of a supernova, some neutron stars spin very quickly. They send beams of radio energy out into space in much the same way as a lighthouse beam. From Earth, these beams appear to flash on and off very quickly as the star spins. These neutron stars are called pulsars.

DO STARS COME IN PAIRS?

Our sun is unusual because it is alone in space. Over half the stars in space are actually double stars, so close together that they appear to be only one. Double stars orbit around each other, held together by the pull of each other's gravity.

WHY ARE BLACK HOLES SO POWERFUL?

IF A STAR'S CORE after a supernova is more than three times the mass of the sun, it will collapse in on itself even further than a neutron star, shrinking into an unimaginably small space called a singularity. Its gravity becomes immensely strong, creating a gravitational well in space. If space was a stretched-out sheet, such as in the diagram on the left, a black hole would create such a steep well in the sheet that any object passing too close would be sucked inside forever. The force is so strong that nothing can escape, not even light.

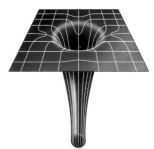

A black hole is so massive that it will create a very deep well in the fabric of space. Objects traveling too close to this well will be drawn toward it and swallowed. Everything that enters a black hole is compressed into the singularity, which is no bigger than an atom.

HOW CAN BLACK HOLES BE DETECTED?

BLACK HOLES emit no light. However, scientists can find them if they are located close to another star. The enormous gravitational pull of the black hole will tear gas from the star, pulling in streams of material. This gas will circle the black hole with such force that its temperature can exceed 100 million °C. This is so hot that x-rays will be released. Satellites such as the RXTE are used by astronomers to detect these x-rays.

The dust cloud around the star becomes a disk. Particles join together and may form planets.

The star will spend most of its life on its main sequence, turning hydrogen into helium.

As its hydrogen fuel runs out, the star expands, becoming a red giant.

The star burns helium, turning it into carbon. Its core heats up, and its surface cools.

When the helium runs out, the star blows off its outer layers to form a planetary nebula.

Once the planetary nebula has blown away, all that remains is a white dwarf.

HOW FAST DOES LIGHT TRAVEL?

Light is the fastest thing in the universe. It travels almost 186,000 miles (300,000 km) in one second. In a single year, light travels 5,900,000,000,000 miles (9,500,000,000,000 km)—or 5.9 trillion miles (9.5 trillion km). This distance is called a light year. It is used by astronomers to describe the enormous distances between stars and galaxies in space.

HOW ARE STARS CLASSIFIED?

THERE ARE COUNTLESS billions of stars in the universe, each at different stages of development. Astronomers use a special chart called the Hertzsprung–Russell (H–R) diagram to help understand the different types of stars better. By plotting stars on the H–R diagram based on their temperature and absolute magnitude, astronomers can sort the stars into groups and learn more about them.

CAN WE LOOK BACK IN TIME?

BECAUSE STARS ARE so far from each other, even light can take billions of years to travel between them. The farther away a star is from Earth, the longer it takes its light to reach us. This means that when we look up at the stars at night, we are gazing back in time. Even the sun's closest neighbor, Proxima Centauri, is more than four light years away, which means that we are seeing it as it was more than four years ago.

WHAT ARE LUMINOSITY AND MAGNITUDE?

THE ACTUAL BRIGHTNESS of a star compared to the sun is called its visual luminosity, which ranges from 100,000 times to 1/100,000 of the sun's brightness. A star's apparent magnitude is how bright it appears from Earth. Brighter stars have low, or negative, magnitudes.

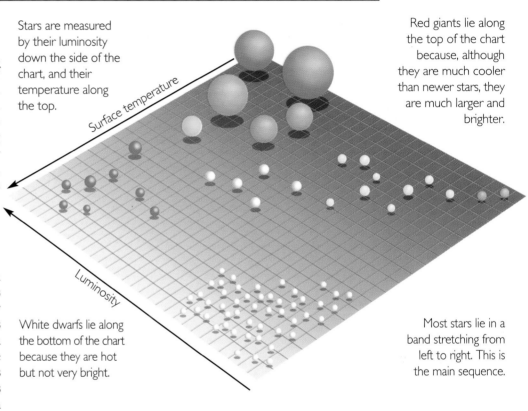

Stars are measured by their luminosity down the side of the chart, and their temperature along the top.

Surface temperature

Luminosity

Red giants lie along the top of the chart because, although they are much cooler than newer stars, they are much larger and brighter.

White dwarfs lie along the bottom of the chart because they are hot but not very bright.

Most stars lie in a band stretching from left to right. This is the main sequence.

WHAT IS LIGHT?

LIGHT IS A FORM OF ENERGY that can travel on its own even through a vacuum. Humans can see visible light, from red to violet, but there are also many other forms of light that cannot be seen with the naked eye. Light consists of energy in the form of electric and magnetic fields, and is therefore referred to as electromagnetic radiation. Light travels like a wave, and light waves come in many sizes. The size of a wave is measured by the distance from one peak to the next, which is called the wavelength. Light waves also come in many frequencies–the number of waves that pass a certain point every second. Gamma rays have the highest frequencies and the shortest wavelengths, and therefore the most energy.

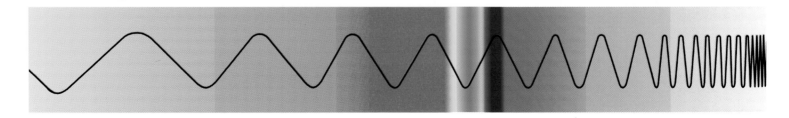

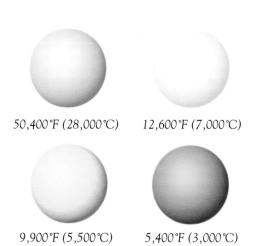

50,400°F (28,000°C)   12,600°F (7,000°C)

9,900°F (5,500°C)   5,400°F (3,000°C)

WHY ARE STARS DIFFERENT COLORS?

STARS IN THE NIGHT SKY appear to glow in a variety of different colors. This is because they have different temperatures and emit light with different wavelengths. Hot stars, with temperatures greater than 50,400°F (28,000°C), glow blue. Stars like our sun, which have a surface temperature of around 9,900°F (5,500°C), appear yellow, whereas cooler stars glow red. Astronomers divide stars into seven spectral types: O (hottest), B, A, F, G, K, and M (coolest).

A spectograph of the sun (right) shows that it is made up of many elements, including sodium, hydrogen, and helium. In contrast, a spectrograph of pure white light (left) will reveal no absorption lines because it contains no elements. Joseph von Fraunhofer invented the spectrograph in the early 1800s.

HOW CAN WE TELL HOW FAR AWAY STARS ARE?

SCIENTISTS HAVE TO KNOW how far away a star is before they can begin to analyze details such as its age, size, temperature, and mass. The most effective way of measuring a star's distance from Earth is called the parallax method. If you are traveling in a car and looking out the window, closer objects seem to pass by much more quickly than distant ones. In the same way, as Earth orbits the sun, closer stars appear to move more quickly through the sky than those farther away. The angle through which a certain star moves over a period of six months is called its parallax. This angle is used by astronomers to figure out how far away the star is.

The position of each star is measured when the Earth reaches opposite sides of its orbit around the sun. Measurements are taken every six months.

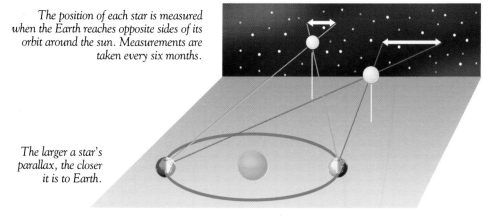

The larger a star's parallax, the closer it is to Earth.

HOW DO WE KNOW WHAT STARS ARE MADE OF?

EACH STAR PRODUCES its own individual light. By splitting the light into a spectrum, astronomers can discover the chemical elements that make up the star. This is because different elements in the star's atmosphere absorb light of different wavelengths. Sodium atoms, for example, only absorb light from the yellow part of the spectrum. A dark line across this part of the spectrum, called an absorption line, tells scientists that there is sodium in the star. By studying the various lines made on the spectrum, scientists can determine what the star is made up of.

fast facts

HOW DOES GRAVITY AFFECT LIGHT?

Gravity affects everything, including light. The Einstein cross appears in the sky as five points of light. However, it is really only one. The light comes from a distant quasar and is bent on its way to Earth by the gravitational pull of a galaxy.

WHAT ARE VARIABLE STARS?

Variable stars seem to get much brighter, then much dimmer over a regular period of time. Cepheid variables are stars that expand and shrink as they become hotter and cooler.

WHAT LIES BETWEEN THE STARS?

MUCH OF THE SPACE BETWEEN the stars may be black, but it certainly isn't empty. Tiny amounts of dust and gas, called interstellar medium, occupy the space between stars. Interstellar medium has an average density of less than one atom per cubic centimeter, but in some places it is concentrated into vast clouds called nebulae. Nebulae come in many different shapes, sizes and colors. Emission nebulae (left) are the most beautiful. Their striking colors come from the presence of hydrogen atoms that release red light. Reflection nebulae (center) are illuminated by light reflected from nearby stars. They appear blue because the light is scattered by dust grains. Absorption nebulae (right) are dark because there are no nearby stars to light them. They can be spotted because they block out the light from more distant stars.

WHAT ARE ISLAND UNIVERSES?

In 1755, the philosopher Immanuel Kant claimed that some bright objects in space were giant collections of stars, and he named them island universes. The work of Edwin Hubble in the 1920s proved that these island universes were galaxies that lay beyond our own. A galaxy is an enormous collection of stars, dust, and gas, held together by its own gravity. Even the smallest galaxies contain hundreds of thousands of stars, and it takes light many thousands of years to travel from one side to the other.

WHAT IS THE MILKY WAY?

THE MILKY WAY IS OUR home in the universe. It is made up of over 200 billion stars, including the sun, as well as large amounts of gas and dust. From above, it looks like a giant spiral, but if it were viewed from the side it would appear as a flat band of stars. This is because the Milky Way is over 100,000 light years long, but only 2,000 light years thick. The center of the Milky Way is made up of a bright nucleus of old, cool stars. Emerging from the central galactic bulge are several spiral arms made up of gas, dust, and young stars.

WHERE IS THE SUN IN THE MILKY WAY?

OUR SOLAR SYSTEM LIES ROUGHLY two-thirds of the way from the center of the galaxy, on the inner edge of a spiral arm called the Orion Arm, or the Local Arm. From Earth, the Milky Way looks like a river of milk stretching across the night sky. This is because we are viewing it from inside. The infrared image above gives a clearer view of the Milky Way as it stretches across space.

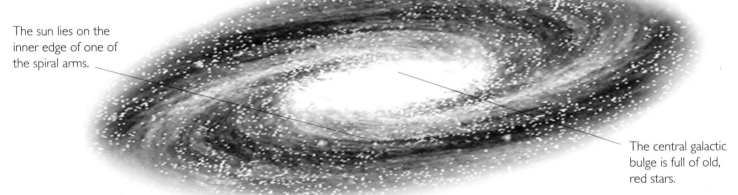

The sun lies on the inner edge of one of the spiral arms.

The central galactic bulge is full of old, red stars.

WHAT ARE SATELLITE GALAXIES?

JUST AS THE SUN'S GRAVITY holds the objects of the Solar System in their orbits, the gravitational pull of the Milky Way keeps two smaller galaxies in tow. The two Magellanic Clouds consist of thousands of star clusters that orbit the Milky Way every 1.5 billion years. The Large Magellanic Cloud (right) is made of the same mix of gas and stars as the Milky Way, but is less than one-twentieth its size. The Small Magellanic Cloud is slowly being pulled apart by the gravity of our galaxy.

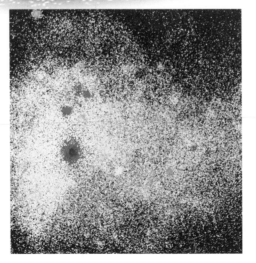

WHAT IS AT THE CENTER OF THE MILKY WAY?

ASTRONOMERS CANNOT SEE what lies at the center of the Milky Way because of the large amounts of dust in the way. Radio waves are not affected by dust, however, so scientists have been able to make detailed maps of the galaxy. They have found that at the center of the Milky Way lies an enormous black hole–as large as Jupiter's orbit around the Sun –which is sucking in matter and pouring out energy with the strength of almost 100 million suns.

ARE THERE DIFFERENT KINDS OF GALAXIES?

GALAXIES COME IN ALL SHAPES AND SIZES, but astronomers divide them into just a few main types. More than half of all galaxies are elliptical, named because of their egglike shape. They are made up of large numbers of old, red stars, and have very little gas and dust with which to make new ones. Around a third of all galaxies are spiral in shape, like the Milky Way. Old stars are packed tightly in their centers, while new stars are continually being born from the large amounts of gas and dust in their spiral arms. Some spiral galaxies are classed separately because their nucleus is elongated into a bar. This bar is made up of stars in motion, and the spiral arms extend from the ends of the bar. Some galaxies cannot be classed as either spirals or ellipticals because they have no recognizable shape. These galaxies are called irregulars, and are full of gas in which new stars are forming.

Elliptical galaxy (E)

Spiral galaxy (S)

Barred spiral galaxy (BS)

Irregular galaxy (Irr)

WHAT HAPPENS WHEN GALAXIES COLLIDE?

GALAXIES ARE NORMALLY SEPARATED by vast, empty gulfs. Occasionally, however, two galaxies can pass close enough to one another to collide. They are traveling at millions of miles per hour, and the resulting impact can be incredible. The individual stars in a galaxy do not collide, but the vast clouds of interstellar gas and dust smash into one another, triggering a ferocious birth of new stars. Only gravity holds these galaxies together, so an amazing battle of strength follows an impact. Sometimes galaxies merge to form even larger galaxies. At other times, galaxies can be distorted, or even ripped apart, by the impact. The Cartwheel galaxy (left) was hit by another galaxy 300 million years ago.

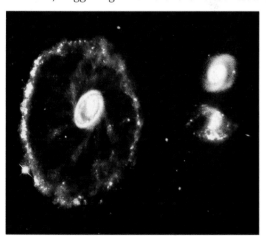

The Cartwheel galaxy used to be a spiral galaxy, but a smaller galaxy, traveling very fast, smashed through its center. The blue ring around the central region is made up of millions of new stars triggered by the impact.

fast facts

WHAT ARE ACTIVE GALAXIES?

Active galaxies are galaxies with supermassive black holes at their cores. Energy created by these black holes forces out giant streams of gas.

WHAT ARE QUASARS?

Quasars are among the most powerful and most distant galaxies in the universe. The radiation from quasars has taken billions of years to reach Earth, so they show us how the universe behaved near its birth.

HOW ARE GALAXIES CLASSIFIED?

GALAXIES ARE CLASSIFIED using a very simple code that describes their basic shape. "E" is used to describe an elliptical galaxy, and a number from 0 to 7 is added to further define its form. An E0 galaxy looks like a ball, whereas an E7 galaxy resembles a short, fat sausage. Spiral galaxies are defined by the letter "S," and barred spiral galaxies by the letters "BS." Both these forms of galaxy are given further definition by the addition of a letter a, b, c, or d. Galaxies with tightly wound arms are labeled Sa, and galaxies with looser arms are labeled Sd.

DO GALAXIES COME IN GROUPS?

GALAXIES THEMSELVES MAY APPEAR to be enormous, but even they do not exist independently in space. They gather together in groups–from pairs to clusters that can contain thousands of galaxies. The Milky Way is only one of a cluster of around 30 galaxies that make up the Local Group, an enormous collection of galaxies that stretches over millions of light years. The largest known cluster is the Virgo cluster, which contains over 2,000 galaxies. Just as gravity causes galaxies to form clusters, it also brings clusters together to form superclusters. These are the largest structures in the universe, stretching hundreds of millions of light years across space.

WHEN DID ASTRONOMY BEGIN?

Astronomy has been around ever since human beings first looked up at the stars and wondered about the sparkling lights above. There is evidence to suggest that people have been charting the skies for over 15,000 years. Cave paintings in France and Spain include maps of star clusters, such as the Pleiades. The Akkadians, who lived in Babylonia 4,500 years ago, kept many astronomical records, including the paths of the sun, the moon, and the planets. Stonehenge, in England, was built in around 3000 B.C. It is a giant astronomical calendar with stones aligned to the sun.

WHO WAS PTOLEMY?

THE ANCIENT GREEKS turned astronomy into a science. Ptolemy (above right), who was born around A.D. 100, published his *Almaghest* in A.D. 140. This was an encyclopedia of the patterns of the stars and planets, and he used it to support his argument that the Earth was at the center of the universe. His "system of the world" claimed that surrounding Earth were seven transparent spheres, each containing a moving object such as the sun, the moon, or a planet. An eighth sphere, which surrounded everything, held the stars. His theory, which we now know to be incorrect, was a very accurate way of predicting the motions of the planets, and was the dominant theory in astronomy for over 1,000 years.

Ptolemy's celestial sphere placed the Earth at the center of the universe, orbited by the sun, moon, and planets.

WHO FIRST SUGGESTED A HELIOCENTRIC UNIVERSE?

NOT EVERYBODY BELIEVED that the Earth was at the center of the universe. Aristarchus, another Greek who lived in the same age as Ptolemy, claimed that the sun was at the center of everything, orbited by the Earth and the planets. This is known as a heliocentric theory. Nobody took him seriously, because he could not explain why, if the Earth moved through space, the stars did not change their positions in relation to each other.

WHO WAS COPERNICUS?

IT WAS NOT UNTIL the 16th century that Ptolemy's system was challenged seriously. A Polish churchman named Nicolaus Copernicus claimed that the Earth and the planets orbited the sun. His ideas were backed up in 1610, when Galileo Galilei used a telescope to view the moons of Jupiter, proving that not everything orbited the Earth.

Copernicus's universe (left), with the sun at its center, is very similar to the Solar System that we know today.

HOW DID THE PLANETS GET THEIR NAMES?

THE NAMES OF THE PLANETS in our Solar System originate from characters they resembled in ancient Greek and Roman legends. Mercury was named after the nimble messenger of the gods because of its fast orbit. Venus was named after the goddess of beauty and love because of its brightness in the night sky. Mars was named after the god of war because of its color. Jupiter was given the name of the king of the gods because of its size, and Saturn was named after the god of the harvest. Planets discovered later were named in the same way–Uranus after the father of the gods, Neptune after the god of the sea, and Pluto after the god of the underworld.

Sun

Earth

WHAT ARE CONSTELLATIONS?

FOR THOUSANDS OF YEARS, societies all over the world have grouped together the brightest stars in the sky to form patterns and pictures called constellations. People have projected characters, natural images and human beings on these groupings– from animals such as the Great Bear to mythological heroes such as Hercules. There are 88 officially recognized constellations in the night sky.

WHAT IS THE ECLIPTIC?

WHEN PEOPLE FIRST BEGAN to study the movement of the sun, they believed that it orbited the Earth. It seemed to move along the same path through the skies every day, and the path was named the ecliptic. We now know that the Earth orbits the sun, and that this line is actually a projection of Earth's orbit around the sun onto the stars beyond (left).

There are so many stars in the night sky that it is possible to find almost any image you like. The brightest stars have been grouped together into similar patterns by people all over the world.

ARE THE STARS IN A CONSTELLATION JOINED?

Despite being grouped together into a recognizable pattern, the individual stars in a constellation have no real link with one another. In fact, they can be thousands of light years apart.

HOW IS LEARNING THE CONSTELLATIONS USEFUL?

Knowing the patterns of the night sky is as useful to an astronomer as knowing the layout of a new town is to a tourist. It is much easier to get to grips with the mass of stars in the sky if you have markings to go by. Sailors used to use the constellations to help navigate their way across the oceans.

WHAT IS THE CELESTIAL SPHERE?

Although the stars extend in all directions, astronomers find it useful to think of them as being on the inside of a giant sphere. The sphere has grid lines that astronomers use to plot the positions of the stars.

WHAT IS THE ZODIAC?

THE ZODIAC IS A GROUP of twelve constellations that lie along the ecliptic. Of the 88 constellations that are officially recognized today, the twelve of the ecliptic are the most ancient. They are regarded as special because the sun appears to pass through them as it moves through the sky. Even today they act as markers in astrology–the belief that human life is affected by the position of the stars and planets.

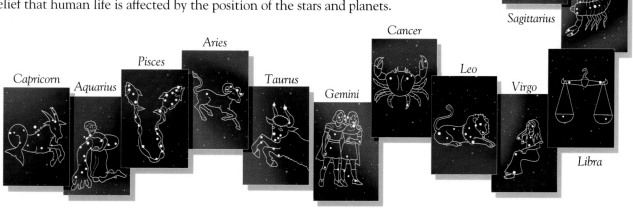

Capricorn Aquarius Pisces Aries Taurus Gemini Cancer Leo Virgo Libra Scorpio Sagittarius

WHO INVENTED THE TELESCOPE?

The first telescope was created by the Dutch spectacle-maker Hans Lippershey in 1608. It was a simple design that could only magnify objects a small number of times, but the idea spread like wildfire through Europe. One year later, the Italian inventor Galileo Galilei was the first person to use the telescope to study the movement of the stars and planets.

HOW DO OPTICAL TELESCOPES WORK?

ASTRONOMERS USE TWO different types of visual telescope: reflectors and refractors. The idea behind both is to capture as much light as possible from distant objects, and direct that light to the human eye, or to data-recording equipment. Refractor telescopes, which are used by most amateur astronomers, work by capturing light through a main lens. This light is then magnified by a second lens, which focuses it into an image. Most professional astronomers prefer to use reflector telescopes (right), which use mirrors to capture light.

The image is formed in the main mirror. Because it is curved, the mirror focuses the image, directing it toward a second mirror.

Light from objects in space enters here and is collected by the main mirror.

The secondary mirror reflects the light of the main image to an eyepiece, or to data-recording equipment.

Data-recording equipment

Unlike the lenses in a refracting telescope, which are limited in size, mirrors in a reflecting telescope can be any size.

DO TELESCOPES ONLY STUDY VISIBLE LIGHT?

VISIBLE LIGHT ONLY MAKES UP a tiny fraction of the electromagnetic spectrum–less than 0.00001 percent. Objects in space emit radiation in many different forms, from radio waves to gamma rays. By studying these forms of radiation, astronomers can learn more about space. Astronomers use different kinds of telescope to study different types of radiation.

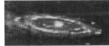

WHAT OTHER TYPES OF ASTRONOMY ARE THERE?

RADIO ASTRONOMY COLLECTS the radio signals given out by objects in space, which can be used to put together a picture of something that cannot be seen with the naked eye, such as volcanoes on Venus (above left). Many objects in space emit energy in the form of infrared waves, such as the Andromeda galaxy (second left). Ultraviolet astronomy is used to track down the hottest stars in space, such as the Crab supernova (second right). Radiation with the highest energy levels is called gamma ray (right).

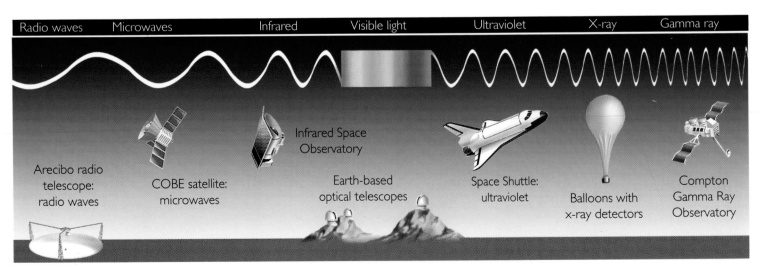

| Radio waves | Microwaves | Infrared | Visible light | Ultraviolet | X-ray | Gamma ray |

Arecibo radio telescope: radio waves

COBE satellite: microwaves

Infrared Space Observatory

Earth-based optical telescopes

Space Shuttle: ultraviolet

Balloons with x-ray detectors

Compton Gamma Ray Observatory

How have modern telescopes been improved?

MODERN ASTRONOMY RELIES AS MUCH on computers as on telescopes. Data collected by telescopes and satellites is processed by computers to produce images that can be stored and studied at leisure. Telescopes are becoming bigger and more powerful. The twin Keck telescopes, built on the 13,780-foot (4,200-m) summit of an extinct Hawaiian volcano, are eight stories tall, with mirrors 33 feet (10 m) wide.

What is the largest telescope?

THE BIGGEST TELESCOPE in the world is aptly named the Very Large Telescope, and is located in Chile. It is made up of four separate 27-foot (8.2-m) mirrors, each over a billion times more powerful than the naked eye. It is so powerful that it is even able to spot an astronaut on the moon. The Arecibo telescope in Puerto Rico is the world's largest curved focusing antenna. Its dish is 1,000 feet (305 m) in diameter, and made up of almost 40,000 aluminum panels.

Satellites such as the Compton Gamma Ray Observatory are carried into space by a space shuttle.

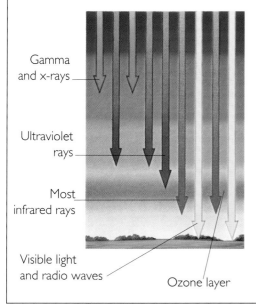

Gamma and x-rays

Ultraviolet rays

Most infrared rays

Visible light and radio waves

Ozone layer

Why do we need telescopes in space?

EARTH'S ATMOSPHERE SHIELDS the planet against radiation from space. Gamma rays, x-rays, and most ultraviolet rays are absorbed by the atmosphere, preventing them from reaching the surface. Because of this, these types of radiation are best studied from space. There are many different satellites in orbit around the Earth, such as the Compton Gamma Ray Observatory (above), which allow these forms of radiation to be studied.

Only visible light, some infrared, ultraviolet, and radio waves reach Earth's surface.

fast facts

Why are refractor telescopes less reliable?

Refractor telescopes use thick lenses to absorb light from distant objects. Lenses focus different parts of the light spectrum at different points, which can blur images and make them difficult to view.

Who invented the reflector telescope?

It was the famous scientist Isaac Newton who first suggested using mirrors in telescopes. He realized that light would always be split up by a lens to produce unwanted colored fringes. In 1668, he produced the first reflector telescope. It used a solid metal mirror made of copper and tin.

Why are mountings so important?

The reliability of a telescope depends greatly on its mounting. Besides having to support the weight of the telescope, which can often be many tons, a mounting must be able to move freely to compensate for the Earth's movement. The most common mounting is called altazimuth, which allows the telescope to move in all directions.

What is the Hubble Space Telescope?

LAUNCHED IN 1990 AFTER nearly half a century of planning, the Hubble Space Telescope was a dream come true for astronomers. It orbits 380 miles (610 km) above the Earth's surface, meaning that its view is not blocked by the planet's turbulent atmosphere. Hubble's main telescope is a reflector telescope, like those used on Earth. This can take crystal-clear pictures of the most distant parts of the universe. Hubble also has many other kinds of telescope, including a faint-object camera, infrared cameras, and a wide-field telescope.

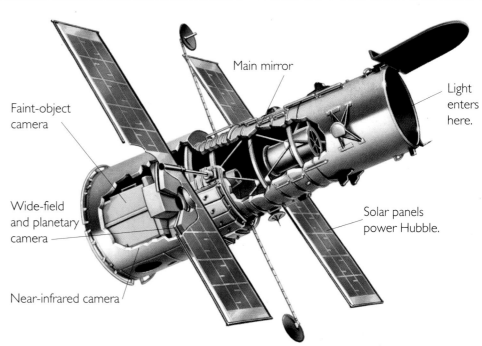

Main mirror

Light enters here.

Faint-object camera

Wide-field and planetary camera

Solar panels power Hubble.

Near-infrared camera

HOW DO SATELLITES GET INTO SPACE?

Everything that enters space, from satellites to astronauts, does so through the incredible power of rocket propulsion. In order to escape Earth's strong gravitational pull, a space launcher has to reach a speed of over 17,500 miles per hour (27,000 kmph). Once the rocket is in orbit, its power is shut off. Although it is still being affected by Earth's gravity, it does not fall back down to the ground, because its speed cancels out the gravitational pull.

WHAT IS PROPULSION?

PROPULSION IS THE act of driving something forward. Rockets, cars, boats, planes, and all other vehicles use some form of propulsion in order to move.

HOW DO ROCKETS WORK?

A ROCKET NEEDS to produce enough thrust to overcome gravity and lift its own weight. Rockets burn liquid hydrogen and oxygen in a specially built combustion chamber. For every pound of rocket fuel burned, a pound of exhaust gas is allowed to escape from a nozzle at the base of the rocket. As the high-temperature, high-velocity gases are fired downwards, they exert an equal, opposite force that fires the rocket upward.

WHAT ARE NEWTON'S LAWS OF MOTION?

SIR ISAAC NEWTON, a scientist who lived between 1642 and 1727, completely changed our understanding of the universe when he proposed his three laws of motion:

1 *An object remains motionless or traveling in a straight line until a force acts on it.*
2 *The acceleration of an object is equal to the overall force acting on it divided by its mass.*
3 *Every action has an equal and opposite reaction.*

This last law is most important in relation to rocket propulsion. When firefighters spray water from a hose, they have to struggle to hold it still. This is because the hose is firing water forward, and the firefighters are struggling against the opposite reaction.

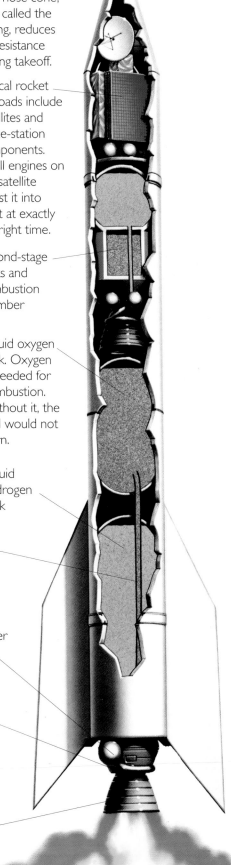

The nose cone, also called the fairing, reduces air resistance during takeoff.

Typical rocket payloads include satellites and space-station components. Small engines on the satellite boost it into orbit at exactly the right time.

Second-stage tanks and combustion chamber

Liquid oxygen tank. Oxygen is needed for combustion. Without it, the fuel would not burn.

Liquid hydrogen tank

Pipes carry the liquid oxygen and liquid hydrogen to the main combustion chamber.

The liquid helium container pressurizes the fuel tanks, preventing leakage.

Main engine combustion chamber. This is where fuel is mixed and ignited.

Exhaust gases are ejected from the exhaust nozzle, giving the rocket lift.

WHY DOES A ROCKET HAVE DIFFERENT STAGES?

ROCKETS HAVE TO carry an enormous amount of fuel in order to make the journey into orbit. So much fuel is needed that most rockets are made up of enormous chambers in which to store the liquid hydrogen and oxygen. Rockets such as the Ariane need maximum thrust for the first few seconds of takeoff, so the main engine and two extra boosters fire at full power. After about two minutes, all the fuel in the two boosters has been used up, so they are jettisoned in order to lighten the payload. The less a rocket weighs, the less fuel it has to use.

WHEN WERE ROCKETS INVENTED?

SOLID-FUEL ROCKETS were first used by the Chinese over 1,000 years ago. They were powered by gunpowder made of sulfur, saltpeter and charcoal, and were used as weapons. In 1926, the American scientist Robert Goddard launched the first liquid-fueled rocket. Long-range rockets were perfected in 1942, when Wernher von Braun developed the powerful V-2 for the German army.

WHAT IS A SPACE LAUNCHER?

SPACE LAUNCHERS ARE rockets that carry payloads into space. Just as there are many sizes of truck to carry different goods from place to place, there are many different space launchers, each suited to different purposes. Rockets such as the Mercury-Atlas (left) were designed to be small and light, since they only had to carry one person. Russia's Soyuz series (middle) are incredibly powerful, able to carry 20 tons into a low-Earth orbit. NASA's Saturn V (right) was designed to be powerful enough to carry three people to the moon.

WHAT HAPPENS AT MISSION CONTROL?

MISSION CONTROL IS a rocket's contact back on Earth. All missions into space require constant technical support from scientists and engineers on the ground. The staff at Mission Control have many important jobs, such as ensuring that the craft is on the right course, maintaining vital communication links, and making sure there is enough oxygen and fuel to complete the mission safely.

WHEN DID THE SPACE AGE BEGIN?

From the early 1950s on, the Union of Soviet Socialist Republics (USSR) and the United States were engaged in a ferociously competitive war of supremacy against one another, each trying to be the country to begin the space age. Vast amounts of money were invested in space exploration, and in October 1957, the USSR launched the world's first artificial satellite, Sputnik 1. It did very little besides transmit a simple radio signal, but it marked a new stage in the history of humankind.

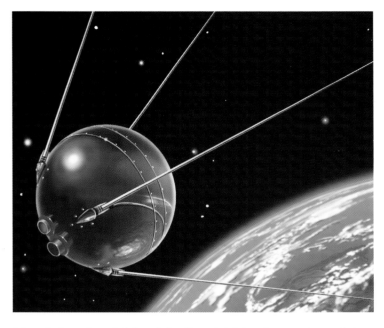

Many frightened people believed that Sputnik 1 (above) was spying on their activities from space. In reality, all the probe did was emit a simple tracking signal for the 21 days that it was in orbit.

WHO WAS THE FIRST PERSON IN SPACE?

THE SOVIET Yuri Alekseyevich Gagarin was the first person to be launched into space. He traveled aboard Vostok 1, and blasted off from Earth in April 1961. After completing one orbit, he returned safely to Earth. John Glenn was the first American to be sent into space in 1962.

Russian cosmonaut Yuri Gagarin was the first man in space.

WHICH COUNTRY WAS FIRST TO EXPLORE THE MOON?

LUNA 2 (left) was launched from the USSR in 1959, and was the first probe to visit the moon's surface, although it did not so much land as crash. Ranger 7, an American probe, also crashed on the moon's surface in 1964. It managed to take over 4,000 close-up pictures. Luna 9 was the first probe to land successfully on the moon in 1966. It sent back television pictures of the barren surface.

WHAT WAS THE FIRST LIVING THING IN SPACE?

LESS THAN ONE MONTH after Sputnik 1 had been launched, the Soviets claimed a second amazing achievement by sending the first living creature into orbit. Sputnik 2, which blasted off from Earth in November 1957, contained a small dog called Laika. The spacecraft was designed especially for the dog, with life-support facilities and a cradle. Laika survived the launch and the journey into space, but died when her supply of oxygen ran out in orbit. Three years later, in August 1960, two more dogs, named Belka and Strelka, became the first creatures to survive the journey into space and return, traveling aboard Sputnik 5.

WHAT WERE THE APOLLO MISSIONS?

THE APOLLO LUNAR PROGRAM was launched in 1961 by U.S. President John F. Kennedy. He ambitiously claimed that human beings would set foot on the moon by the end of the decade. It was one of the most complicated and technically challenging projects of the twentieth century, but resulted in a manned mission being sent to the moon in 1969. A very powerful rocket, called the Saturn V, was built especially for the journey. It was able to carry the 57 tons of equipment needed for a successful visit to the lunar surface. Apollo 8 carried the first men around the Moon in 1968, but it was not until one year later, in July 1969, that humankind first set foot on the surface of the moon.

WHAT ARE CONDITIONS LIKE ON THE MOON?

GRAVITY ON THE MOON is only one-sixth of that on Earth, which means that astronauts can jump several yards effortlessly. There is no atmosphere on the moon, so sound will nor carry, even over a small distance. Radios have to be used for communication over even a few inches. Because there is no weather, the astronauts' footprints will last for thousands of years (below).

HOW DID THE APOLLO ASTRONAUTS GET TO THE MOON?

SATURN V held the Apollo spacecraft, which was made up of three parts–the Command, Service, and Lunar Modules. Neil Armstrong and Buzz Aldrin touched down on the moon's surface in the Lunar Module. Besides providing their transportation, the Lunar Module was the astronauts' home for the three days they spent on the moon. Michael Collins remained in orbit aboard the Command and Service Module. When it was time to leave the moon, Aldrin and Armstrong blasted back into orbit in the top half of the Lunar Module, before docking with the Command and Service Module and beginning the journey back to Earth.

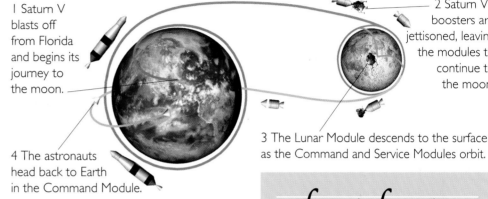

1 Saturn V blasts off from Florida and begins its journey to the moon.

2 Saturn V's boosters are jettisoned, leaving the modules to continue to the moon.

3 The Lunar Module descends to the surface as the Command and Service Modules orbit.

4 The astronauts head back to Earth in the Command Module.

WHAT KIND OF EXPERIMENTS WERE DONE ON THE MOON?

THERE HAVE BEEN SIX APOLLO missions to the moon, during which 12 astronauts have explored its composition and conditions. Thousands of photographs have been taken, and 388 pounds (176 kg) of moon rock were brought back to Earth to be studied. Scientists are interested in finding out what the moon is made of because this may determine its origin and history. Astronauts also measured the amount of solar particles reaching the lunar surface, the amount of dust in the air, and the power of moonquakes, which are slight movements in the moon's crust.

WHAT WAS THE MOON BUGGY?

ON APOLLO 17, the last manned mission to the moon, the astronauts took with them a small buggy called the Lunar Rover. It was battery-powered and could travel at just under 12 mph (20 kmph), enabling astronauts to explore much more of the moon than their predecessors had been able to do on foot. It had a small television camera and a satellite dish that sent the footage back to Earth. The moon buggy, as it is often called, had rubber tires that could not be punctured, and was steered by a small hand control. It could be folded up and stored when it was not needed.

DID THE USSR AND THE U.S. WORK TOGETHER?

Despite their battle for political supremacy, the U.S. and the Soviet Union cooperated on one space mission. During the Apollo–Soyuz rendezvous, the crews docked their craft with one another. Over a period of a few days, they worked together on various experiments.

WILL ASTRONAUTS EVER RETURN TO THE MOON?

Scientists are already considering sending astronauts back to the moon in order to build lunar bases. Astronauts will investigate the moon's surface in order to find suitable locations for constructing laboratories and telescopes.

WERE OTHER ANIMALS SENT INTO SPACE?

The Russians sent at least ten dogs into space after Laika, Belka, and Strelka, in order to test equipment prior to manned missions. The Americans sent several chimpanzees and monkeys into orbit, the first of which was named Gordo. Turtles, flies, and worms have also been on trips into space.

WHAT IS THE SPACE TRANSPORTATION SYSTEM?

Sending a rocket into space is a very expensive procedure, especially considering that each launcher can be used only once. The Space Transportation System (STS), better known as the Space Shuttle, was designed to be the world's first reusable space vehicle.

WHY IS THE SHUTTLE ECONOMICAL TO RUN?

MOST ROCKETS either burn up in Earth's atmosphere or are decommissioned after they have completed their mission. A new rocket has to be built from scratch for the next launch. All but one part of NASA's Space Shuttle returns to Earth intact. After these parts have been checked for damage, they are ready to be used again, therefore saving the cost of rebuilding.

WHAT ARE THE DIFFERENT COMPONENTS OF THE SHUTTLE?

THE STS IS COMPRISED of four main parts: the orbiter is the main section of the Shuttle, housing the crew, the control center and the payload. The orbiter is the only part of the Shuttle to reach orbit, after which it returns to Earth, landing like a plane. An external fuel tank contains the liquid hydrogen and liquid oxygen needed for propulsion. Two solid rocket boosters propel the orbiter to a height of 28 miles (45 km) before they are jettisoned.

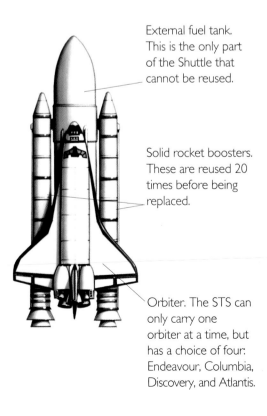

External fuel tank. This is the only part of the Shuttle that cannot be reused.

Solid rocket boosters. These are reused 20 times before being replaced.

Orbiter. The STS can only carry one orbiter at a time, but has a choice of four: Endeavour, Columbia, Discovery, and Atlantis.

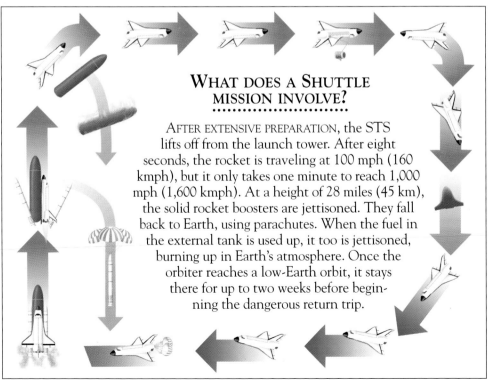

WHAT DOES A SHUTTLE MISSION INVOLVE?

AFTER EXTENSIVE PREPARATION, the STS lifts off from the launch tower. After eight seconds, the rocket is traveling at 100 mph (160 kmph), but it only takes one minute to reach 1,000 mph (1,600 kmph). At a height of 28 miles (45 km), the solid rocket boosters are jettisoned. They fall back to Earth, using parachutes. When the fuel in the external tank is used up, it too is jettisoned, burning up in Earth's atmosphere. Once the orbiter reaches a low-Earth orbit, it stays there for up to two weeks before beginning the dangerous return trip.

WHAT DOES THE ORBITER CONTAIN?

THE ORBITER is the most important section of the Space Shuttle. Although it looks a lot like a small plane, it is actually a high-tech laboratory and storage area, with facilities to hold up to seven crew members for over two weeks. The front end of the orbiter is comprised of three levels: the flight deck, the mid-deck, where the crew lives while in space, and the lower deck, which contains vital life-support equipment. Most of the orbiter is taken up by a vast payload bay.

The flight deck is the equivalent of a cockpit in a normal aircraft. This is the control center for the entire Shuttle—power, communications, lighting, and life support are all overseen from here.

A remote-controlled manipulator arm is used to move cargo.

The orbiter has several different types of engine. The three main engines are used to help the Shuttle into orbit. Orbital-maneuvering engines help the craft move in space. Smaller thrusters allow the orbiter to change its position more accurately.

The orbiter's wings are designed to help the craft land back on Earth.

The mid-deck can be accessed from the flight deck by a ladder. It contains almost everything the astronauts use during the mission, such as the galley (kitchen), bathroom, and sleeping stations.

The lower deck houses life-support equipment designed to keep the Shuttle's environment cool and comfortable.

The payload bay holds the Shuttle's cargo, which varies from satellites to equipment such as the Hubble Space Telescope.

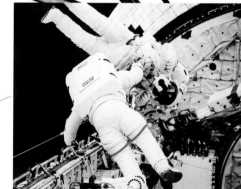

ARE ALL SHUTTLE MISSIONS SUCCESSFUL?

UNFORTUNATELY THERE ARE MANY risks relating to space travel. With the tremendous forces involved, accidents inevitably occur. In 1986, the Challenger orbiter exploded when a joint between two segments of one of the boosters came loose. Tragically, everybody on board died.

WHAT IS THE PAYLOAD BAY?

THE PAYLOAD BAY is where the Shuttle's cargo is kept during flight. It measures 60 feet by 15 feet (18.3 m by 4.6 m), which is large enough to hold two small buses end to end. The two large bay doors can be opened when the Shuttle reaches low-Earth orbit, allowing the cargo to be lifted into space.

WHY DOES THE SHUTTLE HEAT UP ON REENTRY?

EARTH'S ATMOSPHERE IS MADE UP of minuscule particles of rock and gas. When an orbiter reenters the atmosphere, it impacts with these particles, heating up because of friction. Parts of the Shuttle can reach up to 2,732°F (1,500°C), which is hot enough to cause them to melt. Because of this, the nose tip and wing edges are protected by heat-absorbing tiles that prevent the orbiter from getting too hot.

The orbiter is traveling so quickly as it reenters the atmosphere that tiny particles hit it with great force. In the same way that your hands heat up when you rub them together, the rapid movement of particles against the craft causes it to heat up.

fast facts

WHEN WAS THE FIRST SHUTTLE FLIGHT?

The orbiter Columbia was the first Shuttle to enter orbit. It was launched on April 12 1981.

HOW DOES THE SHUTTLE LAND?

The Shuttle begins to slow down half a world away from the landing site in Florida. It is traveling so quickly that it does not need its engines to power it. Instead, it acts in the same way as a glider, using the air to slow it down as it approaches the 2.8-mile-long (4.5-km-long) runway.

WHAT ARE ION DRIVES?

Ion technology is the future of space travel. It is a cheap, efficient form of propulsion that enables crafts to travel at incredible speeds. Ion drives are one of many technologies that are about to change the way we think about space travel, allowing us to travel farther from Earth than ever before.

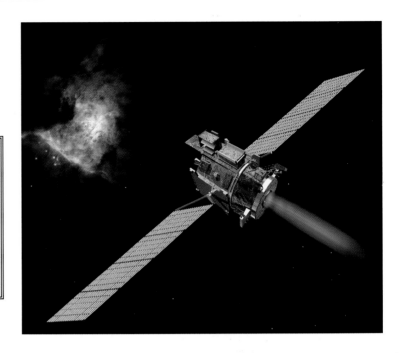

HOW DOES ION PROPULSION WORK?

ION PROPULSION ENGINES WORK using the same principles as conventional rockets–they expel a force in one direction that propels the craft in the opposite direction. However, instead of using liquid propellant, an ion drive works by accelerating and expelling positively charged atoms (ions). These ions are fired at more than 24 miles per second (31 km per second)–much faster than the exhaust gases of liquid-fueled rockets. However, their accumulative mass is so small that it would take a spacecraft with an ion drive many months to reach its maximum speed.

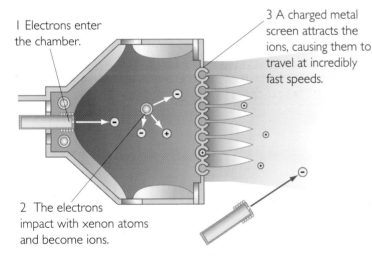

I Electrons enter the chamber.

3 A charged metal screen attracts the ions, causing them to travel at incredibly fast speeds.

2 The electrons impact with xenon atoms and become ions.

WHICH FORM OF PROPULSION IS MOST EFFECTIVE?

WHILE THE PARTICLES expelled from an ion drive travel much faster than the gases from a conventional rocket, they are not massive enough to provide sufficient thrust. Rockets such as the Space Shuttle can produce millions of pounds of thrust at lift-off, whereas, to begin with, an ion drive can only produce around 20-thousandths of a pound of thrust. This is not enough force to escape Earth's gravitational pull. Crafts with ion drives have to be carried into space by a conventional rocket, but once they have left Earth's orbit, their velocity continues to increase, until they reach much faster speeds than rockets. Ion drives are also much more efficient, using only 176 pounds (80 kg) of xenon in a two-year mission.

ARE ION DRIVES ALREADY IN USE?

NASA's DEEP SPACE 1 probe (above), launched in 1998, was the first craft to use ion technology in space. It flew close to the near-Earth asteroid Braille (also known as 1992 KD), guided by an automated navigation system. Afterward, it investigated the comet Borrelly, completing its mission in late 2001. Deep Space 1 is an experimental craft that is also testing several other new technologies, including more efficient solar panels, and an autonomous operations system, which allows the craft to think and act on its own. Its success has made scientists optimistic about the use of ion technology.

WILL CHEAPER ROCKETS LEAD TO VACATIONS IN SPACE?

SOME COMPANIES ARE already taking bookings for pleasure trips into space. In 2001, the American millionaire Dennis Tito was the first "tourist" in space, flying into orbit in a Russian Soyuz rocket. Other firms have already spent millions on designing hotels and condominiums on the moon! As the price of traveling into space goes down, more and more people will make plans to go on the ultimate vacation in orbit.

WHAT IS SPECIAL ABOUT THE X-33?

THE X-33 is a single-stage-to-orbit reusable launch vehicle designed by NASA. It is currently a sized-down prototype of a new rocket design called the Venturestar, which will be built if the X-33 is successful. The Venturestar will be able to travel into space and back in one piece, without jettisoning any boosters or fuel tanks, and will lower the cost of putting one pound of payload into orbit by more than 90%.

IS FASTER-THAN-LIGHT TRAVEL POSSIBLE?

IN 1905, ALBERT EINSTEIN published his theory of special relativity. This stated that travel at the speed of light is impossible. He argued that the faster an object moves, the heavier it becomes, so that an object traveling at the speed of light would have infinite mass, which is impossible. Spacecraft are getting faster and faster but may never be able to reach the speeds needed to travel between stars.

Spacecraft like the proposed warp-drive ship above may be able to fly faster than light by creating bubbles of space through which the ship travels.

ARE THERE OTHER ALTERNATIVES TO CONVENTIONAL ROCKETS?

SCIENTISTS AND ENGINEERS are continually working on new ways to carry expensive payloads into space. The X-34 (below left) is a small rocket designed to be launched by an airplane. It is hoped that the X-34 will be able to minimize the cost of carrying satellites into orbit. The DC-XA (below right) was a new design for a single-stage-to-orbit vehicle. It made four successful flights before crashing. The Roton is designed to work without the heavy technology needed to pump rocket fuel. Its rotor blades spin, literally throwing propellant into the combustion chamber.

HOW DOES AN AEROSPIKE ENGINE WORK?

The Venturestar rocket will be powered by an engine called a linear aerospike. The shape of the engine nozzle, through which gases are released, is designed to allow it to change shape as the rocket changes altitude. This allows the craft to work at maximum efficiency all the way to orbit.

HOW WILL FUTURE SPACECRAFT BE POWERED?

Scientists have suggested giving starships giant sails. Powerful lasers beamed from Earth would propel these craft forward at incredible speeds. Theoretical warp drives are another possible solution. These would work by contracting space in front of a starship and expanding space behind it. Although the ship itself would not be traveling at the speed of light, the "bubble of space" carrying the ship would be.

WHAT ARE INTERSTELLAR CITIES?

One way of being able to travel beyond the Solar System without having to exceed the speed of light is to build enormous space cities. These would be spaceships capable of sustaining thousands of people, animals, and crops for hundreds of years. The journey to other stars would still take thousands of years, but descendants of the original crew would eventually be able to explore distant planets.

WHAT IS HOPE?

The H-II Orbiting Plane, or HOPE, has been designed by the Japanese to carry supplies to and from the International Space Station. It is unique in that it has been developed to fly without a crew. Instead, fully automated systems control the craft on its journey into orbit.

HOW ARE SPACE STATIONS BUILT?

Because space stations are so large, it is impossible to build them on Earth and then carry them into space. Instead, space stations must be built in orbit. This can be a long, difficult, and dangerous process. The International Space Station (ISS) is currently in orbit around Earth. It began construction in 1998, but installation of all 100 components will not be finished until 2006. Over forty space flights will be needed to bring parts and equipment to the ISS, and around 160 space walks, totaling nearly 1,300 hours, will be required to put it all together.

HOW DO SPACE STATIONS KEEP PEOPLE ALIVE?

A SPACE STATION MUST MAINTAIN an atmosphere similar to that on Earth in order for it to be habitable. In the ISS, oxygen is made by electrolysis. A generator splits water into oxygen and hydrogen. Carbon dioxide is collected by special materials and released into outer space. Water is recycled for maximum efficiency. It is collected from various sources including urine, sinks, and showers, and cleaned for reuse. The ISS is heated by all the electronic equipment on board.

HOW IS THE ISS POWERED?

LIKE MANY OF THE SATELLITES in orbit around Earth, electricity on the ISS will be generated by solar power. Eight giant solar arrays collect energy from the sun and transform it into electricity. When the ISS passes through the Earth's shadow it is powered by three rechargeable battery stations. The ISS needs to be boosted periodically in order to prevent it from losing speed and altitude. This is done by small rocket engines mounted on the command modules.

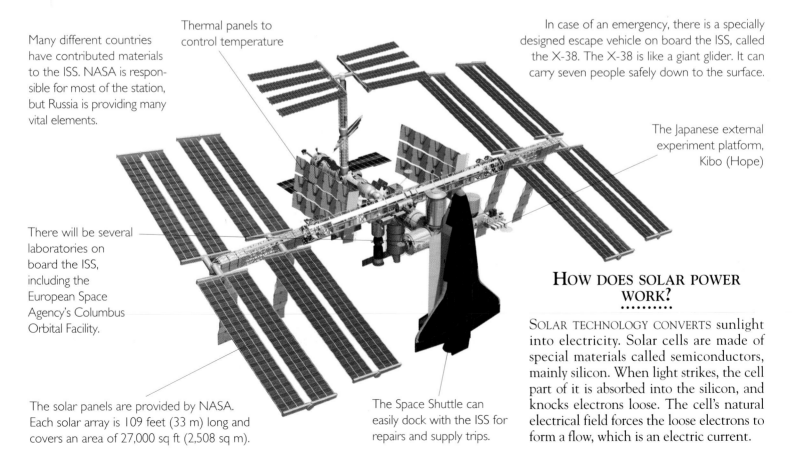

Many different countries have contributed materials to the ISS. NASA is responsible for most of the station, but Russia is providing many vital elements.

Thermal panels to control temperature

In case of an emergency, there is a specially designed escape vehicle on board the ISS, called the X-38. The X-38 is like a giant glider. It can carry seven people safely down to the surface.

The Japanese external experiment platform, Kibo (Hope)

There will be several laboratories on board the ISS, including the European Space Agency's Columbus Orbital Facility.

The solar panels are provided by NASA. Each solar array is 109 feet (33 m) long and covers an area of 27,000 sq ft (2,508 sq m).

The Space Shuttle can easily dock with the ISS for repairs and supply trips.

HOW DOES SOLAR POWER WORK?

SOLAR TECHNOLOGY CONVERTS sunlight into electricity. Solar cells are made of special materials called semiconductors, mainly silicon. When light strikes, the cell part of it is absorbed into the silicon, and knocks electrons loose. The cell's natural electrical field forces the loose electrons to form a flow, which is an electric current.

WHAT IS IT LIKE INSIDE A SPACE STATION?

CONDITIONS ON BOARD A SPACE STATION can be very strange. There is no gravity, which means that astronauts can float in midair and lift heavy objects with ease. In a space station, there is no up or down, which can be very confusing, so the walls, floor, and ceiling are painted different colors to help the crew orient themselves. The lack of gravity means that astronauts can eat or sleep on the walls, or even the ceiling, but it can also cause problems. Scientists have to strap themselves to the walls when they are working to stop themselves from floating away. The planned ISS habitation module is equipped with everything astronauts need to live normally for long periods in space, including a gym, a galley, medical facilities, and a meeting area.

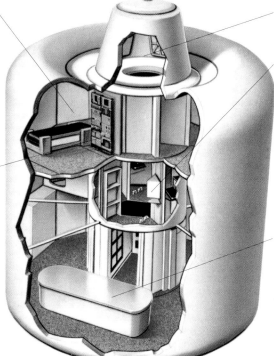

The station gym will be where astronauts work out every day to prevent muscle and bone wastage. It will contain a treadmill and an ergometer (shown below).

The exercise area also contains vital medical equipment.

Although there is no "up" or "down," the ISS will be arranged with carpets, and lights in the ceiling to help astronauts feel at home.

Pressurized tunnel leading to the ISS

The habitation module will sleep four astronauts. The sleeping bags are fixed upright to the wall and are used mainly to keep the astronauts securely in place while they sleep.

The wardroom will be where the astronauts eat and relax. It will contain a large table, a galley area, and storage space for their belongings.

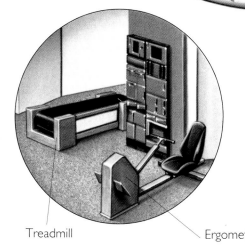

Treadmill

Ergometer

WHY IS EXERCISE ESSENTIAL IN SPACE?

BECAUSE THE BODY does not have to fight against gravity in space, there is a serious danger of it losing bone and muscle mass. Astronauts must exercise every day to prevent their muscles from wasting away. In the ISS there is a treadmill and a stationary exercise bike, but astronauts must remember to strap themselves on, or they will float away.

HOW DO ASTRONAUTS GO TO THE BATHROOM IN SPACE?

BECAUSE OF THE LACK of gravity, going to the bathroom in space can be tricky. Toilets on board space stations are equipped with restraints to hold an astronaut in place. A powerful vacuum pump is used to create a seal between the body and the seat. Waste products are collected. Some are recycled, while solid waste is disposed of safely.

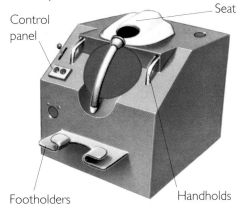

Control panel

Seat

Footholders

Handholds

fast facts

WHAT IS SPACE DEBRIS?

In the same way that humans have discarded many unwanted materials into the ground and oceans, there is now a great deal of pollution in space. Millions of pieces of space debris orbit the Earth, mainly the remains of spacecraft or satellites that have been discarded.

HOW CAN SPACE DEBRIS AFFECT SPACE TRAVEL?

It is estimated that there are over 10,000 items of space debris larger than 4 inches (10 cm) orbiting the Earth. Because craft such as the Space Shuttle move at incredibly high speeds, this orbiting junk can be very dangerous. A fleck of paint traveling in the opposite direction from a Space Shuttle could impact at speeds of 25,000 mph (40,000 kmph). Such an impact could easily smash the orbiter window, depressurizing the cabin and killing everybody on board the Shuttle.

WHAT HAPPENS WHEN A SPACE STATION IS NO LONGER NEEDED?

When a space station is no longer needed, or it is too old to be of any use, it is abandoned and destroyed. In early 2001 the Russian Mir space station, which had orbited Earth for fifteen years, was abandoned. Its rocket engines were fired to slow it down, and it lost altitude. As it entered the Earth's atmosphere, it burned up.

WHAT DO ASTRONAUTS DO FOR FUN?

Early space missions on the Space Shuttle and Mir involved astronauts doing a great deal of work and having no leisure time. This proved to be unhealthy. All astronauts aboard the ISS will have time to themselves, so that they can e-mail friends, play games, read, or just watch Earth from the window.

WHAT IS SPACE SCIENCE?

Space stations have given scientists a unique laboratory that can be found nowhere on Earth—one that is unaffected by gravity. Gravity influences everything on Earth, from the way the human body works to the growth of crystals used in semiconductors for computers. In orbit, however, a space station's speed cancels out the Earth's gravitational pull, so scientists can carry out experiments in weightless conditions.

In a space station, such as Skylab (above), experiments can be carried out in microgravitational conditions. Although there are gravitational pulls present, none are strong enough to affect the scientific tests.

WHAT IS GRAVITY?

EVERY OBJECT WITH MASS has a gravitational pull, even you and I. The more material an object contains, the stronger its gravitational pull. Objects such as a football have tiny gravitational pulls that are barely noticeable, whereas much larger things, such as planets and stars, have very strong forces of gravity. Imagine that space is a thin rubber sheet. If you placed a heavy object such as a bowling ball on the sheet, it would create a dent. Other objects would roll into this dent, toward the bowling ball, if they passed by too closely. In a similar way, stars and planets create deep gravitational wells in space. The more massive or dense the object, the deeper the gravitational well.

Earth creates a moderate gravitational well toward which all nearby objects are attracted. A ball thrown upward will always be pulled back down because the force of gravity pulls it toward Earth's core.

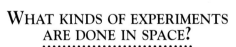

ARE SPACE STATIONS AFFECTED BY GRAVITY?

SPACE STATIONS TYPICALLY ORBIT BETWEEN 120 and 360 miles (192 and 576 km) above the Earth's surface. The Earth's gravitational pull is still fairly strong, even at this altitude. If you were standing on Earth and dropped a ball, it would fall to the ground. If an astronaut on a space station dropped a ball, it would fall, too. However, the ball would appear to float in midair because it, the astronaut, and the space station are all falling at the same speed. They are not falling *toward* the Earth, but *around* it. This condition is called microgravity.

WHAT KINDS OF EXPERIMENTS ARE DONE IN SPACE?

WORKING IN SPACE ALLOWS scientists to explore how different things are affected by gravity. The European Space Agency's Spacelab was designed with two pressurized laboratories where microgravity experiments could be carried out. Special racks held hundreds of different kinds of cells and organisms, including bacteria, lentil seedlings, and shrimp eggs. Tests were run on these organisms, and on human beings, to determine whether they behaved differently in space.

DO HEAVY AND LIGHT OBJECTS FALL AT THE SAME RATE?

IT WAS ISAAC NEWTON who discovered that all falling bodies accelerate at the same rate. His second law of motion states that the greater an object's mass, the greater the force required to accelerate it. A bowling ball weighing 7 kilograms is pulled to Earth by a gravitational force 100 times as strong as a 70-gram tennis ball. However, because the bowling ball's mass is 100 times greater to begin with, the acceleration of the two balls will be exactly the same.

WHAT TECHNOLOGIES HAVE BEEN DEVELOPED IN SPACE?

SPACE SCIENCE HAS LED TO many amazing developments in technology. Scientists have studied combustion in microgravity in order to design more efficient jet engines. We have all benefited from technology that was designed for use in space. Microchips found in digital watches, computers, and cell phones were first developed so that lots of equipment could fit into a small spacecraft. Many household items have come about because of space technology, including airtight cans and tin foil. Technologies such as solar power and keyhole surgery have also advanced largely due to the space program.

WHAT OTHER FORCES ARE THERE IN THE UNIVERSE?

GRAVITY IS ONE OF ONLY FOUR FORCES that govern every event in the entire universe. Gravity binds together the universe, while electromagnetic force is responsible for light and electricity. A strong nuclear force holds basic particles together, and a weak nuclear force causes the decay of unstable atoms. These four forces may have been united during the Big Bang, emitted as one superforce bound by extremely high temperatures. As temperatures began to cool, the superforce was gradually broken down into four separate forces. All four forces are linked with special particles that act like couriers, transferring the force from one place to another. Electromagnetism and gravitation can work over large distances, but the two nuclear forces only operate on an atomic level.

IS THERE A THEORY OF EVERYTHING?

TOGETHER, THE FOUR FORCES can explain everything that happens in the universe. Many scientists are now working to prove that they are all separate parts of the same universal force that once existed at the birth of the universe (see above).

WHAT HAPPENS DURING A NUCLEAR EXPLOSION?

NUCLEAR REACTIONS are the result of the strong nuclear force, which binds together the particles that form atoms. During a nuclear explosion, this powerful force is released, expelling vast amounts of energy.

CAN WE DEFY GRAVITY?

Flying saucers have always been the stuff of science fiction. But a Russian scientist named E. E. Podkletnov recently claimed that the force of gravity could be beaten. His theory states that a spinning, superconducting metal disk loses some of its weight. NASA is now conducting similar experiments with the aim of reducing the cost of sending rockets into orbit.

HOW DOES CARBON DATING WORK?

Several important processes are the result of the weak nuclear force, including the natural decay of Carbon-14 to Nitrogen-14. The isotope called Carbon-14 has a half-life of 5,730 years. All living things on the planet contain carbon, so scientists, such as geologists and archeologists, are able to examine objects to see how much the carbon has decayed. This allows them to estimate with great accuracy the age of ancient objects.

Gravity broke away first as temperatures began to cool. Gravity is responsible for the attraction between matter in the universe.

The electromagnetic force, which binds atoms together into molecules, and the weak nuclear force were the last to separate.

In the extreme conditions of the Big Bang, there may have been only one force.

The strong nuclear force, responsible for atomic fission and fusion, separated next.

WHY IS SPACE DANGEROUS?

From Earth, space can seem calm and quiet, but it is actually deadly. If humans ventured into space without the protection of a space suit they would die almost instantly. The lack of oxygen would mean suffocation. But before this, the lack of pressure would cause gases in the blood to separate as if it were boiling. With no protection from the sun's harmful ultraviolet radiation, the astronaut would be burned to death.

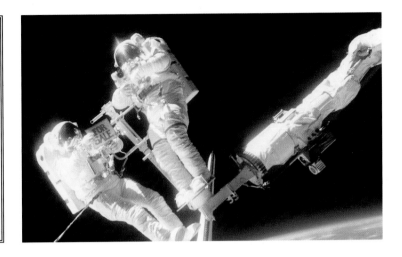

HOW ARE ASTRONAUTS PROTECTED IN SPACE?

EVERY ASTRONAUT who leaves a spacecraft has to wear a specially designed space suit. It is called an Extra-Vehicular Activity (EVA) suit and acts like a miniature spaceship. Layers of material protect the astronaut from the sun's rays, as well as tiny particles of space dust that travel at hundreds of thousands of miles per hour. The suit provides everything that an astronaut needs to survive in space for short periods of time, including oxygen to breathe and water to drink. It also provides heating and cooling, communication devices, and toilet facilities.

WHAT KINDS OF JOBS DO ASTRONAUTS DO?

ASTRONAUTS HAVE TO PERFORM many different duties that involve leaving their spacecraft. The International Space Station, which is currently under construction, requires many adjustments that can only be done by trained personnel. Robotic equipment is used to put the components of the space station together, but much of the construction can only be done by hand. Astronauts also have to make repairs to complicated items such as the Hubble Space Telescope and damaged satellites.

A camera on board the Manned Maneuvering Unit allows scientists and mission controllers to see what the astronaut is doing.

Space suits have shiny, gold-plated visors that protect the astronaut's eyes from harmful solar radiation.

Space suits are heavily insulated with 13 different layers to cope with extremes of temperature. They are white to reflect the sun's light.

Small thrusters built into the Manned Maneuvering Unit allow astronauts to adjust their position very slightly, or to move rapidly through space.

Astronauts wear a large, specially designed diaper, called a Maximum Absorption Garment, to absorb waste products.

Specially designed life-support systems in the astronaut's backpack supply a pure oxygen atmosphere and remove the dangerous carbon dioxide that the astronaut exhales.

Space suits maintain a constant pressure around the body by surrounding it with a giant balloon. Neoprene-coated fibers restrict the outer side of the balloon, keeping the air pressure inside at a constant level.

WHAT IS THE MANNED MANEUVERING UNIT?

MOVING AROUND IN SPACE is a lot like trying to move underwater. Wearing a large suit makes movement even more difficult, and when time is short, an astronaut must be able to move quickly. The Manned Maneuvering Unit was specially designed to allow astronauts to move swiftly and safely through space. The MMU is like an armchair with small thrusters attached. It is operated by a hand control similar to those used in computer games.

HOW DO ASTRONAUTS STOP THEMSELVES FROM FLOATING AWAY?

MOVEMENT IN SPACE is very difficult, because if you push on something, you will move in the opposite direction. Astronauts on the Gemini missions complained that when they tried to use a wrench in space they spun in the opposite direction. Microgravity means that an astronaut is in danger of floating away in the middle of a job, or seeing a vital tool float into outer space. To help astronauts to move around outside, spacecraft are equipped with handles and special footholders into which feet can be locked.

CAN ASTRONAUTS EAT OR DRINK IN SPACE?

BECAUSE ASTRONAUTS CAN BE in their space suits for up to seven hours, they need water to avoid dehydration. Space suits are equipped with the In-suit Drink Bag (IDB), a plastic pouch connected to the inside of the suit's torso. It can hold nearly 32 fluid ounces (0.9 liter) of water that can be accessed via a straw. The helmet also has a slot for rice-paper-covered fruit and a cereal bar, in case the astronaut gets hungry.

WHO FIRST WALKED IN SPACE?

THE FIRST HUMAN BEING to leave the confines of a spacecraft and take a "walk" in space was the Soviet cosmonaut Alexei Leonov. He crawled through the airlock of Voskhod 2 in 1965 and was so overwhelmed by the view that he shouted out the first words he could think of: "The Earth is round!" During his twenty minutes in space, Leonov's space suit expanded, due to the lack of pressure, and he was barely able to fit back in the airlock.

fast facts

HOW MUCH DO SPACE SUITS COST TO MAKE?

Because each EVA suit acts like a miniature spacecraft that can act independently of the space station, each one costs around $12 million to construct.

HOW ARE ASTRONAUTS TRAINED TO SPACE WALK?

Astronauts train to move around in space in enormous water tanks on Earth. They wear a space suit similar to the one used in orbit, and practice space walking and using tools. Water tanks are used because the buoyancy of an inflated suit in water is a very accurate simulation of microgravity.

WHAT WILL FUTURE SPACE SUITS BE LIKE?

Scientists are constantly working on new ways to make suits less expensive and easier to move around in. For the planned missions to send astronauts to Mars, NASA is working on suits that are much lighter than those used by Apollo astronauts on the moon—which were clumsy and heavy. The improved suits should allow the astronauts to explore the planet much more freely.

WHY DO SPACECRAFT NEED AIRLOCKS?

AIRLOCKS ARE VITAL FOR PROTECTING the crew of a space-craft. If there was no airlock in a submerged submarine, the vessel would instantly be flooded with water as soon as the hatch was opened. In the same way, a space station with no airlock would depressurize the instant the door was opened, killing anybody on board who was not wearing a spacesuit. This is because air always tries to remain at a level pressure. If the pressure inside a spacecraft is greater than the pressure outside, air will rush out into outer space as soon as the hull is breached.

Astronauts entering a space station open an outer door to the airlock. Once inside, the airlock is pressurized to a level safe for humans.

Only when the pressure in the airlock is the same as the pressure inside the rest of the space station will the inner airlock door be released.

HOW DOES A SPACE PROBE NAVIGATE?

Space probes are highly advanced robotic craft, often the size of a large car, launched into space to investigate celestial objects. They use radio transmitters to communicate with mission specialists on Earth. All probes have highly sensitive electronic equipment on board.

1 The first probe to visit Neptune was Voyager 2 in 1989. It sent pictures back to Earth that took over four hours to reach us.

2 The Mariner 10 probe passed within 203 miles (327 km) of Mercury's surface when it flew by three times in 1974.

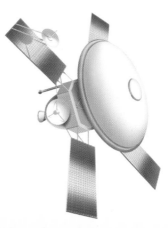

3 The Viking probes that visited Mars in 1976 landed on the surface and took samples of Martian soil for analysis.

ARE THERE DIFFERENT KINDS OF SPACE PROBE?

SPACE PROBES are designed to do different jobs. Some fly by their target at a distance of several thousand miles, taking pictures of the planet's surface and surveying its atmosphere. Other probes are designed to enter a planet's orbit, which allows them to survey the planet in more detail.

The probes that provide the most information about planets are called landers, because they touch down on the planet's surface.

WHEN WAS THE FIRST SUCCESSFUL SPACE PROBE LAUNCHED?

THE FIRST SPACE PROBE to complete its mission was Luna 2. It was launched by the USSR in 1959 and successfully landed on its destination–the moon. Its predecessor, Luna 1, was launched toward the same target several months earlier, but missed by 3,730 miles (6,000 km).

Independent rovers such as the one shown here can travel short distances across a planet, analyzing the terrain.

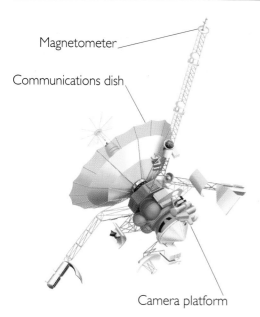

Magnetometer

Communications dish

Camera platform

The Galileo probe used the sun's gravity to catapult it across the immense distance to Jupiter.

HAVE PROBES VISITED EVERY PLANET IN THE SOLAR SYSTEM?

SO FAR SPACE PROBES have visited every planet in the Solar System except Pluto. Venus was the first planet to be investigated as Mariner 2 flew by in 1962. Mariner 10 orbited Mercury in 1975. Mars is the most visited planet in the Solar System, with over five probes landing on its surface. The Pioneer and Voyager probes, launched between 1979 and 1989, investigated the outer planets Jupiter, Saturn, Uranus, and Neptune. The Pluto-Kuiper Express aims to visit Pluto between 2006 and 2008.

DO PROBES ONLY INVESTIGATE PLANETS?

SCIENTISTS have sent probes to investigate many kinds of celestial objects. In 1995, the Ulysses probe was launched toward the sun and took readings of the solar wind and the star's magnetism. The Giotto probe, launched in 1986, battled its way past flying debris and gas into the heart of Halley's comet, taking incredible pictures of its nucleus. Asteroids have also been visited by space probes. The Near Earth Asteroid Rendezvous probe landed on the asteroid Eros in 2001.

WHAT KIND OF EXPERIMENTS DO PROBES CONDUCT?

PROBES investigate as much of their target as they can. Cameras take an assortment of photographs from different angles and distances, while antennas detect magnetism and radio waves. Lander probes, such as the Vikings that touched down on Mars, can take soil samples and analyze the atmosphere.

DO PROBES TRAVEL IN A STRAIGHT LINE?

The Ulysses probe was actually launched toward the planet Jupiter, although its destination was the sun. This was so that the giant planet's gravitational pull could be used as a free source of energy to catapult the probe millions of miles across the Solar System.

CAN PROBES FULLY INVESTIGATE THE SUN?

The sun's intense heat means that it is impossible for probes to fly too close to it. However, NASA's Solar Probe is set to fly within several million miles of the surface, taking measurements from within the sun's corona.

WHAT IS THE FARTHEST DISTANCE A PROBE HAS TRAVELED?

The Pioneer and Voyager probes did not stop when they flew by their target planets, but continued deep into the dark outer regions of the Solar System. They will continue traveling for millions of miles before their power source runs out.

HOW ARE IMAGES SENT FROM PROBES TO EARTH?

Images are transmitted as radio signals that are received by radio telescopes on Earth. There are receiving stations placed around the world so that it does not matter where the Earth is in its rotation when the signals arrive.

HOW ARE PROBES POWERED?

Most probes are powered by electricity generated by solar panels attached to the probe's casing. Others use a nuclear generator. One modern method of propelling a space probe is the ion drive, which uses reactions in a chemical gas instead of combustion.

HOW DOES A PROBE LAND?

A PROBE'S LANDING PROCEDURE is complicated and dangerous. Because scientists do not know everything about a target planet, they can never be sure what the conditions will be like when a probe lands. Mars, for example, suffers from enormous dust storms that could seriously damage a probe descending to the surface. The diagram below shows a procedure for a landing.

1 In orbit, the lander separates from the main body of the probe. Once it is deep inside the planet's atmosphere, it releases a parachute.

2 Despite its parachute, the probe is still traveling at speed when it hits the surface. Probes like Pathfinder have inflatable cushions that ease the landing.

3 Once it has landed, a probe begins its experiments. Pathfinder released a robotic rover called Sojourner to investigate beyond the landing site.

WHAT IS A SATELLITE?

Any object in orbit around a celestial body is called a satellite. Earth has had its own natural satellite–the moon–for billions of years. Since 1957, however, hundreds of artificial satellites have been launched into orbit around Earth, each transmitting a cacophony of radio signals to locations across the planet. Satellites are now vital to modern life and are used in many areas of technology, including communications, entertainment, and espionage.

HOW DO SATELLITES STAY IN ORBIT?

SATELLITES MUST BE LAUNCHED into orbit with enough speed to prevent Earth's gravity from pulling them back down to the ground. Imagine throwing a ball horizontally. Gravity pulls the ball back to Earth very quickly. If the ball could be thrown hard enough, however, it would have enough force to keep on traveling horizontally forever. It would be in orbit. A satellite at an altitude of 120 miles (200 km) must be traveling at 4.8 miles per second (7.8 km per second) to prevent it being pulled back down to Earth.

Although the ball is in free fall toward Earth, the planet's curve means that it never reaches it.

HOW ARE MILITARY SATELLITES USED?

A GREAT MANY of the satellites sent into space by the U.S. and Russia are used for military activities. These range from eavesdropping on important telephone calls to detecting the x-rays and electromagnetic pulses given off by nuclear explosions. Early military satellites were used to take close-up pictures of enemy territory but had to return home to have their film developed. Modern satellites use digital technology to take photographs, so they never run out of film. Amazingly, they can photograph things as small as the headlines on a newspaper.

HOW DO COMMUNICATIONS SATELLITES RELAY INFORMATION?

COMMUNICATIONS SATELLITES are used for many different tasks, including television broadcasts and telephone calls. A telephone call made from England to the United States would be sent to the nearest Earth station, which would use its giant antenna to beam the call into space in the form of radio waves. The satellite would receive these radio waves and beam them back down to an antenna on the other side of the planet.

The American Defense Support Program (DSP) satellites, shown right, are used to detect the launch of enemy missiles. Infrared sensors detect the heat released when a ballistic missile is launched, and a warning message is instantly transmitted to Earth.

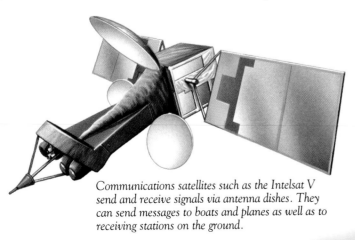

Communications satellites such as the Intelsat V send and receive signals via antenna dishes. They can send messages to boats and planes as well as to receiving stations on the ground.

WHAT KIND OF ORBITS DO SATELLITES HAVE?

SATELLITES FOLLOW one of four different orbits. A satellite in geostationary orbit takes the same time to orbit the Earth as the Earth does to spin, therefore it always remains over the same point on the planet. This orbit is used mainly for communications satellites. Low-Earth orbits, often used by spy satellites, can be lower than 155 miles (250 km) above the planet. Polar-orbit satellites orbit at around 590 miles (800 km), while highly-elliptical-orbit satellites have very low altitudes when they are closest to Earth, but pass far beyond the planet when they are at their most distant.

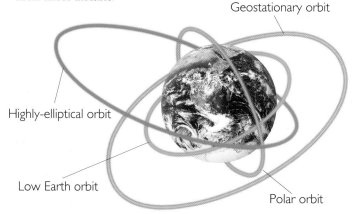

Geostationary orbit

Highly-elliptical orbit

Low Earth orbit

Polar orbit

HOW DO SATELLITES PREDICT THE WEATHER?

METEOROLOGY SATELLITES, which orbit in geostationary and polar orbits, can keep a constant watch over the weather systems at work around the planet. They record data, such as cloud formation and movement, pressures, wind speeds, and humidities, and send them to Earth, where scientists can use them to predict weather in preparation for weather forecasts. Satellites are also used to detect hurricanes–fierce tropical storms with wind speeds of over 80 mph (130 kmph). These storms can strike with very little warning, but satellites can detect them before they hit land, warning people of danger in time for them to take cover.

WHAT ARE EARTH-RESOURCES SATELLITES?

SATELLITES CAN HELP SCIENTISTS learn a lot more about the planet than instruments on aircraft and ships can. They use Earth-resources satellites to monitor every part of the world in order to get information about the planet's condition. Satellites can detect things such as the amount of water in a field of crops, which will give early warning of a harvest failure. They can also detect large areas of deforestation, showing changes over large periods of time.

HOW DO SATELLITES REMAIN STABLE IN SPACE?

A SATELLITE CANNOT do its job properly if it is not stable. A satellite dish must always point toward its location, or signals will be lost in space. In order to keep satellites from flying out of control, some are deliberately designed to spin. In the same way that a spinning top remains stable if it is spinning quickly, a satellite that is spinning will not deviate from its course. Some satellites have small, spinning wheels at various points on their frame. These wheels can be used to realign the satellite if it moves off course.

WHAT IS GPS?

GPS, or the Global Positioning System, is designed to aid navigation around the planet. It consists of 24 satellites in six different orbits around Earth. Their position in these orbits means that any receiver, anywhere on Earth, can always receive a signal from four satellites or more. Using data from these signals, a GPS receiver can work out its position, including altitude, to within a few meters.

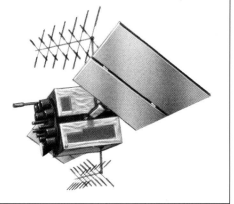

HOW DO GPS RECEIVERS WORK?

GLOBAL POSITIONING SATELLITES beam signals to special receivers on Earth. These receivers, which are not much larger than cell phones, know the difference between when the satellite signal was sent and when it was received. This allows the receiver to work out the distance between each of the satellites and itself, and therefore calculate its position.

fast facts

WHEN WERE SATELLITES FIRST USED?

The idea of transmitting radio signals across the world by beaming them through space was first put to use in 1954. The U.S. Navy sent a message from Washington, D.C. to Hawaii by bouncing a signal off the moon.

WHAT WAS ECHO?

Echo was an aluminized balloon launched by NASA in 1960. It was used to reflect radio signals across North America.

HOW DO SATELLITES AID MINING?

Industry depends on a continuous supply of nonrenewable resources such as oil, gas, and coal. Because most of the easily obtained supplies of these resources have already been depleted, satellites are used to scan the surface for harder-to-spot supplies. Oil can be spotted from space as it seeps into the sea from deposits beneath the seabed.

ARE THERE OTHER SOLAR SYSTEMS?

Four hundred years ago, an astronomer named Giordano Bruno was burned at the stake for suggesting the existence of other Earth-like worlds. Today we know that there are potentially billions of extrasolar planets in the Milky Way. None found so far resemble Earth. Indeed, many are shockingly different from our world. Although none of the planets investigated so far have shown any signs of life, many astronomers believe that it is only a matter of time before Earth's twin planet is discovered.

HOW CAN WE DETECT OTHER SOLAR SYSTEMS?

EXTRASOLAR PLANETS ARE very difficult to see because they are outshone by the light from their parent stars. It can be determined whether or not a star has a planetary system by observing whether or not the star's light "wobbles." As a planet orbits a star, its gravitational pull causes the star's light to bend slightly, and thus to change color. This technique only works for giant planets, however, because an Earth-sized world would have little effect on its parent.

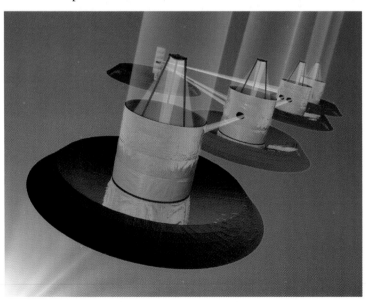

WHAT IS THE PLANET FINDER?

NASA's Terrestrial Planet Finder (above), due to be launched in 2010, will be powerful enough to search the brightest 1,000 stars in the galaxy. It will be able to spot Earth-like planets, and will even be able to detect what their atmospheres are like.

HOW LIKELY IS ALIEN LIFE?

THE ASTRONOMER FRANK DRAKE pioneered the search for intelligent life elsewhere in the universe. He claimed that for intelligent life, capable of communicating over interstellar distances, to arise on a planet, conditions must be perfect. He came up with an equation to estimate the number of civilizations in the galaxy with the means for communicating with Earth:

$$N = R^* fp\ ne\ fl\ fi\ fc\ L$$

N = the number of civilizations with the ability to communicate over long distances.

R = the rate of formation of suitable stars.

fp = the fraction of those stars with planets.

ne = the number of Earth-like worlds in a planetary system.

fl = the fraction of Earth-like worlds on which life develops.

fi = the fraction of life forms that develop intelligence.

fc = the fraction of intelligent life forms that develop electromagnetic communication technology.

L = the lifetime of these communicating civilizations.

HOW CAN WE SEARCH FOR ALIENS?

RADIO ASTRONOMY IS THE MOST effective way to search for alien life. Radio telescopes can be positioned all over the world–because radio waves are not affected by the Earth's atmosphere, and can pick up signals from across the universe. Radio telescopes such as Arecibo (below) in Puerto Rico, and the Very Large Array, enable astronomers to view space in all directions for signs of alien intelligence.

fast facts

WHAT ARE UFOS?

UFO stands for Unidentified Flying Object. Thousands of reports of mysterious objects in the skies are made every year. Over 95% of these can be explained in terms of everyday things such as weather balloons.

WHAT HAPPENED IN ROSWELL?

One of the most famous UFO encounters was in Roswell, New Mexico, in 1948. Several witnesses saw a craft crash next to a military base. A strange metallic material was found next to the crash site. The metal was thin, but was resistant to extreme heat and very strong.

CAN WE COMMUNICATE WITH ALIENS?

BESIDES RECEIVING SIGNALS from outer space, radio telescopes such as Arecibo can also broadcast signals to the entire galaxy and beyond. In 1974, radio waves beamed from the Arecibo telescope carried a message deep into space. The message consisted of 1,679 pulses that, when arranged into a grid 23 columns wide and 73 rows tall, creates an image (below). The message was aimed at a dense ball of stars called M13, which is so far away from Earth that it could take up to 50,000 years to receive an answer.

The message contained information about life on planet Earth, including:

The numbers 1–10 in binary code

The most important elements of life

A strand of DNA, which carries the blue-print of life

The image of a human, the world's population, and the average height of a human

Earth's position in the Solar System

An image of the Arecibo telescope

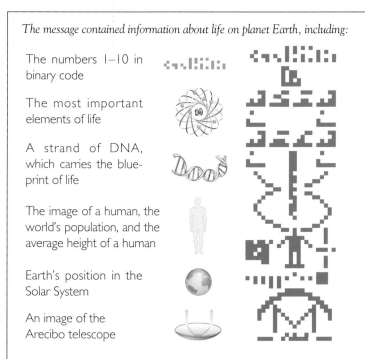

Lights from big cities, burning oil wells, and large fleets of boats are visible from space at night (above). The Pioneer probes each had plates showing a man and woman giving a greeting, and Earth's position in the Solar System.

HOW COULD ALIENS FIND OUT ABOUT EARTH?

IN 1990, THE GALILEO SPACE PROBE began to investigate Earth. It was determining whether it is possible to detect signs of life on a planet when viewed from space. The probe detected that Earth had water on its surface and oxygen in its atmosphere, which told scientists that the planet contained life. In addition, Earth at night is like a glowing neon signpost, alerting aliens to our whereabouts. The Pioneer space probes (above) had special plates engraved with symbols in case the probes ever encountered intelligent life on their journeys into space.

Glossary

Absolute zero The coldest temperature possible, or –459°F (–273°C).

Asteroid A small rocky body orbiting the sun. Asteroids can range in size from smaller than a few feet in diameter to larger than a thousand miles across.

Big Bang A theory of the beginning of the universe which states that it started from a violent explosion around 13 billion years ago.

Black hole The core of a collapsed star with a gravitational pull so strong that nothing can escape from it, not even light.

Celestial body Any object in the sky such as a moon, planet, or star.

Comet An object composed of dust and ice that orbits the sun. When a comet travels too close to the sun, the solar wind melts ice from the comet, thereby forming its tail.

Elliptical A term used to describe an elongated circle.

Galaxy An enormous body of stars, gas, and dust held together by gravity. Galaxies are separated from one another by voids of empty space.

Gravitational pull The mutual force of attraction between masses. The gravitational pull of a planet or star is very strong because of its large mass.

Halley's comet One of the most famous comets to be seen from Earth. It orbits the Earth once every 76 years.

Light year A unit of measurement based on the distance light travels in an Earth year.

Meteor Streaks of light that appear briefly in the night sky. They occur when particles of rock or dust left by comets burn up in the Earth's atmosphere. They are also known as shooting stars

Microgravity Extremely low gravity. Astronauts experience this when floating in orbit, because there are no objects with large enough mass to pull them to any surface.

Orbit The path of one celestial object around another celestial object with a greater mass. For example, the Earth orbits the sun.

Planet A spherical celestial body that orbits the sun, or any star. There are nine known planets in our Solar System.

Quasars Exploding centers of remote, aged galaxies.

Radar Short for RAdio Detecting And Ranging. It works by sending out a short burst of radio waves and then listening for the echo. In this way operators can determine how far away an object is and what it is made of.

Solar flare Enormous and unpredictable explosions that occur in the Earth's atmosphere.

Solar System Everything that orbits our star, the sun. It includes 60 moons, and millions of asteroids, meteoroids, and comets. It also includes the Oort cloud, which is a vast sphere of comets.

Supernova A star that suddenly increases greatly in brightness due to an internal explosion ejecting most of its mass.

Terraforming The process by which a planet's atmosphere can be changed, thereby making it able to support human life.

Total eclipse During a total eclipse, the moon appears (from Earth) to cover the sun completely. Total eclipses occur once every 18 months.

Universe Everything that exists, including humankind, planets, stars, moons, and galaxies.

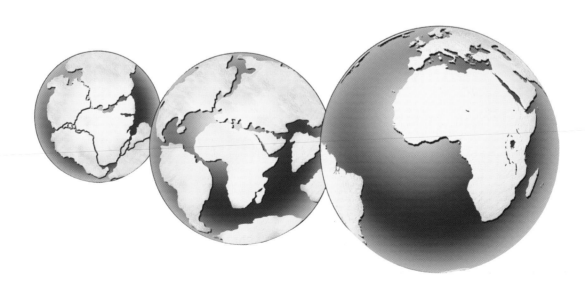

INDEX